Mission. Impossible?

Mission. Impossible?
Taking Christianity to the Congo

by

R. R. HALL

with a postscript by

NORBERT MBU-MPUTU

THE CHOIR PRESS

First published in the United Kingdom in 2023 by
The Choir Press

ISBN 978-1-78963-349-8

Contents

List of illustrations   vii
Preface   xv
Acknowledgements   vii
Abbreviations   xvii

1. Introduction   1
2. The Vision   4
3. The Committee   7
4. The Congo   10
5. Congolese Society and Religious Beliefs   14
6. The Livingstone Inland Mission   22
7. Malaria   35
8. The First Congo Christians   41
9. A Second Dawn   48
10. King Leopold and the Congo Free State   55
11. The Silence of the Missionaries?   67
12. Congo Belge   88
13. Congo Balolo Mission: The Early Years   92
14. The Roaring Twenties   104
15. Thirty Years: 1930–1960   110
16. Independence   121
17. A New Approach   129
18. Simba   132
19. Working in Partnership   138
20. Closure   147
21. Failure?   157
22. Missionary Children: Third Culture Kids   171
23. The Heart of Darkness   193

Postscript by Norbert Mbu-Mputu   203
References   206

List of Illustrations

Fig. 1. Dr David Livingstone. *Getty Images.*

Fig. 2. Rev Alfred Tilly. *In, Fanny E Guinness. The New World of Central Africa. Hodder and Stoughton. 1890.*

Fig. 3. Rev Henry Grattan Guinness & Mrs Fanny E Guinness. *In, Michele Guinness. The Guinness Legend. Hodder & Stoughton. 1989. With kind permission of Mrs Michele Guinness.*

Fig. 4. Captain Tuckey's Voyage in Africa: The Fetiche Rock, looking down the river. *James Fittler, from a sketch by Lieu* Hawkey. In, Captain J.K.Tuckey RN. Narrative of an Expedition to explore The River Zaire, usually called the Congo, in 1816. John Murray, London. 1818.*

Fig. 5. Henry Morton Stanley. *L Hanson.1964. With kind permission of Mrs B Snowball.* This statue has been removed and lies broken in the Institute of National Museums of Congo, Kinshasa.

Fig. 6. Henry Craven, the first missionary to the Congo. *In, Fanny E Guinness. The New World of Central Africa. Hodder and Stoughton. 1890.*

Fig. 7. SS Livingstone on the Lower River. *In, Fanny E Guinness. The New World of Central Africa. Hodder and Stoughton. 1890.*

Fig. 8. Map to show the Lower Congo and mission stations established by the Livingstone Inland Mission. *RR Hall.*

Fig. 9. PS Henry Reed. *In, Fanny E Guinness. The New World of Central Africa. Hodder and Stoughton. 1890.*

Fig. 10. Memorial to the early pioneers of the Livingstone Inland Mission. *In, Fanny E Guinness. The New World of Central Africa. Hodder and Stoughton 1890.*

Fig. 11. John McKittrick, leader of the Congo Balolo Mission. *In, Fanny E Guinness. The New World of Central Africa. Hodder and Stoughton. 1890.*

Fig. 12. Dr Harry Guinness. 1910. *Centre for the study of World Christianity, University of Edinburgh. File CSWC33/059/11.*

Fig. 13. The first party of the Congo Balolo Mission, sailed for Africa April 1889. *Centre for the study of World Christianity, University of Edinburgh. File CSWC33/OS9/8.* *

Fig. 14. King Leopold II of the Belgians. *Image in the public domain.*

Fig. 15. Edmund Dene Morel. *Photograph by Bassano Ltd. 1923. National Portrait Gallery, London. NPGx12218.*

Fig.16. Rev George Washington Williams. *Image in the public domain. BlackPast.org.*

Fig. 17. Daniel J Danielsen. *With kind permission of the Danielsen family.*

Fig. 18. Sir Roger Casement. *With kind permission of the Fenian Graves Association.*

Fig. 19. Stamp to commemorate Daniel J Danielsen. *Issued by the Faroe Islands 1904. With kind permission of Posta Faroe Islands.*

Fig. 20. Mrs Alice Seeley Harris with her camera. *Bodleian Libraries, University of Oxford. MSS. Brit. Emp. s. 24, J46, page 20.*

Fig. 21. Church at Baringa. *Centre for the study of World Christianity, University of Edinburgh. File CSWC33/OS10/49.*

Fig. 22. Yuli, Congo Balolo Mision station. *Centre for the study of World Christianity, University of Edinburgh. File CSWC33/OS38/1.*

Fig. 23. Mr & Mrs E A Ruskin. *In, Mrs E A Ruskin. Ruskin of Congo. Regions Beyond Missionary Union. 1948.*

Fig. 24. Mrs Ruskin with staff of the printing press, Bongandanga. *Centre for the study of World Christianity, University of Edinburgh.*

Fig. 25. CBM missionary staff at annual conference 1928. *Personal collection, Dr E R Wide.*

Fig. 26. PS Livingtone on the Maringa River. *Centre for the study of World Christianity, University of Edinburgh. File. CSWC33/OS10/73.*

Fig. 27. Maps to show the locations of stations established by the Congo Balolo Mission in the Basankusu District of Equateur Province.

Fig. 28. First meeting of the CBM Congolese Pastors' Conference, 1931. *Centre for the study of World Christianity, University of Edinburgh. CSWC33/OS11/15.*

Fig. 29. Students at Mompono Bible School.1939. *Centre for the study of World Christianity, University of Edinburgh. CSWC33/OS37/3.*

Fig. 30. Girls' boarding school, Ikau. 1944. *H J Hall.*

Fig. 31. Students at girls' school, Ikau. 1944. *HJ Hall.*

Fig. 32. Baringa Hospital. 1938. *Personal collection, ER Wide. 1938.*

Fig. 33. A corner of the Lifeta Leprosy Village. 1938. *Personal collection, E R Wide.*

Fig. 34. Dr E R Wide. *Personal collection, E R Wide. 1938.*

Fig. 35. Nursing Staff at Baringa hospital. 1964. *R R Hall.*

Fig. 36. Yoseki Hospital. *R R Hall.*

Fig. 37. Ekwalanga Timoteo. *R R Hall.* Pastor Bofaso Davide. *Centre for the study of World Christianity, University of Edinburgh. CSWC33/OS38/10.* Pastor Lofinda Benjamin. *R R Hall.* *

Backcover. A childhood friend greeting the author on his return to Congo, 1963.

---

* Traditional personal nomenclature in Congolese society comprised a given name followed by the person's father's name and a description of their future capability. For example, President Mobutu (given name) Sese Seko (father's name) added Nkuku Ngbendu Wa Za Banga, which meant "The all-powerful warrior who will go from conquest to conquest". When missionaries arrived in the Congo they gave converts to Christianity a new Biblical name that replaced the father's name. Throughout this book I have used the names known to me or as found in written records, giving the Congolese given name first followed by the missionary addition, if known.

About the Author

———

Reg Hall studied medicine in London graduating in 1962. Born of Protestant missionary parents in 1939 in the Belgian Congo (now the Democratic Republic of Congo) his African name was Kongo. In 1963 he returned to the Congo as a volunteer doctor for one year with the Congo Balolo Mission.

Subsequently, he followed a career as a urological surgeon and cancer specialist in the National Health Service, working, also, with the Medical Research Council and the European Organisation for Research in the Treatment of Cancer in national and international cancer research. Following retirement, he co-founded Cancer Connections, a cancer support charity in the northeast of England where he is still a volunteer.

Preface

One hundred and fifty years ago the country now known as the Democratic Republic of Congo was unknown to the Western world. By the middle of the 19th century European countries had colonised the periphery of the African continent but the interior of the continent remained a mystery. When Henry Morton Stanley completed his historic descent of the Congo River on 9th August 1877 the Kongo and its people, with a civilisation far older than that of Europe, would never be the same again. The first to capitalise on Stanley's achievement were Protestant missionaries. Inspired by Stanley and the missionary-explorer David Livingstone, a group of British Christian visionaries that included a Welsh Baptist minister, some businessmen and a member of the Guinness brewing family, initiated an enterprise that would last for 125 years. The Livingstone Inland Mission (LIM) and its successor, the Congo Balolo Mission (CBM), were the vanguard of late 19th century Victorian Christian expansionism that would take Christianity to the Heart of Africa and a people who they considered to be "lost in darkness".

When I was born my name was Kongo, given to me by the villagers of a remote riverside village in what was then the Belgian Congo. This was a great honour, for Kongo had been a renowned Chief and all great chiefs wore around their necks a leather thong that carried many leopard's teeth, one canine from each of the beasts they had killed. As an indication of their expectations of the new, white man-child I was given a thong with but a single canine; I would have to kill my own leopards to earn their respect.

My parents arrived in the Congo in 1924 as enthusiastic, new missionaries to work with the Congo Balolo Mission, a non-conformist Protestant mission that had adopted an area the size of England in the Central African rainforest. Living with a handful of colleagues in a remote village on the banks of the Lopori River my father assisted in the printing of educational and Christian literature, supervised the construction of schools and churches, and travelled by riverboat and bicycle to preach and teach in the many surrounding villages. My mother, a nurse and midwife, ran a simple hospital and a school for girls. As the only white child all my friends were Congolese and my first language was Lomongo. At the age of five we came to England with no plans to return. Nineteen years later that was to change. In 1963, as a newly qualified doctor I arrived at my childhood home where I would work as a volunteer at one of the mission's two hospitals. Doing so I was afforded an opportunity to meet and learn from the people amongst whom I had been born, and who I came to appreciate and admire.

The stimulus for this book sprang from a desire to learn more about the country and the people of Congo before the intrusion of Europeans; their society, traditions, way of life and religious beliefs. Also, having questioned the only previous published account of the Congo Balolo Mission[1] I wished to explore the contribution of Christian missions to the development of the country that is now the Democratic Republic of Congo.

Many readers will have little knowledge of the Congo as a country, and possibly less of Christian missions in the past. The purpose of this book, therefore, is to provide an overview of the historical, geopolitical and religious context of 19th-century Congo and, by telling the story of a single Protestant mission, to examine the Christianisation of a pre- and post-independence African country in the late 19th and 20th centuries. In doing so the missionaries' vision, good intentions, sacrificial devotion and achievements are presented together with the unanticipated consequences of venturing into a remote, isolated African society of which there was no prior knowledge. The book considers, also, the response of this enterprise when confronted by a fatal disease, a population suffering brutal Western commercial exploitation, independence from colonial rule, and disrupted, personal family relationships.

In recent years overseas Christian missions have been criticised on the grounds that they were inherently racist and predominantly agents of European imperialist colonialism. Such grave charges should not be ignored. Evidence of racism will be apparent during the course of the narrative; the final chapter considers this together with the colonialist nature of missionary enterprise. Recent population studies have recorded that the large majority of people living in the Democratic Republic of Congo describe themselves as Christian. Given the absence of religious awareness in Congolese society little more than a century ago the book concludes by asking what features of Christianity have proved so attractive.

The book is unique in that it is based on detailed study of the archived records of the Congo Balolo Mission together with personal interviews with retired missionaries and missionary children, current leaders of the Congolese church and other previously unpublished personal material. Throughout its writing I have been concerned that it presents only a Western 'white' perspective. That has been inevitable as the only available source material was from missionaries and archived mission records, except for a single Congolese dissertation. I am therefore grateful to Mr Norbert Mbu-Mputu for contributing a Congolese opinion in the form of a postscript.

Acknowledgements

———

Completing this account of missionary endeavour that lasted for more than a century has required the help of many people to whom I wish to extend my gratitude.

For the early years I have depended on a great deal of archived source material held by the collections of the Centre for the study of World Christianity, University of Edinburgh; Antislavery International; the Bodleian Library, Oxford; the London School of Economics and Adam Matthew Digital. When personal access was not possible during the Covid pandemic the staff of these institutions were especially helpful. Seeking information about Alice Seeley Harris and Daniel J Danielsen I met new friends in Judy Pollard Smith and Oli Jacobsen both of whom have been generous and encouraging throughout. Dean Pavlakis corrected some early errors and Kevin Grant, Jos Erdkamp and Michael Prichard led to the true identity of Mrs Harris' camera.

Written information about the latter years of the Congo Balolo Mission and the Regions Beyond Missionary Union was less plentiful but retired missionaries John Bruce, Bob Hunt, Richard Martin, Robert and Dorothy Dear, Hanni Gruenig, Cath Ingram, David Pouncey, Shirley Bull (nee Marks) and the late Elsa Morgan all came to the rescue. Their contributions were invaluable. Geoffrey Larcombe directed the mission during its latter years, ably assisted by Judith Hymer. Their recollections of the final weeks were moving; Geoff's concern for the future of the widespread mission family was exemplary. Communications with rural Democratic Republic of Congo are not always easy but thanks to Francis Hannaway in Basankusu and CADELU senior staff Bokombe Jean Denis, Richard Iyema, and Samuel Menga it has been possible to bring the story up to date.

Recalling one's childhood brings back many memories, some of them long forgotten. The experience of missionary children growing up in a foreign land, often in remote locations, followed by long periods of separation from parents, is a subject that has been seldom considered. For sharing your very personal experiences, to Evelyn Garland, Paul Hanson, Frances Grindell,

Beryl Snowball, Morag Drew, Dugald Campbell, Barbara Robertson, Josephine Higgs, Ruth Thomas, Beverly Johannson, Edwin Manning and Val Walling: thank you.

The skills of an experienced editor will improve any manuscript. For this I am undoubtedly indebted to Allison McKechnie. Although my research set out to explore my own origins and trace the narrative of the Congo Balolo mission I have, inevitably, reflected on the role of British Protestant Christian missions in an African society. Except where obvious in the text the opinions expressed are my own, as are any residual errors. The paucity of Congolese opinion remains a concern. I am, therefore, particularly grateful to Rene Lingofe for his contribution and to Norbert Mbu Mputu for his postscript.

R R Hall.

Abbreviations

ABIR – Anglo-Belgian India Rubber Company
ABMU – American Baptist Missionary Union
AIM – Africa Inland Mission
ANC – Armée Nationale Congolaise
APL – Armée Populaire de Libération
APS – Aborigines' Protection Society
BMS – Baptist Missionary Society
CADELU – Communauté des Eglise Evengelique de la Lulonga
CBM – Congo Balolo Mission
CDCC – Communauté des Disciples du Christ au Congo
CEHC – Comité d'Etudes du Haut-Congo
CIM – China Inland Mission
CMA – Christian Missionary Alliance
CMS – Church Missionary Society
CPC – Congo Protestant Council
CPRA – Congo Protestant Relief Association
CRA – Congo Reform Association
DCCM – Disciples of Christ Mission
DRC – Democratic Republic of Congo
ECC – Eglise du Christ du Congo
ECMB – Eglise Chrétienne Missionnaire Belge
EUSA – Evangelical Union of South America
HMS – Henry Morton Stanley
ICC – Institut Chrétien Congolais
ICM – Institut Chrétien de la Maringa
ITB – Institut Théologique de Baringa
JRS – Jesuit Refugee Service
LIM – Livingstone Inland Mission
LMS – London Missionary Society
MAF – Missionary Aviation Fellowship
MNC – Movement Nationale Congolais

MSA – Mission Suédoise Americaine
MSF – Médecins Sans Frontières (Doctors Without Borders)
RBMU – Regions Beyond Missionary Union
SAB – Société Anonyme Belge
SECB – Synod of Evangelical Churches in Belgium
SMG – Schweizerische Missions-Gemeinschaft (Swiss Missionary Fellowship)
SUM – Sudan United Mission
UFM – Unevangelised Fields Mission
VEM – Vareinte Evangelische Mission

1

Introduction

———

The Congo Balolo Mission first started its work August 1889, one of many foreign missions that were the outcome of the evangelical revival in Britain during the 19th century. Most of the periphery of the African continent was known to the Western world but the centre was a mystery. Several of the great rivers of the continent were thought to originate there and attempts had been made to determine their source. Some explorers had succeeded in crossing the continent, but the origins of the Nile and the Congo remained the subject of hot debate. Of even greater concern for the leaders of churches in "the homeland" was the realisation that although pioneering missionaries had taken Christianity to much of Queen Victoria's British Empire there were millions of people living in the interior of the continent who remained in ignorance. The plight of these unknown souls could not pass unchallenged: the centre of "the Dark Continent" had to be opened to the light of the Christian Gospel.

One man who attempted to right this situation was a Scotsman, David Livingstone. Growing up in relative poverty, largely self-educated but trained in London as a medical doctor, he joined the London Missionary Society. When his intention to work in China was prevented by the Opium War of 1839 he had a significant meeting with Robert Moffat, a missionary from South Africa.[2] He was also influenced by the views of Sir Thomas F. Buxton MP, a social reformer and abolitionist, that the African slave trade might be destroyed through the influence of legitimate trade

Fig 1. Dr David Livingstone

1

and the spread of Christianity. Livingstone arrived at the Cape in early 1841.

With the passage of time it became clear that the usual way of missionary life was not his metier; he felt constrained, unable to explore the reasons for his dedication to Africa. His desire to address the slave trade and open the unknown continent to the benefits of Christianity and European civilisation were more important than living in a local community to preach and minister to medical needs. Central to his thinking was the concept that the introduction of industrious Christian men and their families would be the best way to bring the benefits of civilisation and the Christian gospel. They would be men with practical skills, not the ordained clergy, who would live and work in African society and would teach by example rather than preaching. Secondly, he proposed a seminary for training African evangelists who would be best suited to convey the Christian message to their fellow men and women.[3] Thirdly, if these objectives were to be achieved a satisfactory route for access to the interior of the country would be essential. This he set out to find. Leaving the London Missionary Society he embarked on solitary exploration of Central Africa accompanied only by African followers, among whom he sought to live by Christian principles. Livingstone built neither churches nor hospitals but sought to "Introduce to the knowledge and sympathies of the Christian church an entire continent. The end of the geographical feat was the beginning of the enterprise."[4] By the time he died in 1873 at Ilala in present-day Zambia, he had explored the Zambezi River, named the Victoria Falls and, mistakenly, identified the upper reaches of the Congo River as the source of the Nile. After his death he was lauded as a hero and his remains were laid to rest in Westminster Abbey.

As a devout Christian but stubborn loner Livingstone would not be considered a role model for future missionaries. However, his intentions were clear: "The spirit of missions is the spirit of our Master; the very genius of His religion. A diffusive philanthropy is Christianity itself. It requires perpetual propagation to attest its genuineness."[5] Florence Nightingale wrote of him, "Dr Livingstone stood alone as the great Missionary Traveller, the bringer-in of civilisation; the pioneer of civilisation to the races lying in darkness".[6] Through his writings, his meeting with Henry Morton Stanley, and his subsequent fame, Livingstone was the undoubted inspiration for many who followed him to the centre of Africa, among them a small group of friends in London. "Africa is open; enter it with the gospel! Did we not deserve David Livingstone's reproach for standing trembling and shivering on the rim of the great continent, instead of plunging bravely into the vast interior, where myriads were waiting in vain for the words of eternal life."[7]

And plunge they did. The first Christian mission to the interior of the continent was founded: the Livingstone Inland Mission. The first word recalled an example, the second an aim.[8]

2

The Vision

The vision was the brainchild of Rev Alfred Tilly, a Baptist minister in Cardiff. Tilly was a member of the Baptist Missionary Society that had been sending missionaries to India, Asia and Africa since 1793. He had a deep concern for the welfare of the people affected by the transatlantic slave trade and had reached the conclusion that the Baptist mission would not address his concern for the people of the Congo interior.[9] He therefore discussed his ideas with Messrs Cory (Cardiff businessmen who offered financial assistance), Mr James Irvine of Liverpool (well acquainted with Africa), Mr Henry Grattan Guinness (a Protestant evangelist and member of the Guinness brewing family) and his wife Mrs Fanny Guinness.

Fig 2. Rev Alfred Tilly

Tilly's suggestion was for an initiative that would take the benefits of Christianity to the interior of the African continent, specifically the people living along the banks of the Congo River. Speaking of Henry Morton Stanley's epic descent of the river he declared "All through these thousands of miles … Stanley did not meet one single Christian, or see a solitary man, woman, or child who had ever heard the gospel!"[10] And, in the opinion of Mrs Guinness, "We fully believe that no part of the world has so strong a claim on the energies of the Christian Church at this time as the continent of Africa, and especially its central regions".[11]

Accordingly, Tilly and friends formed an impromptu committee in the spring of 1877 "resolved to lose no time in sending forth some volunteers to introduce to the vast Congo Valley as many Christian evangelists as possible". How that was to be achieved was not clear, but Stanley's published letters suggested their objective was a realistic possibility.[12] Bearing in mind David Livingstone's concept of mission, their vision was clear: "To plant Christian communities all along the course of the Upper Congo and its tributaries."[13]

It is not sufficient merely to preach the gospel ... We must endeavour to show them a better way in everything; to teach them the arts of peace, to initiate them into a superior way of living, to heal all the sicknesses and mitigate their sufferings ... We must convince them that godliness hath the promise of life that now is, as well as of that which is to come. To plant self-sustaining and self-extending missions in Central Africa is our great object.[14,15]

Anticipating how the mission would function they recalled Livingstone once again and the following practical principle was agreed:

As it is believed that land and native labour can be secured at small cost the agents of the mission shall be men willing to avail themselves of these advantages, and, resolved to be as little burdensome as possible to the funds of the mission. No salaries are guaranteed, but the committee, as far as the means of doing so are placed in their hands, will supply the missionaries with such needful things as cannot be produced in the country.

Another innovative enthusiast for the evangelisation of Central Africa was Robert Arthington, an eccentric, wealthy bachelor from Leeds. Living in a single room of his large, inherited home he supported a variety of Christian enterprises. Combining his extensive knowledge of geography with a strongly held belief in the imminent return of Christ, he made strenuous efforts to facilitate anyone who would carry the Gospel across the whole unmapped centre of Africa; his aim was a chain of Christian missionaries from coast to coast. He offered £50 towards the expenses of the proposed new venture "but we reluctantly declined ... the expense would exceed fifty pounds by fifty multiplied by ten".[16]

Not to be daunted Arthington gave instead to the Baptist Missionary Society (BMS). He believed that there was a navigable river traversing the central region for which a boat would be necessary. The outcome was a brief, preliminary exploration of the lower reaches of the Congo River, in January 1878, by two BMS missionaries, George Grenfell and Thomas Comber. The conclusion was to approach the King of Kongo to the south of the river with a proposal to settle in his capital, São Salvador (now Mbanza Kongo, Angola), with a view to reaching the Central Basin by an overland route. By this means they hoped to avoid the numerous cataracts that were known to obstruct access to the upper reaches of the river.

The objectives of the Tilly-Guinness committee were well intentioned. Putting them into practice in an unknown, underexplored, tropical land, 4,000 miles distant, proved to be far, far more difficult and dangerous than they ever imagined. The Livingstone Inland Mission (LIM) would have a limited lifespan and would not fulfil its objective, but in its remarkable six short years on the banks of the lower Congo it succeeded in establishing a secure foothold from which its successor could sail along many thousands of miles of the Upper Congo River where it would flourish and remain for 114 years: the Congo Balolo Mission.

Hardly had Grenfell and Comber departed from the river but two young men, Henry Craven and a Danish sailor, Mr Strom, arrived at Embomma, a small trading post served by Portuguese and British ships, ninety miles upstream from the mouth of the Congo River. These two men were the pioneers of the Livingstone Inland Mission, the first Christian mission to settle in the Congo. Their express instructions were to advance as speedily as possible up the mighty river to the interior of the country, carrying the Christian gospel to the centre of the continent.

3

The Committee

To widen the basis of the new mission's Council the group was joined by the Right Hon Lord Polworth, Mr T. Coates of Paisley, Mr John Houghton of Liverpool and Mr T. Berger from Cannes. All were volunteers; there were to be no salaried officers. Alfred Tilly acted as secretary, the others provided support as promised and a few other friends joined the cause, but very soon the day-by-day task of establishing and running this entirely new, uncharted venture fell to the devoted and indefatigable Mrs Fanny Guinness, who was already responsible for a different Christian enterprise in the East End of London.

Fanny Emma Fitzgerald was born in Ireland in 1831. Her father led a distinguished career in the British army and became a journalist but when his wife died he struggled to care for his five children. When Fanny was eight he killed himself. However, before taking that final step he wrote a letter in the hope that whoever should receive it would care for the children. Remarkably, Arthur West, an actuary in London, and his wife Mary, both Quakers, responded to the strange request. Placing her siblings with friends, they took Fanny into their own home where she grew up enjoying the independent thinking of the mid-19th century Quakers. In the summer of 1860 she was introduced to Henry Guinness, a well-known non-conformist preacher who she married a few months later.[17]

Fig 3 . Rev Henry Grattan Guinness & Mrs Fanny E Guinness.

Henry Grattan Guinness enjoyed a privileged and very different upbringing,

7

having been born in Dublin in 1835 the grandson of Arthur Guinness the founder of the St James' Gate brewery and the international Guinness brewing dynasty.[18] The family was of non-conformist Protestant persuasion. Both his parents were Congregationalist, his mother being particularly devout.[19]

Henry was an unusual young man. When he experienced a sudden personal religious awakening he started preaching to his neighbours, opposing the oppression of Roman Catholicism. Aged twenty he went to England to study theology at New College, London, where he also developed his preaching skills in local churches and on street corners. New College and the study of theology was not a success and he left after a year. Guinness sought to model himself on George Whitefield and John Wesley, the renowned non-conformist Christian preachers of the 18th century notable for their open-air preaching but, unlike them, he was not an academic. Henry's fellow Irishman and friend, Thomas Barnardo, expressed his Christian concern by founding by a ground-breaking home for destitute and orphaned children in the East End of London that thrives today as the Barnardo's charity. Henry's focus was solely evangelism; as Fanny Guinness remarked of her husband on a later occasion "his mind is in heaven". On his 21st birthday his diary recorded his life's ambition: "to live preaching and to die preaching". The mid-19th century was a time of evangelical revival when churches were full and a handsome, eloquent preacher was in great demand. Declining an invitation to become the minister of the prestigious Moorfields Tabernacle, Whitefield's church in London, Guinness embarked on preaching tours of France, Switzerland, North America, Wales, Scotland and Ireland where he modified his earlier theme: "Protestants were in as much need of conversion as their Catholic compatriots."[20]

Michelle Guinness has provided a vibrant account of the couple's early years together, but sufficient for our purposes is to note their meeting in Dublin, in February 1866, with the missionary-explorer Hudson Taylor who had attracted wide attention for his work in China. Having arrived in China thirteen years previously he had set up the China Inland Mission and on hearing of this work Harry and Fanny expressed an interest in joining him. To their dismay he declined their offer. Because they were over thirty they would find acquisition of the Chinese language too difficult. However, recognising their disappointment and knowing of Henry's previous work, he suggested that they should remain in England to train other young men and women to take the gospel to China and other corners of the globe.

It would take another six years before Hudson Taylor's suggestion took root but in 1872 the vision for a training institute for prospective missionaries took shape. It would be in London and combine both theological teaching and practical crafts, as well as evenings spent in public preaching on the streets. All of this would be in the insalubrious environment of London's late 19th century East End, which he considered would prepare young men for the rigours of life in foreign countries. Furthermore, it would be an enterprise of faith and students would receive their training free of charge.

His wife understood Henry's vision but knew only too well that Henry was a visionary. He had no idea what it would take to make his vision possible, and the practical details were left to her.[21] The Stepney Institute was born, later to become the East London Training Institute for Home and Foreign Missions. Students from far and wide commenced their studies. They were mainly young working men with little previous education, including several from overseas. Henry continued as before, travelling, preaching and recruiting men for the Institute. The enormous task of funding, running and maintaining this extraordinary venture was left almost entirely to his wife Fanny, aged forty-one and the mother of six children.

The Institute was a great success. After a year it moved to much larger premises at Harley College, London. Within a few years there were seventy students and a staff of thirty, and before long it was expanded to include a women's college nearby (Doric Lodge) and a subsidiary, Cliff College, in the Derbyshire countryside. Students wishing to undertake medical work alongside evangelism studied part-time at the London Hospital Medical School. In 1875 the first graduates left to work in Burma, China, France, India, Japan and South Africa. By its sixth year over 1,000 hopeful applications had been received, more than 200 had been accepted and 106 had completed the course. Of these, nineteen started work in England and Scotland, ten in Europe and the remainder in distant lands.[22] In 1878, it was the East London Institute that provided the first two missionaries who would sail into the mouth of the Congo River and establish the Livingstone Inland Mission on African soil: Henry Craven and Mr Strom.

4

The Congo

———

There lies the Congo Kingdom, great and strong,
Already led by us to Christian ways;
Where flows the Zaire, the river clear and long,
A stream unseen by men of olden days.[23]

In the 1870s Congo was a single region that now comprises the Democratic Republic of Congo (DRC, Congo Kinshasa) and the Republic of Congo (Congo Brazzaville). Encompassing more than 900,000 square miles it was almost the size of Europe, was the largest country in sub-Saharan Africa and the eleventh largest country in the world. To the east were the snow-capped mountains of the Rwenzori mountain range, to the north extensive grasslands, to the south open plateaus and savannahs, and in the centre a vast, dense tropical rain forest.

The Congo River, the expected passageway to the interior, was the deepest and second largest in the world. At 2,920 miles in length it was fed by another 13,000 miles of tributaries that drained the 300,000 square miles of the great Central Basin. This region, the objective of the mission, was covered by rainforest and large areas of swamp. The gentle westward flow of the thousand-mile central portion of the river would be easily navigable. It then widened to form a long lake, the Malebo Pool known previously as Stanley Pool. This was fifteen miles wide and now separates Kinshasa, Capital of the DRC from its neighbour Brazzaville, capital of the Republic of Congo. Thereafter the river descended a thousand feet through deep canyons and thirty two cataracts over a distance of 232 miles before resuming a relatively tranquil flow for its final 140 miles to the sea.

King Dom João II of Portugal (1481–1495) is credited as initiator of geographical exploration in the interior of Africa.[24] At his behest the notable Portuguese navigator Diogo Cão explored the west coast of Africa and, in

1482, was the first European to enter the Congo River. During the course of his first voyage down the west African coast, he observed "a strong current setting from the land, the waters of which were discoloured, and when tasted, found to be fresh … So violent and so powerful … forcing a broad passage that for the space of twenty leagues [69 miles] it preserves its fresh water unbroken by the briny billows which encompass it on every side." Claiming the river and the land for Portugal he erected a padrão, a stone pillar, at Shark Point, the seaward point on the south bank.

In the autumn of 1485 he returned and progressed 140 miles up the river, reaching the Falls of Yellala (Lelala), 12 miles upstream from what is now the town of Matadi, and the highest navigable point of the river. Here he erected another padrão: "Here reached the ships of the enlightened king John II of Portugal, Diogo Cão." The explorer commenced trade with the people of the Kingdom of Kongo on the river's southern shore, but he died before reaching Portugal again. A century later the Portuguese explorer Duarte Lopez visited the coast in 1578, sailed up the Congo River as Cão had done, and then stayed at the coast for twelve years. His very detailed account of the way of life in the ancient Kingdom of Kongo was published subsequently by Filippo Pigafetta in Rome in 1591, although a translation into English appeared only in 1881, three years after Craven and Strom's arrival at Boma.[24] The following century saw the Dutch conquest of the region in 1641. Their occupation was short-lived and the Kingdom of Kongo returned to Portuguese control seven years later. Based on information gleaned during this time the Dutch writer Olfert Dapper published a map that showed a very large river extending a thousand miles further upstream than that known by Cão, although no attempt to explore the river was recorded.[25]

Over the following two centuries slave traders from Portugal, France and elsewhere in Europe, including dealers from England, visited the coast in increasing numbers. In the early 19th century two British naval expeditions explored the navigable lower reaches of the river where they both encountered English, Spanish, Portuguese and Brazilian ships engaged in the illicit slave trade dealing with local chiefs to export two thousand enslaved Congolese per year. The river was also known as "Zaire", a name probably derived from the Portuguese adaptation of the Kikongo word meaning "the river that swallows all rivers".[26] The second British expedition, led by Captain J. K. Tuckey in 1816, ventured a further 160 miles on foot towards the interior.[27]

Fig 4 Captain Tuckey's Voyage in Africa: The Fetiche Rock, looking down the river.

Of the Congolese there was no written language, their only clock was the sun and their calendar the moon. Beyond the Yellala Falls the river was said to extend hundreds of miles towards the interior but of the people nothing was known. The river itself was narrow and at intervals interrupted by rapids and cataracts that could be raging torrents. The riverbanks were mostly steep, the only discernible path being the intermittent tracks made by passing groups of enslaved men, women and children on their way to the coast. At the furthermost reach of the exploration Tuckey recorded that the people had never seen a white man before and concluded "This excursion convinced us of the total impracticability of penetrating with any number of men by land, along the sides of the river … The idea of civilizing Africa appears to be utterly useless." Most of his men succumbed to fever. He died a few days later.

In 1858 the German ethnologist Dr Adolf Bastian visited the mouth of the Congo briefly[28], but the next source of information was a visit by British consul Richard Burton,[29] who paid a semi-official visit in the hope of regaining his health in the highlands above the river. Leaving the valley the countryside was very different: populous villages, huts of wicker-work, trees and a variety of crops. It was near here that, twenty-five years later, the early missionaries would create a successful settlement that formed the focus for the young Livingstone Inland Mission. Speaking of Congolese beliefs Burton observed that "Christianity has entirely disappeared, despite the prodigious efforts of the sixteenth and seventeenth centuries."

On 3rd August 1877 the residents of Boma were surprised to receive a hand-written message, brought by a Congolese carrier, from someone calling himself H. M. Stanley. Requesting urgent supplies and assistance this unknown explorer was at a place called Nsanda, 200 miles upstream, where he was exhausted and unable to travel any further. The letter was addressed "To any gentleman who speaks English at Embomma" and concluded "The supplies must arrive within two days or I may have a fearful time of it among the dying. PS. You may not know me by name: I therefore add that I am the person that discovered Livingstone in 1871. – H.M.S." There were similar messages written in French and Spanish.[30]

Supplies and men were dispatched and Stanley completed his descent of the Congo River on 9th August, 999 days after

Fig 5 Henry Morton Stanley.

his departure from Bogamoyo near Zanzibar on the African east coast. Of the 359 people who started with him three years before only eighty-two survived, plus six children born on the journey. Fifty-eight were killed in battles with tribesmen; forty-five had died of smallpox; nine had starved to death, and fourteen had drowned. The other 151 had succumbed to ulcers, typhoid fever, overdoses of opium, crocodiles and other causes. Within days Stanley took ship and was on his way, first with his faithful colleagues to Zanzibar, and then to England. Stanley's account of the journey and his observations of the country and its people were published in 1878. For the mission pioneers this was a few weeks after their departure from England. Henry Craven and his colleague were heading for an unknown land.

5

Congolese Society and Religious Beliefs

On arrival on the west coast of Africa in the 15th century the Portuguese found a large Kingdom of Kongo, ruled by a powerful monarch, the Manikongo (Mwane Kongo), with a capital at Mbanza Kongo (São Salvador). The kingdom occupied many hundreds of square miles of the coastal region that now lie within northern Angola, western Democratic Republic of Congo, Republic of Congo and southernmost Gabon. The Portuguese invaders were followed by Roman Catholic missionaries who arrived in 1491; they were welcomed, the King was baptised and Catholicism was adopted as the national religion. Churches and a cathedral were built and a strong priesthood developed, supported by Kongolese lay teachers. Many Christian texts were translated into Kikongo, the Bible was called Nkanda ukisi and the church Nzo a ukisi – "ukisi" meaning a charm but also holy.

The Christianity that developed in the kingdom was syncretic in that it incorporated traditional African beliefs and practices. In 1684 a young woman of high nobility, Dona Beatriz Kimpa Vita, was born. She was baptised, formed her own Christian movement and taught that God was only concerned with believers' intentions, not with sacraments or good works. She also opposed the Portuguese Catholic church because of its participation in the slave trade. For her opposition, she was burned at the stake at the age of twenty-two. In just a few years Kimpa Vita had developed a strong following, partly underpinned by her belief that Jesus was born of a Kongolese family. Her teachings, that became known as Antonianism, died out during the 18th century but, in the opinion of some, have connections with Kibanguism which has attracted more than twenty million adherents in the DRC since 1921. By the beginning of the 19th century, however, only a few remnants of distorted Catholicism were to be found amongst the people of the lower river. When British missionaries became established at Malebo Pool (Stanley Pool) they learned that life on the upper river was very different from the Kingdom of Kongo.

The population of Congo, currently more than 90 million, was estimated at the turn of the 20th century to be more than ten million. There were more than 250 different ethnic groups who spoke 240 different languages, and even more distinctive dialects. These Bantu languages shared a common, distant, origin indicative of a past sophisticated society. "The Bantu languages are soft, pliant, and flexible, to an almost unlimited extent. Their grammatical principles are founded on the most systematic and philosophical basis ... they are capable of expressing all the nicer shades of thought and feeling, and perhaps no other languages of the world are capable of more definiteness and precision of expression."[31]

The people of Congo encountered by the first European missionaries were part of the Bantu-speaking expansion from West Africa that commenced around 3500 BC and is thought to have reached the Central African basin by 500 BC. Living in villages, some with more than 1,000 inhabitants, organised and large enough to be considered towns, they remained isolated, surrounded by many miles of swamp and impenetrable forest. On the uplands, grasses growing as high as an elephant covered much of the landscape, broken up only by deep ravines and fast-flowing rivers. Thus, the Bantu society that had developed over many millennia, remained isolated from any external societal influence until the arrival of Arab ivory hunters and slavers from the east in the eighteenth century. In addition to the isolation the tribal groups were fiercely warlike; on many occasions both Livingstone and Stanley had to endure many miles of unwanted detours during their travels to avoid becoming embroiled in fearsome conflicts. It was for this reason that elaborate attempts were made to disguise village entrances to make access as difficult as possible. At the mouth of the Lulonga River village houses were built on platforms in the water rather than on the riverbank, residents hiding their valuable elephant tusks out of sight in the water beneath their homes. Inter-tribal warfare was essential as a source of women for wives, food by stealing crops, and slaves for labour, meat and ritual sacrifice. Battles were planned very carefully and enjoined only when needful and likely to succeed. Riverine villagers would only attack neighbours living upstream of their own location. At the conclusion of a fight a speedy retreat was essential. Paddling their canoes against the strong current would be slow and invite costly retaliation; returning downstream, aided by the current, would ensure a safe home coming. Also, wars were of planned duration. Capturing territory or domination of other tribes was not the objective; they were not fought to the death or for outright victory. Neighbours would be essential for the future to supply continuing needs. As soon as sufficient women, goods and slaves had been taken, retreat was honourable.

Each village existed under the separate government of its own chief or head man who exercised considerable authority, although his opinion would always follow the formalised discussions of a "palaver" in which all the men of the village would participate. But, despite this defined social structure, it was the nganga, or witch doctor, who exercised a far superior power over the lives of the people. "Every village has its nganga nkissi and it is the superstitious dread in which the people hold him, owing to his supposed secret understanding with the spirit-world, that enables him to influence affairs of public importance as well as to be supreme in those of a domestic nature."[32] From infancy children wore charms tied around the wrist by parents anxious to do all within their powers to protect their offspring from harm. As time passed, more and more such miscellaneous objects were worn or placed around the family hut to fend off evil, sickness and attacks from wild creatures. "No man ever goes on a journey, no matter how short, without a string of charms about his neck, to ward off death ... death from wild animals ... at the hand of strangers ... the death curse."[33] Should these fail and someone became ill the nganga would be called. If somebody died it could not have been due to natural causes; someone, in this life or the next, must have caused the fatality. On the assumption that it was someone in the local community the nganga would consult his magic, a culprit would be named and a trial by drinking poison arranged. If the suspect died he or she was obviously guilty, if not they were considered innocent. It was more than likely that the outcome could be determined by suitable payments to the nganga in advance, but the sums demanded were affordable only by the wealthy. Cannibalism, too, was characteristic of many of the Congo Bantu tribes although it was not practised on the lower river.

In 1889 the Congo Balolo Mission would become established in the region of the Lulanga (Lulonga), Lopori and Maringa tributaries of the Congo River and it was here that Herbert Ward, appointed by Stanley as an officer of the Société Anonyme Belge in 1884, commanded a fortified station among the

Balolo people. Here he witnessed cannibalism almost weekly[34] but reported subsequently that cannibalism had been repressed in the vicinity of the State post and was not universal among the Balolo tribes.[35] Human flesh was considered a delicacy. When missionaries remonstrated with local people the reply was simple, "You kill your goats and no one finds fault with you; let us kill our meat". Human meat had special qualities that were very desirable. Common belief held that the spirit of a man would be imbued by eating his flesh; a renowned warrior would be thus become a spiritual feast.

Ritual human sacrifice was also practised. This was not a religious practice to appease the gods but a practical provision for the wellbeing of the dead in their afterlife. It was carried out in honour of only the wealthiest and therefore the most eminent and renowned men, after whose death a variable number of slaves, and sometimes wives, would be beheaded in a highly ritualistic ceremony. The bodies would then accompany that of their master or husband in the expectation that they would provide for his needs in such afterlife as there might be. As in life, so in death.

Life expectancy was probably little more than thirty years. Human life was counted of little worth. For Ward it was the everyday cruelty that left a lasting impression:

The white man can never, as long as he may live in Africa, conquer his repugnance to the callous indifference to suffering that he meets with everywhere, in Arab and Negro. The dying are left by the wayside to die. The weak drop on the caravan road, and the caravan passes on. Life is for the strong and the powerful, and the slave – well, perhaps he is fortunate if left undisturbed to await death, which brings him freedom from countless miseries.[36]

However, Ward was able, also, to acknowledge and appreciate incidents of kindness and affection between adults and toward children. Among the cannibal tribes of the interior "I have observed more frequent traits of affection for wife and children among them than are exhibited in the conduct of the people of the lower country. A native of the upper river will embrace his wife ere he sets out on a fighting expedition, or will fondle his child, and even give the child its morning bath in the river if the mother is unable to perform that act."[37]

In the villages and towns of the upper river the task of the menfolk was to maintain the protective stockades, build and repair their simple houses, hunt from time to time, kill elephants as necessary, engage witch doctors if anyone was ill or died, spend many hours discussing palavers, wage war on neighbouring tribes and celebrate victory for days on end. Men did not generally participate in childcare until teenage boys required teaching and training in ritual camps deep in the forest. In the home, men ate separately from their wives and children.

In the view of Ward:

The condition of the Congo native, after putting aside his chances of being murdered and eaten, or taken as a slave, is greatly superior to that of the poorer classes in some parts of the civilized world. His wants are few, and they are easily satisfied, with slight physical effort. Fish abound in the rivers; game can be trapped in the forest; all the necessary materials for hut-building and canoe-making are at hand. A genial sun shines upon him daily, and at night he coils around his fire in the hut with no care for the morrow's victuals and no heart-breaking prospect of misery in the coming winter for want of meat and shelter.[38]

Although there was some truth in this balmy view, Ward was ignoring the lot of Congo women whose role was far more arduous. Girls became wives and mothers in their early teens. When a baby girl was born there was always great rejoicing because she would become a source of income for her parents. Enquiries from potential husbands were negotiated from a very early age and the girl would usually be betrothed by the age of five. Regular dowry payments from the future husband started immediately. The girl would be married at twelve and pregnant by fourteen. Thereafter she joined in the tasks of every village woman. Each morning, with her child on her back, she walked to the nearby stream to collect water for the day before going to tend her garden, gather nuts, fish from the riverbank, prepare cassava, cook and bring up her children. Maintaining a garden to grow the staple cassava root required the constant clearing of encroaching forest; heavy work for the women whose menfolk declined to help. When a man died his son inherited his father's wives, it being his responsibility to take them into his household and care for them. The daily domestic chores demanded of every woman were repetitive, laborious, grinding tasks for which slaves were ideal. Thus, the capture of slaves was a welcome contribution to family life. It also kept the gene pool refreshed as female slaves were often taken to become wives. Stealing a wife from another village or tribe was cheaper than buying a local woman whose complex dowry payments could be demanded life-long.

John Harris, one of the early CBM missionaries, was singular among his colleagues in his study of Congo society. For his fellow missionaries inter-tribal fighting, the universal practice of polygyny, domestic slavery and other social mores were of great concern, being immediate and obvious examples, to them, of the darkness in which they perceived Congo society was mired. For Harris, equally devoted to the task of evangelising a pagan people, it was, nonetheless, important to "probe the mind and thought of the African".[39] To this end when travelling and finding himself alone, he would stay in the hut of a hunter or with fisherfolk in their sheds on the riverbank where he found a welcome and an opportunity to be the student rather than the teacher. Concerning warfare Harris's conclusions were enlightening: "Most African tribes set the civilised world an example in their unwritten methods of preventing war, or after war has been declared, of bringing it to an early termination." Thinking of the British Empire and the behaviour of his home country's European neighbours he opined that the Foreign Ministers of the Great Powers of Europe could do well to learn from studying the peace principles of so-called "barbarous tribes".[40]

Accepting that missionaries were uninvited guests in a foreign community, he was keenly observant of the daily life of his newfound village neighbours.[41] Speaking of women, he noted "After sweeping the hut and opening the chicken coop the garden is her first charge ... then fishing ... or hunting in the forest for caterpillars ... to provide and cook the daily meals. Older women remain at home to make clay cooking pots, weave baskets and mats, crack palm kernels. There is no country whose women are so continuously industrious." When it came to travelling through the forest it was the woman who carried the load as her husband walked in front, but as Harris explained "To the uninitiated European it may seem callous for a man to walk in front of a woman struggling along with a 50-pound load on her head." However, "The African knows his business when on a journey: to protect his family from the ravages of wild animals no less than the violence of hostile tribes and must, therefore, always walk in front unencumbered by a load." Concerning polygyny:

The woman regards polygamy as a desirable condition. The position of the husband is gauged by his possessions ... she prefers being the wife

19

of a man who can afford to keep more than one. If a man possesses several wives the burden of agriculture, fishing and the domestic duties is proportionally lighter upon each individual. On the whole, the lot of the African woman is a hard one … but in her old age … it is the joy and privilege of the younger generation to support her.[42]

Commenting on the response of other missionaries to local customs he noted that in one mission no native was permitted sit down to Holy Communion if their hair was braided or oiled or if they used camwood powder on their bodies. In another mission, cicatrising and the extraction of eyelashes were sufficient reason to warrant suspension from church membership. In a few cases newly converted Christian men had been obliged to put away wives inherited from a deceased relative, but the women concerned had then experienced the disgrace of being outcasts from the social life of the tribe. "How far these simple customs should be checked has always seemed to me a matter of doubt … they cause serious dissensions among the [mission] staff … some missionaries seem to feel called upon to place these old-time customs almost on the level of criminal offences. There is enough that is evil in humanity … without arbitrarily introducing non-essentials which make it grievous to be borne."[43] To what extent these views were shared and practised by his fellow missionaries and later CBM staff will be considered later. Such was the way of life of the people amongst whom the missionaries hoped to live, but what of their religious beliefs?

Given the ancient origins of the Bantu people in West Africa and their subsequent isolation in the Central African rainforest the philosophy of late 19th century Congolese people would have been pre-Christian, pre-Jewish and pre-Hindu. Summarised by Baptist missionary W. Holman Bentley in 1893 the only Congolese idea of a god was a Being known by various names by the different tribal groups, none of which had any apparent specific derivation:

There is nothing that can be said to take the place of a religion throughout the whole region of the Congo. There is no idolatry, no system of worship; nothing but a vague superstition. The people have a name of God but know nothing further about him. The idea is not of an evil thing or they would wish to propitiate him. Hence, as they fear no

20

evil from God they do not trouble themselves about him in any way – never even invoke Him.

Some commentators interpreted the word "nkisi" to mean an idol, but McKittrick concurred with Bentley. "It is my firm belief that they had no idols previous to the introduction of Roman Catholicism. There are many fetich idols but the Congo people do not worship their idols, nor do they pray to them. They are really not objects of worship, but are used as charms, as means of protection in time of danger and to ward off evil spirits."[45] "The natives of the Congo are not idolators, and as they have no means of communicating with Nzambi (God), they betake themselves to charms."[46]

Suffice to say that the word has a sense of greatness and conveys the idea of a Supreme Being... The name of God is all that they know and certainly they have no notion of any means of communication between God and Man. They regard him as the Creator and the sender of rain but would never think of their voice being heard in heaven. They have a very decided idea of a future state; but as to what and where, opinion is much divided. There is not the remotest notion that death can be a cessation of being. If anyone dies they think that someone, living or dead, has established a connection with the unseen world, and somehow, and for some purpose, has 'witched away' the deceased ... There is a natural fear of death – the spirit world is an unknown land – but there is no apprehension of meeting Nzambi, nor is there a burden of sin. There is a sense of right and wrong. To steal, to lie, or to commit other crimes is considered wrong, but only a wrong to those who suffer thereby – there is no sense of God in it.[47]

Thus, Bentley was able to summarise the opportunity presented to the missionaries. "The knowledge of the name of God gives us a good basis to work upon. We can tell them that we bring them a message from Nzambi Himself, not a story of a white man's God, but their God and ours." Missionaries, of whatever calling, would find a blank page on which to write, a vacuum of religious belief that might be filled. The Pew Research Center has estimated that, in 2010, 95.8% of the Congolese population considered themselves to be Christian.[48] When Craven and Strom stepped ashore at Banana 140 years ago there were none.

6

The Livingstone Inland Mission

————

When Craven and Strom arrived at Banana they were offered hospitality by a European merchant who transported them upriver to Boma. While attempting to negotiate local assistance for their onward journey the two men became gravely ill with fever and were saved only by the prompt action of a European trader.

The Guinnesses were aware of the Tuckey expedition of 1816 and knew that most of its members had perished. Despite this, Craven and Strom sailed for the unknown, poorly equipped and ill prepared. The mission statement of the Livingstone Inland Mission comprised fine sentiments and words. The reality was different: despite their confidence that God would bless the endeavour the mission was, very nearly, a disastrous, short-lived failure.

Having survived this initial setback the two men succeeded in establishing a small base at Matadi sixty miles upriver, a journey upstream that took three or four days and would have to be repeated several times. As progress further upriver was prevented by the Yellala Falls they sought a more suitable location for their first mission settlement away from the river at Palaballa, a high plateau on the upper slopes of the Palaballa Mountains overlooking the river. It was here that a friendly King gave them land and was willing to countenance the presence of white men. Their accommodation was made with poles, matting and long grass for thatch. They also planted local fruit and a vegetable garden; no mean achievement given that the climb from the river to 1,600 feet was steep and the terrain extremely difficult.

Individual cataracts obstructing the river did not fall more than twelve feet, but the depth of the water ensured great ferocity. "The river came on gliding smoothly … until, as if exasperated by repeated checks, it lashed itself into white and roaring fury."[49] Of the hillsides bordering the river the British explorer Henry Johnston wrote in 1883: "The background is a wild jumble of hills, clefts and ravines in which the forest hides from the constantly recurring bush fires that sweep over the country when the grass is dry."[50]

Fifteen years later when it came to constructing a railway from Matadi to Malebo Pool it took an army of engineers and labourers four years to traverse twenty-six miles through these hills.[51] For the rookie missionaries this was slow, grinding work in an exhausting climate. "It is very damp at Palaballa. Morning and evening a thick mist surrounds everything and renders the place clammy and unhealthy ... the vegetation is very rich ... there are decided traces of Portuguese influence and many words of that language are introduced into the local dialect ... the natives are disposed to be impudent and even aggressive towards white men."[52] Mary Kingsley, an independent traveller who had spent several years exploring southern, central and west Africa, had different memories of Palaballa: "Those truly horrible Palaballa Mountains ... burning heat ... At the nights, the whole earth exhaling a heavy, hot breath."[53]

Within a few months Craven's colleague Strom was found to be unsuited for African service and returned home but two new recruits arrived, both from the East London Institute. Their arrival was invaluable in creating a more substantial settlement, but within two months Craven and Johnson found themselves burying their young colleague Telford, who had succumbed to fever. The mission's first death on the Congo.

Before any attempt at evangelism could be made there would have to be many months of practical labour, transporting supplies by boat and on foot, clearing plots of land, house

Fig 6. Henry Craven.

building and growing food. Livingstone's precept that the vanguard of Christian civilisation would require "practical men with practical skills" could not have been more true. Thanks to Henry Guinness's intuition, the students recruited by the East London Institute were mainly young men with artisan experience: a builder, carpenters, coach-builder, surveyor, sailors, a cattle farmer, mechanical engineers, as well as a customs-house officer, a soldier who had seen service in Zululand, a seaman on the teaching staff of

Greenwich Naval College, an architect, a doctor and a linguist.[12,54] For female students the theological curriculum also included cookery, dress-making, domestic economy, dispensing, general minor nursing, lectures in tropical medicine and for some, specific training in midwifery.[55] All of these different skills would be essential for the success of a pioneering mission and it was a credit to the tutors at the Institute that such an innovative approach had been adopted.

In addition, there was the question of language. With no teacher to guide them the process of learning a completely new, tonal, unwritten tongue was slow, but without it survival on the Congo would be impossible. With commendable determination significant progress was made and the beginnings of the Livingstone Inland Mission were established although progress was far slower and more complicated than any had imagined. As Mrs Guinness was to write several years later:

> The valley of the Congo is not, like South Africa or Natal, a sphere suited to Christian colonists. Agriculture is out of the question for Europeans, and the only means of possible support is trade. To carry on trade not only requires capital, as well as much time … it inevitably obscures the true character of a Christian mission … Not knowing fully the circumstances, we could not realise this at the outset. Our principal qualification for the task was a deep conviction that obedience to Christ required the attempt, and a confidence that He would bless the endeavour.[54]

Not in the least discouraged, the pioneers pressed on and were joined by Craven's wife, a nurse, and four others. They brought with them donkeys from Madeira and a gang of "Kroo-boys" recruited from the Cote d'Ivoire. Krumen were a particular ethnic group who had worked for many years as sailors on slave ships. They became renowned for their strength, commitment to work if well paid, and for their ability to work as porters in the western and Central African climate. Having grown up in a malaria-endemic region they were also considered to be "fever resistant". With these added resources Richards and his wife were able to trek a distance of fifty miles up the Cataract Gorge to Banza Manteka (also known as Banza Manteke) where they planted crops and raised pigs, goats and fowls. Towards the end of the year two more recruits arrived.

In England, by 1880, the enormity of the task faced by the embryo mission was eventually recognised by the London Committee. The initial volunteers had done remarkably well but it became increasingly obvious that a larger, coordinated team was needed, provided with more plentiful supplies, building materials and barter goods. In addition, the meagre funds available initially would have to be supplemented considerably. This was going to be a costly venture but in March 1880 such a team, better organised and better supplied, sailed for Congo.

The leader was Adam McCall, an architect and surveyor who had spent six years in South Africa travelling thousands of miles and visiting remote mission stations of the London Missionary Society and French Protestant missionaries. A recently converted Christian, he had completed a year's study at the East End Institute. He also paid for his own voyage, equipment and supplies.[56] Everything possible was done to ensure that nothing needful would be forgotten. Funding from British churches met the cost, and the Royal Geographical Society and the king of the Belgians made grants of scientific equipment. McCall's intention was to disembark men and provisions as quickly as possible at Banana, and proceed with all speed by boat to Banza Manteka from where they would make a single determined advance on foot to reach Malebo Pool before the end of the dry season. It was a bold plan, based on his experience in South Africa and the Zambezi rather than the Congo. The likelihood of achieving this objective was remote. They would have only five months to reach the upper river before the rainy season commenced. Illness among his colleagues and the delayed arrival of supplies were not encouraging. On reaching Boma the new recruits learned of the death of Petersen. Left alone unintentionally at Banza Manteka he had become ill and by the time help arrived it was too late. It was the Mission's second death in two years.

By the end of May a station had been established by the Yellala Falls but bringing up the rest of the party and supplies took until the end of September. The dry season was over and the rains were about to start. Undeterred, McCall pressed on. Stanley had descended the left bank of the Congo round the cataracts but on his return he had chosen the north bank, which McCall decided to follow in the expectation that it would be an easier route. Progress was slow, however. Furthermore, the imported donkeys were unsuited to the terrain and the climate of the Congo. Most died and their loads were transferred to the Kroo-boys. By 27th October McCall reached

Manyanga, which was about two-thirds of the way from the coast to Malebo Pool. Here he negotiated with two of the local kings and purchased a plot of land on which to build with well-populated villages nearby. Their arrival was welcomed cautiously because Stanley had preceded them and his men had behaved badly, but recognising McCall's intentions the villagers permitted him to stay. Welcoming him, they soon provided "an abundance of provisions". This station would become known as Bemba and play an important role in the early life of the LIM. Four colleagues were ill[57] and Mr & Mrs Vickers had fallen out with their colleagues and had returned to England.[58]

"The main difficulty to be overcome is transport of goods and supplies, the farther we get from the coast the greater this difficulty becomes. So much of our work this season has been only preparatory to the future work. Large allowances must be made for climate, sickness, native slowness and hindrances of various kinds. However, everything is in the Lord's almighty and loving hands. He can, and will, help us."[59] Considering how to proceed to Malebo Pool McCall concluded that the best way would be by the river wherever possible, but it was not to be. Adam McCall would not make that journey, nor would he see the Upper Congo that had been his dream. When exploring the Zambezi he had contracted amoebic dysentery which now recurred. He left for England and died en route on the island of Madeira on 25th November. Mrs Guinness's tribute summarised the vital contribution McCall had made to the mission: "He infused new hope and courage into its members who were, at the time of his arrival, somewhat cast down and discouraged by the difficulties of various kinds".[59]

In the course of the first four years twenty-six young volunteers had started work with the mission, including four wives of missionaries. Of these, three proved unsuited to the work, two had been invalided home and five had died. Writing several years later Mrs Guinness recalled "It was foreseen that the difficulties would be great, though how great none of us at the time realized. Had we done so we might never have attempted the mission".[60] So much time spent on the mundane practicalities of everyday life left little for the far more important tasks of mission. Funds in Britain were donated for improved transport and a new boat, constructed on the Thames, arrived. The *Livingstone*, the fastest steamer on the river, transformed the lives of the missionaries.

By this time LIM missionaries were by no means the only Europeans

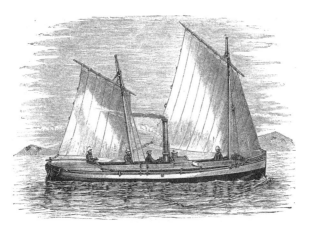

Fig 7. SS Livingstone on the Lower River.

hoping to establish a presence on the Upper Congo. The Baptist Missionary Society, also seeking to take the gospel to the African interior, had tried unsuccessfully to find a route to Malebo Pool from São Salvador, the capital of the Kingdom of Kongo. Realising that they would have to follow the LIM example, George Grenfell arrived in 1880. In a completely different context H. M. Stanley had also returned, this time in the employ of King Leopold II of the Belgians. Under the guise of a philanthropic venture, the Comité d'Etudes du Haut-Congo (CEHC), he was charged with the task of establishing a chain of trading and supply posts from Boma to Malebo Pool that would secure a rapid and reliable route to the interior for the King's covert commercial ambition. Furthermore, the French Government had ambitions for the Congo and their envoy, the Italian explorer Savorgnan de Brazza, had reached the north bank of the Pool from the east coast in 1880. Here he negotiated a treaty with local chiefs, established a French settlement at Mfoa, later to be called Brazzaville, and laid claim to the north bank of the river on behalf of France. On 29th January 1881 it was two BMS missionaries, Thomas Comber and H. E. Crudgington, who were the first to reach Malebo Pool. Stanley followed six months later,[61] accompanied by the first Roman Catholic missionaries.[62]

As 1882 dawned a clearer strategy emerged from the deliberations of the mission leadership in London. The year would be devoted to consolidating the position on the lower river by building a sixth and seventh station equipped with workshops and stores sufficient to support a party who would build a promised steamer on the upper river, the *Henry Reed*. A new recruit, Dr Aaron Sims, would establish a medical mission and more missionaries would be recruited in readiness for the expected advance to the interior of the country. However, a letter received in London in March of that year reported that excellent progress had been made already. The sixth station had been established on the south bank and school teaching commenced, and a seventh station followed thirty miles further upstream. Later, Stanley complimented the missionaries on their achievement. "I wish my chiefs had seen this pretty little station ... the mission cottage as dainty as any residence need be ... a spacious garden, a well-kept court ... surrounded by storerooms, kitchen and schoolroom ... my sojourn for twenty hours was enjoyed with the most exquisite pleasure."[63]

A small but increasing European settlement, named Leopoldville (now known as Kinshasa), had become established on the south bank of Malebo Pool, stimulated by Stanley's activities to develop commerce on behalf of King Leopold. The countryside around the Pool was very different from the lower river. "A beautiful lake with its forest-clad islands, its placid waters and its wooded cliffs. On ascending the river higher than Stanley Pool [the former name for Malebo Pool] the scenery becomes much more tropical ... we are at last in the great central basin of Africa and in the dense forest belt."[64] With several villages and large cassava fields nearby there was a regular market selling food, fish and cloth, all traded using brass rods as currency. Recognising the potential of this location Sims obtained from Stanley an eight-acre parcel of land on which to build a mission station including a small hospital, the first in Congo. By the end of April 1882 there were twenty-one missionaries, albeit that some were in England recovering their health and others were engaged in other activities on behalf of the mission while on furlough. Having reached Leopoldville a secure base had been created, and a reliable supply route from the coast was operating successfully. Evangelism, the essential objective of mission, had commenced. In addition, the British Baptist missionaries had built their own separate station on the banks of the Pool. Once again Stanley was most complimentary: "We live well and happily here at Leopoldville I have no reason to regret having given ground to your mission ... I may say the most complete affair I have seen on the Congo. There is no necessity for me to reiterate the assurance of my keenest sympathy with mission work. Every assistance I can give will be ungrudgingly given to the cause for which, I believe, we are all working."[65]

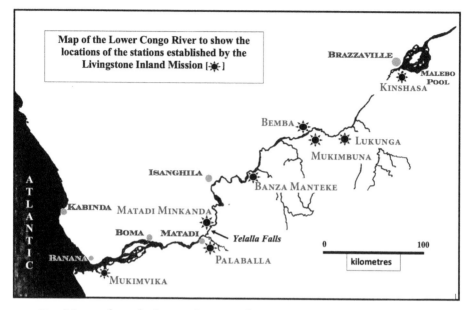

Fig 8 Map to show the Lower Congo and mission stations established by the Livingstone Inland Mission. *RR Hall.*

The first objective of the Livingstone Inland Mission, a Christian presence in the interior of Congo, had been accomplished. However, "We have all along felt that, while to reach the Upper Congo must be our first endeavour, Stanley Pool must be regarded as the starting point. This interior plateau is the future sphere of the Livingstone Inland Mission."

Barely had they settled at Leopoldville but Sims was anxious to make a start on exploring the upper river. "I am constantly thinking of the 'regions beyond' of whose inhabitants we hear and see plenty here. The country is quiet, the men fully occupied with trade and the women planting." Late in 1882 he spent two months travelling by canoe, visiting many places and reaching as far as Bolobo, some 120 miles upstream from Leopoldville. "I came back with Mr Stanley, who has arrived here from his great journey of five months exploration and work past the Equator ... practically open right up to the Stanley Falls ... to his credit, as well as to God's glory, without lifting a gun. With other dangerous and savage tribes he has concluded treaties thus opening the river to all. His kindness to me has been very great."[66]

Before the year was out they had built a station, known as Equator Station, near Wangata (now Mbandaka) at a distance of 400 miles upstream from

29

Leopoldville. More importantly Equator Station was well within the territory of the Balolo people, one of the largest of the Bantu tribes in the Congo. The first LIM missionaries were at work on the Upper Congo.

Stanley had already established a commercial station there. It was a centre for the many different tribespeople of the interior and gave ready access to many rivers and villages in the interior:

> The district is very thickly populated but we know nothing of the country beyond a few miles inland owing to the timid suspiciousness of the people. We have not yet been able to do much systematic study of the Kayansi language … they speak three different languages and we have ordered a small printing press so that we may be able to print short reading lessons in each. We feel assured that our presence here is already influencing the people for the good, though we are so little able as yet to communicate to them the gospel.[67]

After all the setbacks of the first four years this was progress indeed. New recruits arrived from England, languages were mastered, simple school teaching, village visiting and preaching had commenced. And they worked in close collaboration with the Baptist missionaries. George Grenfell travelled more extensively upstream. "Through the efforts put forth during the last year we know much more about the tributaries of the Congo and the people inhabiting their banks than we formerly knew. Mr Grenfell has done the largest share of this important work."[68]

In London, thought had already been given to the practical requirements of transport on the upper river.[69] The *Livingstone* was giving sterling service on the lower river but the craft needed for the upper river would be a very different and expensive undertaking. "While we were pondering and praying about this matter one morning, there reached us, from the Antipodes, a promise of the gift of just such a steamer as should be needed for the upper Congo. Mrs Reed [of Tasmania] presents a steamer to the mission and wishes it to be called in memory of her late husband, the Henry Reed." The cost of transporting the boat to Congo was met by an American supporter[69]; the construction would be tested on the Thames, dismantled and shipped to the Congo where it would be carried piecemeal by more than 1,000 porters from Boma to Malebo Pool and reassembled by amateur engineer-missionaries on a slipway built previously by the BMS for the construction of their steamer the *Peace*.[70]

Fig 9 PS Henry Reed.

Prior to the arrival of the *Henry Reed* Sims had accompanied Grenfell on a 4,000-mile exploratory journey on the upper river. Both missions intended to work in the interior, so the purpose of the voyage was to locate the most populous neighbourhoods, the extent over which certain languages prevailed, and strategic positions for future stations. Initially they observed signs of cannibalism: villages where paths were marked out with human skulls and the villagers wearing necklaces of human teeth. Some towns numbered 10,000 inhabitants; most were friendly and gave the explorers food and firewood, but others were hostile. Nearing the Stanley Falls they entered the territory of the Arab slave traders led by the powerful and notorious Tippu Tip, also the hunters of ivory plundering the elephant population to make their wealth in Zanzibar. On the banks of the river there were villages destroyed by fire, and on the water hundreds of canoes filled with fugitives creeping along by day and night, wreckage floating by, the property of cruelly destroyed towns. The missionaries could do nothing but return downstream better informed and wondering at the magnitude of the task to which they were now committed.[71] This was their introduction to "The Interior" where the millions who "lived in darkness" needed to hear the Christian gospel. Having reached the upper river the Livingstone Inland Mission was on the brink of fulfilling its dream. More than a dream, it was what the founders believed to be God's intention, for which thirty-three volunteers had devoted all their energies and for which eight had died. In

London, however, the fulfilment of that vision had become somewhat less certain.

In 1880 Alfred Tilly resigned as Secretary, finding that the busy life as pastor of a large church precluded further involvement with the mission. After long deliberation Henry and Fanny Guinness agreed that the East London Institute should adopt the LIM and take over responsibility for its recruitment, organisation and funding. Mrs Guinness was appointed Secretary.[72] Over the next few years she received a great deal of help from colleagues within the Institute and from the missionaries on furlough. The generous support of churches and individuals met the escalating costs, but the responsibility lay heavily with Mrs Guinness; she was fifty-four and had suffered a facial palsy. Founding the Livingstone Inland Mission had been an inspired vision but there were growing doubts concerning its sustainability under the aegis of the East London Training Institute and her direction.

During previous visits to the USA the Guinnesses had made the acquaintance of Dr J. N. Murdock of Boston, secretary to the American Baptist Missionary Union. This missionary society, founded in 1813, had 240 missionaries working in seventeen different locations in Asia, Africa, Europe and America. On learning that the ABMU were seeking an opening in Central Africa, representatives of their executive committee were invited to London to discuss the future of the LIM. Correspondence explains the thinking behind this approach. "The thought immediately occurred to me that if the American Baptist's Union is wishing to undertake a mission in Africa it would be better to transfer it [the LIM] to some larger and well organised society. If the American Baptists were willing to undertake it I would gladly surrender it to them. They have resources sufficient to enable them to carry it on vigorously, and the English Baptists would probably welcome their cooperation."[73] Agreement was reached that the ABMU would take over the staff of the LIM, its members having consented to the transfer, together with all the stations, steamers, and property of the mission.[74] The reasons given for choosing the ABMU to take over the future work of the LIM were threefold. Although the LIM was a non-denominational mission all its missionaries practised adult baptism by immersion. The evangelical stance of the ABMU was closely allied to the principles of the LIM so there would be no doctrinal difficulty if the two societies should be merged. As the only other society working in the Congo was the English BMS there would be a common approach to evangelism, church organisation and worship.

Fig 10 Memorial to the early pioneers of the Livingstone Inland Mission.

Furthermore, given that the *New York Herald* had sponsored Stanley's search for Livingstone "There seemed something appropriate in an arrangement which placed in American hands the first mission established on the great river opened up to the world by American capital and enterprise. But for the New York Herald the Congo River might have long remained as unknown as during past ages."[74]

On 9th September 1884 the Livingstone Inland Mission ceased operations.[75] It had not been an easy decision but one driven by practical necessity. Mrs Guinness would write several years later "It was not without some measure of pain that we took this important step for the Livingston Inland Mission was very dear to our hearts. It was not because we were weary of it that we parted with it, but for its good."[76] What the missionaries in Congo thought of this decision is not recorded but they would, no doubt, have felt immense gratitude for Mrs Guinness. There was no question that their work in Congo would be interrupted, none gave up the work to which they had committed themselves. At the time of the transfer the LIM had twenty-four missionaries. Henry Craven, the first of the pioneers who with Strom had established the first station at Palaballa, died just five weeks after the transfer to the ABMU had been agreed. Messrs Frederickson and Westlind, not being Baptists, formed a new Swedish mission on the Congo.[77] The stations at Matadi and Bemba had been closed, leaving Palaballa and Banza Manteka on the lower river; Lukunga in the cataract region; Leopoldville on the south shore of Stanley Pool, and Equatorville on the Upper River. Banza Manteka had the honour of being the site where the first Protestant Church in Congo was gathered and the first permanent building for Christian worship erected. After six years and nine months on the "mother of rivers" the Livingstone Inland Mission was no more. However, within five years the Congo Balolo Mission would follow to implement the original vision for the Upper Congo.

7

Malaria

———

The greatest impediment to any European colonisation of the Congo in the late 19th century was malaria. Causing prolonged periods of debilitating malaise and fever, it cost the lives of many early missionaries.

When Tuckey and his crews first arrived in the Congo his ship remained moored away from the shore, where he noted there were very few mosquitos. However, as soon as the party disembarked at Boma Tuckey's colleagues started to fall ill with fever. The symptoms described by the assistant surgeon to the expedition, Mr McKerrow, suggest that the problem was malaria.[78] Later when Mrs Guinness wrote of the health risks in the Congo she was well aware of previous experience. "Do we not all know about 'Tuckey's expedition' of which not one returned to tell the tale? Did not our own mission lose twelve out of fifty in seven years? Has not the sister mission [the BMS] been even more severely tried?" Mrs Guinness also noted the behaviour of mercantile companies that "count upon the fatality of service in these regions and give higher pay". She then draws the conclusion, so common at the time, "Can there be any question at all that the climate is a murderous one? The deadly nature of the climate of equatorial Africa is an undeniable fact."[79]

Stanley drew similar conclusions. Having suffered over 120 fevers and observing those of 260 Europeans it was his view that the sickness was due to three causes: droughts, malaria, and drink.[80] We should also recall that the 19th century was, in Europe, the era when people "caught a chill" and died, while others died of "exhaustion". Mrs Guinness concurred. "While I do not deny that there is a certain quantity of miasm in the air, bad air, malaria, my belief is that it was not the least of the evils from which the members of our expedition suffered. If our dear missionary friends can guard against these two things, frequent exposure to chills, and the constant presence of bad air … they will be fairly safe on the Congo."[81]

The cause of malaria and its transmission by the bite of an infected mosquito was not understood until the research of Ross and others published in 1897.[82] However, the illness it caused had been known to travellers for centuries. Known by a variety of names including periodic fever, remitting fever and, at its most serious, haematuric fever, it caused recurrent attacks of fever, debilitating fatigue and death. Treatment with an extract from the bark of the South American cinchona tree had been known to be effective since the 17th century. From this the drug quinine had been manufactured in large quantities since 1820 and Warburg's Tincture (a secret concoction which included quinine) had been widely available in Europe since 1834. Information published by the Government in India in 1866 reported that 99% of cases of malarial fever could be cured with quinine.[83] More recent reviews suggest that cure rates depended on the amount of quinine taken, but we can conclude that for the majority of fevers experienced by the missionaries, quinine could have been curative.[84] Furthermore, the decimation of troops on both sides of the American Civil War (1861–1865) by malaria had received widespread attention, together with the finding that quinine given prophylactically was most effective.[85] The *Colonist's Medical Handbook*, published in 1890, the same year that Mrs Guinness published her account, recommended the use of prophylactic quinine: "Quinine is nearly everywhere obtainable. It is always a good safeguard, when in marshy or malarious districts ... Never go to work in the morning without taking a little quinine."[86]

Mary Kingsley's views on African life were sometimes provocative but her observations on malaria were informative:

> Other parts of the world have more sensational out-breaks of death from epidemics of yellow fever and cholera, but there is no other region in the world that can match West Africa for the steady kill, kill, kill that its malaria works on the white men who come under its influence ... The prophylactic action of quinine is its great one ... by taking it when in a malarious district in a dose of five grains a day, you keep down the malaria which you are bound, even with every care, to get into your system.[87]

Quinine powder was so bitter that British officials stationed in early 19th-century India and other tropical posts began mixing quinine powder with soda and sugar, and a basic tonic water was created. The first commercial tonic water was patented in 1858 by Erasmus Bond followed by Schweppes' "Indian Quinine Tonic" in 1870. These products were aimed specifically at the growing market of the overseas British who, every day, had to take a preventative dose of quinine. When the British population started to mix their medicinal quinine tonic with gin the now ubiquitous "G&T" came into fashion. Stanley was not a teetotaller but both he and Mrs Guinness seem to have ignored the reports of the British army and numerous expatriates living in India and elsewhere that a daily "Gin & Tonic" was an excellent prophylaxis against malaria. Many years later Winston Churchill is reputed to have observed that G&T saved the British Empire. In her chapter on the health risks of the Congo Mrs Guinness adopted Stanley's "Fourteen Rules for a life in Central Africa" but introduced total abstinence alterations. Rule 7: "Observe the strictest temperance and drop all thought of tonics." Why she and her colleagues could not recognise a distinction between G&T and the use of tonic water for medicinal purposes is a mystery. Mary Kingsley was of a definite opinion: "Take the case of the missionaries, who are almost all teetotallers, they are young men and women who have to pass a medical examination before coming out, and whose lives are far easier than those of other classes of white men, yet the mortality among them is far heavier than in any class."[88]

David Livingstone did not die of malaria[89] but he did lose his wife to the disease, in 1862. He was, therefore, well aware of the danger. When exploring the Zambezi he administered a daily dose of quinine to fellow Europeans to ward off the African fever.[90] Writing in 1874 of Livingstone's experience Horace Waller was uncompromising: "It cannot be too strongly urged on explorers that they should divide their more important medicines in such a way that a total loss shall become well-nigh impossible ... and, above all, the supply of quinine."[91] When Mrs Richards died from malaria after just eighteen months at Banza Manteka, Mrs Guinness recorded that her supply of quinine had run short and "there was great room for regret that better precautions has not been taken to preserve this precious life".[92]

Livingstone was also well aware of the benefit of using a mosquito net whenever possible, as well as taking quinine. It was known that the "jungle fever" could be prevented by sleeping under a fine net or guarding the entrance to tents or accommodation with a fine screen. Mary Kingsley again: "The best ways of avoiding the danger of the night air – sleep under a mosquito curtain whether there are mosquitoes in your district or not."

Quinine and sleeping nets were not known to Tuckey's expedition in 1816. However, this information should have been known to the LIM committee in London and to Craven and his fellow pioneer missionaries. One may understand their commitment to temperance but the regular, prophylactic use of a quinine containing tonic, or simple powdered quinine was clearly known to be beneficial. Quinine was taken by the young missionaries amongst their supplies and we know they used it when a fever developed[93] but too frequently the missionaries allowed themselves to become separated from their supplies or allowed supplies to run out.[92] The first reference to the use of protective mosquito netting in the mission archive is found only as late as 1905.[94] The undoubted lack of informed planning and adequate practical provision told their own tale.

The LIM was not the only mission to experience such high mortality. The Church Missionary Society (CMS) lost fifty-three missionaries in the first twenty years of their work in Sierra Leone.[95] The BMS suffered similarly; there were periods when the rate of missionary mortality equalled or even surpassed the rate of recruitment.[96] In addition to the deaths, the letters from Congo told repeatedly of recurrent fevers and debilitating illness that interrupted and prevented meaningful work for weeks at a time and delayed the transport of personnel or essential supplies. The experience of these committed young men and women was a tragedy but a tragedy that could have been mitigated and sometimes avoided. Is it, therefore, pertinent to ask why it was not?

The death of James Telford within three months of his arrival in 1878 was a great shock, but his family and fellow students recalled his words at the farewell service before leaving England: "I go gladly and shall rejoice if only I may give my body as one of the stones to pave the road into interior Africa, and my blood to cement the stones together so that others may pass over into Congoland." A young student at Harley College who planned to replace Telford was warned "These heavy tidings come in time for you to change your mind, if you wish, and refrain from taking a young wife to that deadly climate". But his reply confirmed his unwavering determination, they were ready to go and die if it was the will of God. When Charles Petersen died less than two years later Mrs Guinness reflected the sentiments of all those involved in the mission: "How all our hearts sank on receipt of the news. This enterprise was going to be as costly in lives as in money … did not poor, bleeding Africa need to be rescued from death and misery, even at the cost of self-sacrifice?" The news of the third death in Congo, that of Hugh McKergow, arrived in England the day before two new recruits were due to set sail. "Being greatly shocked by this intelligence and the fresh illustration it afforded of the fatal nature of the climate, we felt as if we could not let these dear brethren go forward to this fever-stricken land. We could not have blamed them had they wished to delay their departure till the more healthful interior country was reached. But no such thought seemed to cross their minds. Their courage did not fail, but seemed, on the contrary, to rise with danger." Writing in her account, euphemistically entitled "Some are fallen asleep", Mrs Guinness wrote "Widely scattered over our globe are the mortal remains of these, who are now rejoicing together in the presence of the Lord … We have had to bow the head and say… 'Even so, Father, for so it seemed good in Thy sight; Not as I will, but as Thou wilt' … we have heard, amid our tears, a voice from heaven whispering, To depart and be with Christ is far better."[97]

Reading these words more than a century later there is an important lesson to be learned for present-day missions and the many charitable non-government organisations that recruit and send young volunteers to remote locations where malaria and other diseases are endemic. Some of these young people's lives continue to be endangered by lax administration on the part of the recruiting agency or local organisation. It is, therefore, essential that such bodies ensure they remain fully informed of all potential risk and take every possible measure to protect the health and wellbeing of their volunteers.

Other readers may be disturbed, not by the risks but by the reaction to the fatal outcome. Other missions to West Africa suffered a similar fate yet continued to attract recruits who shared a similar, almost suicidal, determination to follow what they believed to be the call of God. "The very fact that losses by death were so heavy, they proved to be a stimulus to interest at home … there were those who were ready to condemn what appeared to be a complete waste of life, but generally this was not the effect produced. Letters poured in … subscriptions were doubled, and volunteers pressed forward to replace those who had fallen."[98]

To understand this it may be relevant to recognise the way that Victorian Britain remembered its heroes, giving prominence to those who died rather than those who survived. It is Nelson who stands on a column in London's Trafalgar Square rather than Collingwood, who won the battle and survived.

It is Captain Scott and his colleague Oates who died on their return from the South Pole who are remembered rather than Shackleton's heroic efforts that saved his men when trapped by the Antarctic ice. In her book, Mrs Guinness devoted more pages to her missionary volunteers who died than the memory of those who laboured hard and survived.

Henry Guinness had always lived by the principle that when God calls He will also provide. Alas, this proved not to be the case. It was the inspiration of Livingstone's letters, Stanley's achievement descending the Congo River, Henry Guinness's millennial beliefs, his charismatic preaching and that of his fellow evangelists on both sides of the Atlantic, that combined to create an urgency that was the dominant, determining force that drove the overseas missionary endeavour. The words spoken by the pioneers at valedictory meetings were heartfelt and carefully chosen. The grief that followed was real. However, if we are to understand how these events could have occurred it has to be recognised that the social climate and, in particular, the depth of Christian conviction engendered by the evangelical surge that swept through British churches, was something that is unknown to us in the 21st century. The missionaries who witnessed these deaths and were left to continue the task of reaching the Congo interior wrote home "We are not in the least daunted by these deaths! Forward is the order, and, by God's help, forward we go."[99]

8

The First Congo Christians

For Dwight L. Moody, the Guinnesses and the Billy Grahams of this world, preaching their brand of Christianity for the thousandth time before an expectant American or British audience was a simple, albeit tiring, task for the gifted evangelist. For students at the East London Institute confronting unemployed drunks and poverty-stricken wives on the streets of London was more challenging. However, neither could compare with standing before an excited crowd of inquisitive but potentially aggressive men, women and children gathered beneath the searing sun on the banks of a Congo river. Uninvited yet hoping to convert the listeners who had no significant sense of a god and no feeling of need or desire to become acquainted with one, the newly arrived missionaries faced a thought-provoking dilemma. Speaking with an uncertain and incomplete grasp of the audience's language, where could the missionary start?

Within a year of their first arrival Henry Craven had learned sufficient Fiote to commence preaching. He translated the Old Testament's Ten Commandments, which produced a marked effect. "By the King's desire ... the people were ordered to get their water and gather their sticks for two days, so that they might rest on the Sunday; and the next day the whole town came to a service. They were advised to give up their fetishes and turn to the living and true God." However, a difficulty seemed to be the question of health. What should they do in sickness? Would the white man give them medicine if they burned their fetishes?[100] Craven visited some sick villagers who were cured quickly. A simple medical practice sprang up. Neighbouring villages requested a visit from the white teacher, some slave children were ransomed and adopted, and a school started. The women seemed thankful to have the deception of the medicine men exposed. The local King had reputedly killed eighty people with his witchcraft since he began to reign, but Craven was soon able to write "When we first arrived the fetish drum was ever going, now months pass without its being heard at all. The palaver house used to be filled with charms; now all have vanished. Our presence here has not been without effect."

H. H. Johnston recorded his impressions after staying at Palaballa: "After dinner I followed the missionary to attend prayers. The missionary prays in Fiote and in English and also reads a chapter of the Bible. The subject is generally badly chosen, being wearisome records of Jewish wars. All the while the black congregation sits stolidly unmoved, although the missionary strives to infuse the greatest interest. After this follows a hymn in Fiote ... a fairly sensible prayer finishes up the whole thing." On another occasion he noted:

> The people may be said to patronize Christianity. When the missionary holds a service, some twenty or thirty idlers look in to see what is going on. They behave very well and imitate with exact mimicry all our gestures and actions so that a hasty observer would conclude they were really touched by the service. They kneel down with an abandon of devotion and say 'Amen' with deep ventral enthusiasm. The missionary gave a short sermon in Fiote, marvellously expressed considering the short time he has been studying the language. The king took up constantly the end of some phrase to show he was attending.[52]

Ward was also somewhat pessimistic that the missionaries would make any significant impact. Speaking of George Grenfell of the BMS, Ward observed "I cannot help feeling that the trading disposition is too strongly ingrained in the people for a missionary to cause any speedy reformation of their lives".[38]

Initial attempts with spiritual work gave very little encouragement. The teaching skills the missionaries had learned at the East London Institute were not, perhaps, suited to the entirely different situation that confronted them in Congo. However, offering simple medical care that challenged the use of fetishes and the power of the medicine men yielded significant success. Combining religious teaching with addressing a serious social problem that affected everyday living proved more effective. Nonetheless, "It is no small thing to put a stop to the cruel and bloodthirsty practices of these people, but we cannot rest till we have taught them the gospel".[101] Initially, a common opinion was that "The white man's country must be a very bad one since they prefer coming here to live with us, though our climate kills them". Slowly, this perception changed to a recognition that the missionary presence was an example of Christian concern. However, their difficulty in reaching this understanding was that there was no word in the local language for "love", and the concept of a loving Supreme Being was entirely foreign to them. Hugh McKergow's death in 1881 caused perplexity. The Congolese on the mission station asked "If these men are servants of God, if their God is strong and good, why does he let them die?" Other questions followed. Who made God? Who is stronger, God or the spirits in the forest? Why does God not prevent the evil one from tempting us? All of these are questions that can still be heard anywhere today, but they illustrate the developing comprehension of Congolese listeners responding to early mission teaching. On the other hand, from Banza Manteka, Charles Harvey wrote, "I spoke to them about the creation, the fall, and sin and guilt. It is difficult to make them believe that they are wicked, for they all assert that they are good."[102]

A different approach was adopted by opening elementary schools at each station. Initially education was not considered of any value by the villagers but as the boys demonstrated their ability to write and read it proved popular.[103] The missionaries soon recognised that the children were more amenable to Christian teaching than their adults. Simple hymns were translated which the children sang instead of their native songs. Small churches were built at each station where services were conducted daily as well.[104]

In the summer of 1881 Mr and Mrs Craven returned to England with two Congolese boys, N'dambi and Pukamoni. Staying at Harley College, surrounded constantly by the intense Christian atmosphere, it is hardly surprising that these vulnerable teenage boys professed their faith, although it is rather more surprising that they were considered suitable to be baptised. In doing so they were the first two Congolese to profess their Protestant Christian faith through the influence of the Livingstone Inland Mission.[105] During their stay they helped Henry Craven and Henry Guinness senior to compile the first dictionary in the Fiote language, highly complimented by Johnson as "the present standard of the Congo tongue" and recommended to the authorities in Brussels.

N'dambi and Pukamoni were accompanied by a very young girl, Launda, the daughter of the old chief of Palaballa. She, too, adopted Christian ways and requested baptism but was deemed too young. On returning to Congo she died of tuberculosis that she contracted in England. Congolese children accompanied several other missionaries while on furlough and benefited from the experience, from the Christian point of view. Vemba and Nkoiyo, who spent a year in England, made a significant contribution in later years. Vemba became an evangelist and powerful Christian orator. Nkoiyo travelled to America to complete his education and subsequently translated the book of Acts and John's first Epistle into Ki-Congo. Apart from these few examples, progress through evangelism was slow. After five years of intense effort the missionaries summed up their achievements thus: "We feel assured that our presence here is already influencing the people for the good, though we are so little able as yet to communicate to them the gospel. The work may proceed very slowly but we doubt not that God will bring it to a successful issue".[106] After a few years their hopes began to be realised.

Following the transfer of the mission to the ABMU the missionaries continued as before. As several years passed the effect of their living and teaching became increasingly evident. "At most of the stations there were converts; many of these sought themselves to spread the gospel; gradually the movement became more widespread. Candidates for baptism came forward, not by units but by tens, and at one station even by hundreds ... at Banza Manteka ... a revival has begun." The gospels of Mark and Luke were translated to Fiote.

> This evening two converts returned from a preaching tour in several villages. They met with a good deal of opposition ... some people threatened to shoot them but they were not afraid ... Our work is having such a marked effect on the young men, the older men are displeased, and we get daily notices that we will be killed. All the youths want to live with us; they are beginning to see the reasonableness of the teaching ... the man whom I had stopped from shooting his wife the next day came and told that he had given himself to Christ.[132]

One of the ABMU missionaries reported "Opposition is principally on the part of the Ngangas who fear losing their living ... Even this difficulty is dying away. The chief and Ngangas are losing their hold of the people. The revival has done much to set the native mind from the superstition in which it had been held."[107]

We do not have to take the missionaries' words alone concerning the changes that had taken place. C. R. Kakansjon, an Officer of the Congo Free

State, was most impressed. "When I reached the top of the hill above Banza Manteka I was changed in a moment when I saw before me the pretty villages and green ravines ... the whole impression was one of peace. I was not wrong. Arrived here I could not believe my eyes! I beheld Mr Richards preaching in the middle of a large number of men and women throwing away their 'nkissis' (charms). I have been witness to an event of great importance: Banza Manteka will be distinguished in the future Congo history as the first Christian parish – today already more than six hundred Christian people."[107]

If we are to consider how such dramatic change came about, Henry Richards' opinion was very clear. "I went to work the wrong way at first, to teach the heathen the folly of idolatry and superstition, the nature of God, duty and morality and such things, as well as about Christ. I noted what the Apostles did and began to follow their example. First, they preached Christ and Him crucified; they made the people feel their guilt in killing and rejecting Him, in not resembling him, in not caring and coming to Him."[108] Richards was also clear about his long-term vision. "I greatly object to any attempt to Europeanise Africans ... I do not want to make them like children depending on me. I am intensely anxious to develop them as rapidly as possible into a self-governing and self-extending church."[109] That would take some time but within a decade the Livingstone Inland Mission had succeeded in bringing about significant change in the Congo.

The two explanations by Richards are enlightening. They illustrate, firstly, his discovery that the instinctive desire to challenge the Congolese way of life was counterproductive, as a consequence of which he reverted to the simplistic evangelistic methodology learned at the East London Institute. Acknowledging the Congolese way of life, he did not consider it his role to adopt the commonly held European paternalistic approach to the local people. Thirdly, his purpose was to enable his converts to establish an indigenous, evangelical church structure. This he considered to be in keeping with Pauline principles from the first century. What is apparent from reading the accounts of the LIM is that the missionaries tended to work as individuals, sometimes living alone for significant periods. Coming from very different backgrounds their thinking and approach to mission were not always the same. Also notable is the absence of any mention of the traditional spiritual beliefs of their audience. As there had been only a brief and unsuccessful encounter with Portuguese Catholicism three centuries before, the Congolese were considered to be in spiritual darkness. Whatever beliefs they may have held they were, at best, irrelevant and at worst, wrong. Whether a deeper understanding of Congolese philosophy would have assisted the initial mission methodology is unknown but, given its eventual success, there must have been some attractive elements to the missionary message.

In the course of one of their early journeys Mr Ruskin asked one of the bearers who also excelled on the talking drum (lokole) to send a Christian message on his behalf to any who might listen. That evening the drum spoke:

The creator who made men, the owner of the forest, sent his only son to die on a tree and he also received a spear wound. He died for us because he loved us. Those who grip spear and shield. Those who bear child and for those who recline in chairs, and for those who run about with pattering feet. He is not dead now he is alive and with us. When you go into the forest he accompanies you. Love him in your heart. Speak to him in the forest or by the stream. He hears you. He never leaves you. He is with you wherever you may be, always.[110]

We have seen, also, that the first appealing factor was social, not spiritual. Life expectancy was short and fatal illnesses were commonplace. The life of every Congolese person was dominated by the fearful power of fetishes and the nganga. Before his preaching could have any meaningful effect on the residents of Palaballa, Craven's use of his simple medical skills was evident for all to see. Children with fever no longer died, wounds could be dressed and healed. The missionary had powers greater than the medicine man that were appreciated immediately and had a profound effect on their daily existence. Fetishes were burned and the nganga's controlling influence was undermined, something appreciated especially by the local women. The women would have observed the relationship between the married missionaries and their wives, and some may have thought how their lives might be different. A few slave children were ransomed and cared for, and a simple school was started. The value of being able to read and write opened remarkable new opportunities which were welcomed enthusiastically by the young men as well as the children; the young men wanted to live on the mission station. This would become a major feature of later mission development throughout the Congo. Mission stations became the focus of new villages. Encouraged, initially, to house freed slaves who had lost all contact with their home villages a thousand miles distant, for people attending for medical care or seeking Christian education, the proximity to the mission provided a degree of protection from the nganga and the worst abusive practice by the State and trading companies. The missionary homes also offered employment and a more secure food supply.

The people were perplexed that missionaries should want to stay in their country without the inducement of riches from the slave trade, when the climate and diseases were so inhospitable. What they could not have understood was the overwhelming sense of being called by God to promote the Christian gospel in the Congo, a factor that should not be underestimated. However, from the Congolese perspective, whatever the missionaries' motivation, the potential improvements to everyday life that would follow from adopting the missionaries' teaching was very appealing. Richards said that he objected to any attempt to Europeanise Africans but unwittingly, by their very presence, the missionaries were changing Congolese social mores and introducing European aspirations.

None of this was in keeping with the intentions of Livingstone, whose vision was to open men's minds to a personal faith through the settlement of Christian families; nor did it reflect Robert Arthington's urgent quest to evangelise the world as speedily as possible to expedite the Second Coming. Even the founders of the LIM probably had no concept of what might develop; having no knowledge of Congolese society they sought only to introduce to the country as many Christian evangelists as possible. Notwithstanding the primary social appeal of the missionary teaching a growing number did develop a genuine desire to learn about Christianity. The church built by Aaron Sims in 1891 is still in regular use today by a thriving Christian community.

The BMS recorded its first baptism in March 1886 and the first Baptist church was formed in São Salvador in December the following year. It was perhaps inevitable that the earliest converts were young men who had been to England or were employed by the missionaries to help with the new stations and were thus witnessing the new way of life and hearing the daily Christian teaching.[111] A Congolese Church had been planted and some of the new converts had started the process of church-extension through indigenous evangelism. The widespread adoption of Christian beliefs and the creation of an organised Protestant church would be a slow process. Self-government of that church would take nearly another eighty years to be fully realised.

9

A Second Dawn

———

Irishman John McKittrick arrived in Congo in April 1884, one of the last group of missionaries to join the Livingstone Inland Mission at Equator Station where he continued with the American Baptists. In 1888 he was due for furlough but, before leaving, he obtained permission to make a special exploratory journey along the Upper Congo. Seeing for himself the territory visited previously by colleague Aaron Sims and BMS's George Grenfell and recalling their unfulfilled plans for mission "in the regions beyond", his long-held hopes for evangelising the interior were re-ignited. This was the Lulonga region, between Equator Station and the Stanley Falls, delineated by the thousand-mile-long horse-shoe bend of the Congo River, home to the Balolo people.[112] Perhaps, after all, the vision of Alfred Tilly and the Guinnesses could be realised.

Aaron Sims still held similar views and, years later, would build a station at Stanley Falls.[113] At the time, however, the ABMU was not interested. Their principle for mission was "concentration with radiation" from a central focus, a pattern of work not considered suitable by the LIM on the basis that the topography of the Congo River would be served best by a series of mission foci forming a chain along the rivers. There was, also, the matter of language. The ABMU preferred to work at Leopoldville and along the cataract region in an area with but one language; moving further upriver would involve several languages. The Swedish Mission was still small and the BMS, although they had selected sites upriver, would be unable to occupy them all for the foreseeable future.

On arrival in London McKittrick found that there was still a great interest in the work started by the LIM. As an old student of the East London Institute he returned to Harley House where he discovered that there had been significant change. Henry Grattan Guinness Jr. had assumed the Directorship. Dr Harry, as he was known, had expressed the hope of becoming a medical missionary.[114] While studying medicine at the London

Hospital, Whitechapel, he lived with his parents and participated in the work of the East London Institute. Here he developed his skills as an evangelist. He was handsome, charismatic, highly sociable, and considered by colleagues as a born leader. In January 1885 he qualified as a doctor but a career in medicine was not his immediate concern; within a few weeks he was on his way to Australia to stay with a widowed family friend. This was Mrs Reed, who had funded the steamer *Henry Reed* in memory of her husband. Harry demonstrated that he shared his father's talent as a popular evangelist, preaching in all the major cities and attracting huge crowds wherever he

Fig 11. John McKittrick, leader of the Congo Balolo Mission.

went. He also became engaged to Mrs Reed's daughter Annie. Returning to England two years later he found that the task of overseeing the East London Institute was proving too arduous for his mother. The idea of taking over the "family business" did not appeal, but slowly he conceded. He and his wife Annie assumed the management of the Institute.

When John McKittrick travelled back to England he was accompanied by Bompole, a Congolese boy from the Bololo tribe of the upper Congo. Some eighty years previously the peaceful Bantu dwellers in the densely forested region had been displaced by a much stronger tribe, the Balolo, that brought new customs and a new language and came to occupy an area nearly five times the size of England. They cleared the forest around their villages for gardens where maize and manioc were grown. They were expert in smelting and working brass for agricultural implements and decorative bracelets; knives, a spear and shield were carried by the men. Their towns were well organised with streets and a central place for "palavers"; women held equal status as the men. Despite their dominant, warrior history they were deemed industrious, intelligent and friendly. They had never been attacked and exploited by the Arab slavers from the east and never before had they been contacted by Europeans from the coast.[115] These were the people that attracted Aaron Sims and John McKittrick.

Congolese children had been brought to England by missionaries in the past. The motivation for this was never stated but their presence at public meetings certainly stimulated interest in the mission. Bompole was about sixteen years of age and learned English with apparent ease. During his year-long stay he was introduced to numerous churches where he was an undoubted attraction; in Victorian England a teenage Congolese boy on the platform with a Congo missionary or a renowned gospel preacher would have caused a stir. When asked to speak he was very clear: his people were anxious for missionaries to be sent to them with the Christian gospel. Before leaving England he wrote a letter in English for all to read: "My people want missionaries to teach them what bad, what good."[116]

Fig 12. Dr Harry Guinness.

Within a few months it became increasingly apparent that John McKittrick's desire to carry the vanguard of Christianity beyond Leopoldville, to Bompole's Balolo people, was gaining widespread support. There were already fifty-five missionary societies at work elsewhere in Africa but still none in the very centre.[117] McKittrick's old classmate, Harry Guinness, became convinced by the argument. Furthermore, he agreed that the East London Institute should embark, once again, on a new venture in the Congo. As a precaution, agreement was reached with the ABMU that should difficulties arise in the future they would maintain what had been started. However, with the nationwide growth of the evangelical movement, few doubted that it could succeed and flourish, provided, of course, that lessons were learned from the LIM experience. An international authority on Christian missions had been very critical;[118] the planning, direction, organisation and funding would need to be much improved and made more secure than previously. That would be Harry's responsibility.

In terms of enthusiasm and the likely availability of both volunteers and financial support, there could not have been a better time than the last decades of the 19th century to embark on a second bold Christian adventure. With the continuing progress of the industrial revolution provincial towns and cities expanded and the burgeoning suburbs established new parishes and many new non-conformist churches.[119] The Religious Census of 1851 revealed that about half of the population of England and Wales attended church.[120] The second half of the century then saw the impact of the evangelical revivals of 1859 and the 1870s. In Newcastle in the northeast of England the Brunswick Methodist Chapel recorded 1,400 professions of faith in one year and the Bethesda Chapel across the river in Gateshead was nicknamed "the Converting Shop".[121] The East End Tabernacle, the Metropolitan Tabernacle, Westminster Chapel, Shoreditch Tabernacle, all in London, together with Charlotte Chapel in Edinburgh and others elsewhere, attracted thousands every Sunday. The post-millennial beliefs of previous years had been overtaken by the more urgent pre-millennialism of which Henry Guinness senior was a vocal and prolific supporter.[122,123] Many were convinced that it was the task of the church to evangelise the whole of the known world as soon as possible. Supporting foreign missions had become an integral part of evangelism. The Church Missionary Society, for example, recruited more than 1,000 new missionaries in the last fifteen years of the century, 45% of them women.[124]

Within the year a new team was ready. The new mission would be called the Congo Balolo Mission. As before, it would be "interdenominational, simply Christian, and thoroughly evangelical". It would offer "no attractions in the way of good salaries or other earthly advantages ... a work of faith and labour of love, seeking the co-operation of men and women willing to endure hardness and, if need be, to lay down their lives for Christ's sake and the gospel's."[125] The latter statement was no idle, pious platitude. Any volunteer would know very well what had happened to too many previous young missionaries. At the farewell meeting at the great Exeter Hall in London there were several speeches but the most persuasive was that from Bompole himself. His people wanted the gospel: "Isn't it a shame – shame to keep the gospel to yourself? Not meant for English only! Isn't it a shame?"

In April 1889 John McKittrick and his new wife Dora set sail, together with Bompole, James Blake, Lily Mary de Hailes, Gustave Haupt, John Howell, James Todd and Peter Whytock. On arrival they were met at Boma by Joseph Clark from the ABMU with whom they stayed at Palaballa, McKittrick renewing acquaintance with old colleagues before the hard six-day trek past the cataract region to Malebo Pool where ABMU's Billington captained the *Henry Reed* and transported the group up the Congo River. McKittrick had identified a possible site for missionary activity on his last exploratory visit, a village called Bonginda, thirty-five miles from the confluence of the Lulonga tributary with the main river. Dora wrote her own account of the memorable day on board the *Henry Reed* when they saw, for the first time, the river, the country, the place and the people that would become her home.

August 24th 1889 was a memorable day in the annals of the Congo Balolo Mission. Were we not on the verge of entering the country to which God had called us? Of its people, their numbers, their habits and language we knew almost nothing, though many stories of their warlike character, their ferocity and cannibalistic tendencies had been related to us by the natives down river.

As we approached the place where the Lulanga flows into the Congo we discerned indications of large settlements on the bank of the river and steaming slowly up could see immense crowds standing on the left bank as far as the eye could reach. No women or children were visible; only men fully armed had come out to gaze upon the mysterious "smoke-canoe" and we did not need our interpreter to tell us that these large crowds wore a distinctly hostile attitude, and that it would be dangerous to attempt landing or even to slacken speed. We bade him salute these fierce looking warriors in our name, tell them that our mission was a peaceful one, and ask for food. But the only response was threatening looks and wild gesticulations with spear and bow. So putting up our arrow-guards we went on our way. Just beyond the towns we cast anchor for the night in midstream and determined to make friends before going further. In this we were successful, and were able to buy some provisions, though we could not induce the women to come out of their hiding places.

The following day we proceeded up river. Our behaviour at the mouth of the river had apparently disarmed suspicion for there were no more warlike demonstrations. The news of our arrival was 'telephoned' from one village to another and our interpreter was able to tell us some of the messages beat out on the drums – "The white man, Englesa, has come to sit down with us". At last we came to a halt at the town of Bonginda where dwelt the most important Chief on the river, a man who had once seen a missionary and had asked for teachers. But as we neared the landing place, the noise and smoke of the steamer terrified the poor folk and they fled en masse into the bush. Some hours passed in unavailing attempts to get at them. Then we threw a handful of beads on the ground in front of the steamer and by degrees a few of the bolder spirits ventured out into the open to pick them up. With these men we made friends and in less than half an hour the beach simply swarmed with men, women and children, while the Reed was surrounded by an eager chattering crowd in their shaky-looking canoes. Fear and distrust seemed to have vanished completely and it was only when darkness fell that we could get rid of them.

Work began in earnest the next morning. The old chief came in state to visit us bringing a long train of wives and slaves, and invited us to land. This we promptly did and were accompanied everywhere by a gaping and gossiping crowd. The women were clothed in short grass petticoats but the men in tiny pieces of bark cloth. The bodies of all alike were covered with a mixture of palm oil and camwood and decorated with a variety of tattoo marks. The chiefs were distinguished by their head-dresses, made of monkey skin. A great palaver was arranged and attended by more than a thousand of these wild-looking people. A heated discussion took place as to whether we were to be allowed to settle among them. We, of course, could not understand what was said, but the expressive gestures of the orators told us plainly if they were speaking for or against us. The matter was decided by the king's chief speaker, old Mata Lokota, who, amidst furious excitement declared in our favour. Presents were exchanged and we took possession of our new home. Then, for the first time, we had an opportunity of declaring our message to these Balolo people. As our interpreter finished a murmur of assent went round and our hearts were thrilled as Mata Lokota rose up and replied: "These words are good, white man; you shall be our father and we will be your children." And so we had been brought to the haven we had sought for and were filled with rejoicing. In the months and years which followed the work was often fraught with difficulty, sometimes with danger, but the joy and privilege of carrying the gospel into these "Regions Beyond" more than atoned for all.[126]

After intense negotiation McKittrick paid 1,500 brass rods, 10 spoons, 10 knives,1 large bottle, 10 mirrors, 5 deep plates, 6 pieces of cloth, 1 basket of cowries and 1 red coat for a plot of land that would become their first mission station. The Congo Balolo Mission had secured a presence in the hinterland of Congo and would remain there for the next 114 years.

Mr. James Blake. Mr. James Todd. Mrs. McKittrick. Miss de Hailes.
Mr. John Howell.
Mr. Peter Whytock. Bompole. Mr. John McKittrick. Mr. Gustav Haupt.

Fig 13. The first party of the Congo Balolo Mission, sailed for Africa April 1889.

10

King Leopold and the Congo Free State

———

The modern kingdom of Belgium came into being on 21st July 1831 with the inauguration of the first King of the Belgians, Leopold I of Saxe-Coburg-Saalfeld. Leopold was the brother of Princess Victoria of Saxe-Coburg-Saalfeld, mother to Britain's Queen Victoria. Leopold was her uncle. He was popular in Britain, had considerable influence over Victoria during the early years of the young queen's reign, and brokered her marriage to Prince Albert. After his death in 1865 he was succeeded by his son Leopold II, Victoria's cousin. Prior to his accession the young king had served in the Belgian army and reached the rank of Lieutenant General. He had also been a member of the Belgian Senate, where he took an active interest in the development of Belgium and its trade, and urged Belgium's acquisition of colonies. In a later letter to his brother he summarised his ambitions as monarch: "The country must be strong, prosperous, beautiful and calm, and therefore have colonies of her own."[127]

By the time Leopold met Stanley after more than a decade as sovereign, his broad experience of politics, international diplomacy, trade and the military made him ideally placed to seek the fulfilment of that ambition, the personal fiefdom of a wealthy colony. If he sought any guidance he needed only to look across the Channel to his cousin's growing empire. As monarch

Fig 14. King Leopold II of the Belgians.

55

he could not oversee or control developments directly, but like his cousin he could seek to exert considerable influence. For Leopold that influence would focus on the accumulation of personal wealth.

When Stanley returned to Congo on 14th August 1879 his purpose was to establish, on behalf of King Leopold II, the basis for a commercial enterprise in this newly available country, to acquire a colony in Africa for his country. The British government showed no interest, France was content with de Brazza's quiet progress to the north of the Congo, and neither England nor France favoured any extension by Portugal. Quiet acquiescence with Leopold was an acceptable diplomatic position. Furthermore, Leopold's intentions were stated to be entirely honourable and unselfishly philanthropic. For the new country he would offer all the benefits of European civilisation and for the world he would offer free access to enriching trade. Both France and Portugal imposed strict regulations in their colonies that prohibited international access and in Gabon France prohibited any instruction in the native language, closing Protestant mission schools and driving out American missionaries.[128] Leopold was promising full freedom for missionaries, both Catholic and Protestant. By 1879 the trans-Atlantic slave trade had come to an end but the Arab slave trade, focused in Zanzibar and gaining access to eastern Congo, was still operating unchecked.

The obvious person to deliver the king's desire was Stanley. Since Livingstone's death, not only was he the only European to have traversed the African interior and the length of the great river, but he had demonstrated his physical and psychological prowess. To fulfil his dream Leopold would need to gain control of the whole new territory, its marketable resources, and the indigenous manpower required to support future commercial activities. The task was a formidable one. The objective was threefold. Firstly, to secure a trade route beyond the cataract region. Secondly to acquire free access to as much land adjacent to the Congo River and its tributaries as possible. This, in turn, would require engagement with the Arab slavers, which was necessary to achieve the third objective, the ending of the slave trade.

Throughout Europe there was support for Leopold particularly because his stated intentions promised peaceful, munificent civilisation for a country that was so obviously needful:

The time and influence of white men of upright character, as missionaries, traders and government officials, dwelling among them, will effect great changes in the people of the upper Congo. As civilisation spreads and the ways of the white men become known to the dwellers of the far interior, a desire to imitate the more agreeable modes of living then presented will spring up in the breasts of these poor African savages by that time, let us hope, freed from the devastating scourge of Arab slave raiding in their midst.[129]

To achieve these objectives Leopold proposed the creation of the Association Internationale du Congo. Stanley's first task was relatively straightforward. With a team of generously funded, well equipped and trained men, marching past the cataract region was not particularly taxing. Having reached his eponymous Pool he negotiated land and built a primitive settlement with little difficulty.

To achieve the second objective, just like the aspiring missionaries, he would need a series of trading posts at frequent intervals on both banks of the river. This he achieved by a busy programme of personal visits during which he negotiated with local chiefs. Responding to his persuasive words the village leaders thought they were agreeing to treaties of friendship for mutual benefit. In reality the chiefs, unable to read the documents proffered for their mark, would later discover they had agreed not only to the presence of white men on their land but had sold, in exchange for beads, some brass rods, a few rolls of cloth and the occasional firearm, all rights to the ivory and other produce from the forests and soil. "All roads, waterways running through this country, the right of collecting tolls on the same, and all the game, fishing, mining, and forest rights, are to be the absolute property of the said Association, together with any unoccupied lands as may at any time hereafter be chosen."[130] Stanley is known to have exaggerated his achievements on occasions and the veracity of the contract described by him is in doubt,[131] but the outcome was, in effect, that he had succeeded in buying both the country and its people for the personal ownership of his employer Leopold.

With the rapid growth of this enterprise Stanley needed men to staff the trading posts he had established. The treaties signed by their chiefs notwithstanding, the appearance of more white men with clear intentions of taking over local village economies was not welcomed by many local tribespeople. Angry resistance arose in several places and the employees of Leopold's International Association had no compunction in using force.

Stanley's epic voyage down the Congo had not been a peaceful adventure. For several possible reasons he had acquired the name "Bula Matari" – "Breaker of Rocks". Fighting broke out and many Congolese were killed or wounded; knives and spears offered little protection from European guns. Herbert Ward was a young Englishman who served with the International African Association for several years. He recounts several such encounters with considerable gung-ho enthusiasm, despite the slaughter of numerous Congolese and the loss of some colleagues.[129] The acquisition of the Congo for civilisation and commerce was not a peaceful process. Communication and transport on the river was also a necessity. Several boats were soon plying the waterways and the *Henry Reed* and the BMS *Peace* were but two among a growing fleet on the river.

Stanley's approach to his third objective, the elimination of the Arab slave trade, was more unusual. Hamad bin Muhammad bin Juma bin Rajab el Murjebi, otherwise known as Tippu Tip, worked for a succession of sultans of Zanzibar where he was the recognised leader of the slave and ivory trades controlling the supply route to Zanzibar with armed forts manned by Congolese recruits. Stanley recognised that an attempt at armed expulsion of the whole trade from many thousands of square miles of densely forested country would be a difficult, prolonged and expensive process. Furthermore, given that it was closely linked to the ivory trade that was profitable to many of the Congolese, the likelihood of complete suppression was small. He therefore adopted a novel strategy, appointing Tippu Tip as Governor of the Stanley Falls province in the hope that political pressure could subsequently be applied that would result in winding down the trade in human lives. The outcome was not as he had wished and only after a three-year war between Leopold's Force Publique and Tippu Tip's militia did the slave trade come to an end in January 1893. With the closure of the trade route east to Zanzibar the consequence was just as Leopold had planned. The only route for trade of any description was now downriver to the Atlantic coast through territory over which he had sole control.

While Stanley had been consolidating Leopold's position on the Upper Congo, Portugal and France had been doing the same at the coast. They claimed the south and north banks of the river mouth respectively for themselves, so that access to the river, and the whole interior, was threatened. Germany, too, was annexing along the African west coast. Some form of international consensus was required to regularise the situation. The

Conference of the Great Powers met in Berlin on 15th November 1884 under the chairmanship of Otto von Bismarck, first Chancellor of Germany. No African representatives attended. Discussions were concluded on 26th February 1885 and the General Act of the Berlin Conference was published. This confirmed the formal division of Africa amongst European colonial powers, the so-called Scramble for Africa[132] which replaced African autonomy. Or, as Kwame Nkrumah reputedly described it, "The old carve-up of Africa". In 1870 10% of the African continent was under the control of European governments; by 1900 Europeans controlled 90%.[133]

Henceforth, Leopold's acquisition would be known as the Congo Free State. There were conditions, however. The conference insisted, in keeping with Leopold's own stated intentions, that the whole of the Congo Basin should be open to all countries for free trade without any restriction and the aborigines were to be protected in the peaceful possession of their rights and property. In addition, religious liberty and freedom of worship was to be guaranteed, together with special favour and protection for all missionaries, religious and scientific enterprises.[134] Nonetheless, so far as Congo was concerned, Leopold was granted supreme power and authority over the whole territory drained by the Congo River and its tributaries together with twenty-three miles of coastline at the mouth of the river to guarantee access.

Initially, amongst the churches in Britain, this conclusion was greeted with gratitude and enthusiasm: "We cannot fail to see the hand of God in this result. Those who have been watching the development of affairs can but wonder at the marvellous Providence which has guided all. Now, with such a Sovereign, and such a charter of Freedom, we can but look forward with the fullest hope to the future of l'Etat Independent du Congo."[128]

Thousands of miles away the Congo had been "discovered", a way to its centre had been found and opened. But little did the missionary organisations and their supporters understand the implications of that remarkable feat. Congo was no longer the unknown, inaccessible heart of Africa that held such mysterious fascination for Europeans. Instead, it was now a rich commercial resource waiting to be exploited by the rest of the world. The innocent Congo of Craven, Strom and their colleagues, waiting in ignorance for the Christian gospel, was no more. They had taken Christianity to the Congo but the gospel had been accompanied by 'civilisation' and that would be accompanied by unintended consequences.

At a later date Leopold gave a very clear account of his approach to colonisation:

The task which the State agents have to accomplish in the Congo is noble and elevated ... Face to face with primitive barbarity, struggling against dreadful customs their duty is to gradually modify those customs. They have to place the population under new laws, the most imperious as well as the most salutary of which is assuredly that of work. In uncivilised countries, a firm authority is, I know, necessary to accustom the natives to the practices of civilisation, which are altogether contrary to their habits. To this end, it is necessary to be at once firm and paternal. But if, with a view to the necessary domination of civilisation, it be permitted, in the case of need, to have recourse to forcible means.[135]

"Forcible means" were not new to colonising powers.

Since time immemorial the strong have overcome the weak and stolen their lands. During the sixty-four years of Queen Victoria's reign there was not a single year when British forces were not engaged in what Rudyard Kipling called the savage wars of peace.[136] While Craven and Strom were establishing themselves at Palaballa, British forces were invading Afghanistan for the second time. As the new LIM missionaries were settling at Palaballa, British-led troops overwhelmed the Zulus and another part of Africa fell under British domination.[137] Just a few months later the British started their first war with the Boers, a conflict to protect trade routes to India and gain access to immense mineral wealth in southern Africa. By contrast with such universally aggressive British behaviour Leopold's mission was, ostensibly, peaceful. His vision was commercial. Leopold's intentions were altruistic, he said he had no desire to dominate or humiliate; there was no reason to suspect that his proviso concerning forceful means would be called upon.

Ivory was the highly prized commodity from the Congo that Tippu Tip had exploited and was the prime natural resource that Leopold planned to trade. The Congolese killed elephants to protect their livelihood and their food sources. They were also glad to trade their tusks for a modest income. Initially, international commercial returns for Leopold were promising but it soon became apparent that they would not satisfy his expansive expectations. The cost of establishing the Congo Free State had been greater than anticipated, and an additional source of income was required. To his and everyone else's surprise an innovation from an unlikely source would meet that need.

Natural rubber is a latex that can be extracted from a variety of plants. Archaeological evidence suggests that its first use was by the ancient cultures of Central America that tapped the latex from Hevea trees. In 1770 Englishman Joseph Priestley found that the rubber latex was good for erasing pencil marks, hence the name "rubber". In 1888, John Boyd Dunlop invented the pneumatic tyre, and in March the following year the Irish cyclist Willie Hume was the first member of the public to purchase a cycle fitted with the new tyres. Having witnessed their superiority Dublin-born cycling enthusiast and entrepreneur Harvey du Cros acquired the patent rights and by 1901 was managing director of the Dunlop Tyre Company. At the same time the motor car industry was developing rapidly. Demand for the product grew but the only source of the latex in the early 19th century was Central and South America. An alternative source was the latex of the Landolphia woody vines that are indigenous to tropical Africa, where they scramble to great heights over the largest trees in the rain forest, a very common sight in the Congo Basin. Congo became Leopold's domain at a time when the potential importance of rubber had been recognised but a full decade before large-scale production from Hevea plantations in other countries. The decline in Leopold's income from ivory coincided with the sudden demand for rubber and he found himself in the enviable position of owning the source material that could meet that demand ahead of any competition. Between 1891 and 1892, in direct violation of the Berlin treaty, he imposed decrees that limited access to the country's resources by other nations. There was, however, a problem.

Vines growing in profusion deep in the equatorial rain forest were one thing; extracting the valuable sap and transporting it 1,000 miles to the West African coast for shipment to Europe was an altogether different matter. To export from Belgium a very large workforce unaccustomed to the Congo climate would be impracticable as well as expensive. On the other hand, Leopold believed that Stanley had secured a Congolese workforce for him through the treaties he had agreed with the many local kings and village chiefs. Had not Tippu Tip enrolled the services of numerous Congolese who assisted in his successful ivory trade, and had there not been many more who collaborated with him in supplying slaves? Indeed, but rubber was not the same as ivory and human bodies. For the Congolese, killing elephants was a part of everyday life, as was inter-tribal warfare and the capturing of slaves. Supplying Tippu Tip with tusks and slaves required no significant change in the way of life of the Congolese population. Rubber, however, was different. Although the Congolese were well aware of the rubber vines in their forests they had never made any collective attempt to harvest the latex for the simple reason that it offered nothing of value or practical use. Even more of a deterrent was the difficulty of collecting it. The vines could not be grown in their gardens and the only way to obtain the latex was to venture into the forest and climb trees, something no Congolese woman, man or child would think of doing without a very compelling reason.

Taxes have been imposed by monarchs on their subjects for millennia so a similar practice by Leopold to develop the structure of the new colony would not have been unreasonable. The Berlin conference anticipated such a need: "Taxes must only be sufficient to compensate for the expense of keeping the river navigable and of keeping up the establishments placed on its banks."[138] Taxes, however, require currency and some form of income for the populace from which to pay the tax. Neither existed in Congo at that time. Food was bartered in the markets, a wife was bought with a goat and other simple goods and the only currency usable by the newly arrived Europeans comprised beads, brass rods, and lengths of cloth. The men hunted, fished, constructed houses and village palisades. Women worked their gardens to produce sufficient food for their needs. The people had no need for any other form of employment or income. Work for commercial purposes was unknown and it was this work that Leopold required if he was to profit from his colony's natural resources. Realising that his new subjects might not be enthusiastic about such a radical change in their way of life, he came up with a special measure. Leopold would introduce payment of tax in kind with rubber. The principle of the tax was simple. Wherever rubber grew every man would be required to harvest a stipulated amount of rubber each week which would be taken to collection points administered by the new, mainly Belgian administration. It would be the responsibility of village chiefs to ensure that their community adhered to this requirement and thereby contributed the mandatory tax. The rubber would then be brought to the lower river, processed and exported to generate the income necessary for the development of the colony.

At the Berlin Conference Leopold committed his Congo Free State to improving the lives of the Congolese people, but to achieve the fortune he desired Leopold ignored these conditions from the outset. When resistance from the population arose he ran his colony using a ruthless, mercenary Force Publique comprising Congolese and other African recruits overseen by a relatively small administration staffed primarily by Belgians. He re-invented slavery in a new guise.

Meanwhile, the new Congo Balolo Mission was born in 1889, barely four years after Leopold assumed ownership of the country. In 1892 the Congo Free State established ten concession companies to undertake the extraction of the rubber, nine of them ostensibly independent but all, indirectly, channelling profits to his benefit. To display some concern for international involvement one of these companies was the Anglo-Belgian India Rubber Company, later known as ABIR.[139] Established with British and Belgian capital and its first president being the British entrepreneur Col. John T. North, the new company received exclusive rights to all forest products from the Maringa-Lopori basin for 30 years and all land within twenty miles of eight designated posts. This was almost exactly the area adopted by the CBM. As a consequence the CBM missionaries, after less than four years of their arrival, found themselves living and working on the banks of the Lulonga, Lopori and Maringa rivers surrounded by the ABIR concession company.

The sites of the first three CBM stations were chosen for their ease of access to the rivers and the proximity of large, thriving village communities. It was therefore inevitable that they should be joined by the first of the ABIR posts for the same reasons. The Free State supplied the guns, ammunition and soldiers required to establish their posts and the ABIR had police powers within the limits of the concession. Two State employees were ordered to establish the first of these at Basankusu, but the local villagers resisted and killed both men.[140] Several armed conflicts ensued, greatly increasing the native opposition, but the ABIR's superior arms soon gained complete control of the local population. Each post maintained a census of all the males in every village and implemented the rubber tax of eight kilograms of wet rubber to be collected by each man per fortnight. To oversee this, each post had a force of more than sixty Congolese armed village sentries, often ex-slaves, whose sole purpose was enforcing the collection of rubber. Although, in principle, the villagers were paid for their collection with brass rods, the overriding incentive quickly became fear of the sentries who, in turn, were obliged to achieve the stipulated amount of rubber from their village. Before long the ABIR would acquire the worst record for cruelty and oppression in the Congo. "ABIR created no structural relationships ... The ABIR was a plundering and tribute-collecting empire of the cruelest sort ... and departed leaving a legacy of death, disease, and destruction."[141]

The amounts of rubber demanded were excessive; it became increasingly difficult to gather the quantities demanded. Unlike the process of tapping rubber trees, which preserved the trees for decades, the vines were cut across and thereby killed at the first harvest. As the vines closest to villages were destroyed the men had to penetrate further and further into the forest which increased the danger and the time spent away from home. If a man failed to meet his quota one of several punishments followed. He might be sent back to the forest and his wife would be taken hostage, imprisoned and starved, until the quota was met, with no provision for care of the children. Alternatively, he would be flogged with the chicotte, a whip made from knotted hippopotamus hide, which many men did not survive. Many were shot without question. If a village did not meet its quota the chief would be killed or the whole village burned to the ground. This became the norm, not just for the ABIR but for the whole of the Congo.

The population of Congo in 1885 was estimated to number twenty million. By 1924 the population was counted by the Belgian administration to have fallen by 50%. It is true that several factors contributed to this alarming decline. There were epidemics of smallpox, sleeping sickness and influenza, and the Europeans had brought tuberculosis, pneumonia and other diseases previously unknown in Central Africa. However, whole villages living close to Angola and French Congo moved across the borders to escape the brutality of Leopold's agents. The Rev A. R. Williams of the Christian Missionary Alliance reported "There used to be very large towns and villages. They are now quite abandoned, the natives preferring the rule of the Portuguese, which is none of the best, to the rule of the Belgians which is far worse."[142] And Mr Hall of the ABMU explained "When I first went to Irebu in 1889 the population was estimated at 5,000. When I left in 1897 it only amounted to about three or four hundred ... large towns on the banks of the river – now they are all wiped out, and the natives, because of the oppression to which they are subjected, have crossed into French territory. The native plantations and gardens have all disappeared."[143] Writing in 1903

Rev J. Whitehead of the BMS reported "The population in the villages of Lukolela in January 1891 must have been not less than 6,000 but by December 1896 I found only 719". The cause? Famine as a consequence of rubber slavery.[144] Finally, over three decades, by enslaving a whole nation, millions, including women and children, were starved, mutilated and killed in Leopold's pursuit of the riches he could accrue from the export of rubber from his colony.

The cruelty employed by the Leopold regime was nothing new; British slave owners had been perpetrating similar abuses on the sugar and cotton plantations in the Caribbean and American southern states until only a few decades before.[145] By 1898 there were no longer any British shareholders in the ABIR. Nonetheless, it was British capital that largely financed the company at its outset. In 1906 American financial support followed when entrepreneurs J. P. Morgan, John D. Rockefeller, Thomas F. Ryan and Daniel Guggenheim invested in Leopold's Congo.[146] The Viscount Mountmorres from Ireland, who visited the ABIR and CBM area in 1906, concluded "No words can convey an adequate impression of the terrible and callous inhumanity which marks the methods of the territorial companies, nor of the abject misery and hopelessness of the native population".[147]

Eventually, international outrage and diplomatic pressure forced Leopold to relinquish his ownership of the country and its people, and it was one final act of mutilating cruelty that led to his downfall. The village sentries and troops of the Force Publique were obliged to account for every cartridge expended in their control of the population. Each was assumed by Belgian administrators to have been used with a fatal human outcome rather than for hunting animals for food. Proof was demanded, in the form of a hand cut from the slaughtered victim. Hands were, also, cut off as a form of punishment when insufficient amounts of rubber were collected. Years later it was photographs of these hands, collected in baskets for counting by the authorities, and other photographs of children as well as adults with missing hands, that aroused the British public and demanded an end to Leopold's reign. On 15th November 1908 the Congo Free State became a colony of the Belgian State: Congo Belge.

For nearly sixteen years the communities amongst whom the CBM and other missionaries were working were ravaged by Leopold's forces. The missionaries were, unavoidably, witnesses to these atrocities. Further downstream the BMS, the ABMU, the Swedish mission and Roman Catholic missionaries from Belgium were all active with well-established stations along the banks of the main Congo River[148], and the ill-gotten gains of the rubber concessions passed daily before their eyes en route to Europe and America. How was that possible? Did nobody express their concern at such a flagrant breach of the Berlin Agreement? Did none of the missionaries attempt to protect their Congolese neighbours?

In the only previous account of the Congo Balolo Mission the author Joseph Conley concluded that they did not: "The early silence of the missionaries in the face of these atrocities eludes explanation ... For some, silence became the price of ministry."[149] More recently, Grant has levelled the same accusation: "Missionaries, merchants, and British officials all had particular interests that prompted them to mute their public criticism. Missionaries regarded the conversion of Africans to Christianity as their priority, and they worried that if they publicly embarrassed the Congo Free State, it would refuse to grant them additional station sites upriver ... This was of special concern to Protestant missionaries, who observed that Leopold, a Catholic, favoured Catholic mission."[150,151] These are astonishing conclusions. The next chapter will consider the evidence.

11

The Silence of the Missionaries?

Although the earliest reports of misrule in Congo became known to the wider world in 1890, observers were disinclined to believe that the sovereign of the Congo Free State could have sanctioned the physical abuse of his Congolese subjects. It was not until six years later, when further abuses continued to be reported, that the Aborigines' Protection Society (APS) in London raised the matter with the British Government but "its appeal fell on deaf ears"; the Prime Minister replied only that "these representations should be borne in mind". The following April Sir Charles Dilke initiated a debate on the subject in the House of Commons and spoke at a public meeting. Although extensive press coverage ensued no political or diplomatic action was stimulated.

In 1901 the APS reported to the Legislature in Brussels, but the Belgian Parliament was coerced to abandon any significant debate. The following year a further detailed report was submitted to the British Government, another public meeting held and a major debate took place in the Commons that did result in a note to the other signatories to the Berlin Agreement but to no avail. During the intervening years disquiet concerning the situation of British subjects in Congo had been raised on several occasions but Colonial Secretary Joseph Chamberlain had been unable to persuade his cabinet colleagues of their importance.[152] Seeking to alert the world to what were, by then, undeniable accounts of widespread enslavement and cruelty, the secretary of the Aborigines' Protection Society, H. R. Fox Bourne, published *Civilisation in Congoland: a Story of International Wrong-doing* in 1903.[153]

Several years previously the Polish-born novelist Joseph Conrad had published a story based on his personal experience as a riverboat captain on the Congo, during which time he had witnessed at first hand many of the atrocities committed in Leopold's name. Appearing as a three-part serial in the Edinburgh-based *Blackwood's Magazine* in 1899 the "Heart of Darkness"[154] attracted a limited readership and was subsequently re-published as a novella in 1902.[155] In 1905 Samuel L. Clemens, under the pseudonym Mark Twain, followed with an American pamphlet, "King Leopold's Soliloquy", a polemical satire that sought to expose the king's exploitation of the Congolese.[156] In 1909 Sir Arthur Conan Doyle published *The Crime of the Congo*.[157] These popular authors certainly contributed to the general public's awareness of Leopold's activities, on both sides of the Atlantic, but public awareness led to no significant British or international diplomatic action. As Mark Twain is reported to have said "The war in Congo is like the weather; everyone talks about it but no one does anything about it". And Conrad remarked, "It is an extraordinary thing that the conscience of Europe which seventy years ago has put down the slave trade on humanitarian grounds tolerates the Congo State today. It is as if the moral clock has been turned back many years … and the Belgians are worse than the seven plagues of Egypt."[158]

Fig 15 Edmund Dene Morel.

Georges Edmond Achille Morel de Ville was born in Paris in 1873 but settled in England at the age of eighteen, adopting the name Edmund Dene Morel. In Liverpool he found employment as a clerk to Elder Dempster & Company Ltd., a premier shipping company that served the trade to the West Coast of Africa including a contract with the Leopold enterprise.

Promoted to Head of the Congo department, Morel documented the company's numerous voyages between Antwerp, Banana and Matadi. He found information that revealed the supplies imported to the Congo from Brussels were not goods for trade but large quantities of arms. Stimulated to explore further he discovered that the records of shipments he compiled were not those published by the company. Observation at the Antwerp docks confirmed that 80% of the articles sent to Congo "were remote from trade purposes". Furthermore, the profits accruing from the sale of rubber and ivory "greatly exceeded the amounts indicated in the Congo Government's returns". In summary, very little was going into the Congo Free State to pay for the huge profits that were being made. "From what he saw in Antwerp, and from studying his company's records in Liverpool, Morel deduced the existence of slavery."[159] He reported his findings to the head of Elder Dempster, Sir Alfred Lewis Jones, who was also Honorary Consul in Liverpool of the Congo Free State, who assured him that he had spoken with Leopold and the King had given assurances that reforms were in progress; the Belgians needed time "to set their African house in order".[160] Dissatisfied, aged twenty-eight, Morel declined financial inducements to keep silent and resigned his position determined to expose the wrongdoing he had discovered. After a brief period working for a British newspaper where his findings about the Congo Free State were once again supressed, he became an investigative journalist. One influence on Morel was Mary Kingsley, who shared her concern that traditional African communities were being destroyed by European invasion. Obtaining financial backing from John Holt, a businessman and philanthropist from Liverpool, and the support of Henry Fox Bourne, secretary of the APS, he founded his own newspaper, *The West African Mail*. As an illustrated weekly journal this provided him with a vehicle to expose King Leopold's duplicity. He also became a prolific writer publishing a series of books[161,162,163,164] which left the reader in no doubt as to the dishonesty of the Congo enterprise and the unending supply of the weapons of brutality. In 1903 he met Roger Casement, who persuaded him to establish the Congo Reform Association.

Morel dated the start of the struggle against the misrule in Congo to September 1896 "when the Aborigines' Protection Society appealed to the British government. From that time onwards Mr. H. R. Fox Bourne, the society's secretary, stimulated by the published diary of Glave, by the disclosures of the Swedish missionary Sjoblom, the Irish missionary Murphy and by reports from other sources, has waged a gallant fight against Congo State methods."[165] In all of this Morel and Bourne were dependent upon sources of information wherever they could be found; both men were prohibited by Leopold from visiting Congo in person. Who was Glave? Who were Sjoblom and Murphy? Who were the other sources?

Edward James Glave was a young Yorkshireman who had been employed for six years by Stanley during his initial work of establishing access to the Upper River. Later he returned to Africa as an independent traveller during 1894 and 1895. The shocking content of his diaries published in April 1897 corroborated the early complaints of the missionaries.[166] Of the Equateur Region where the missions had their stations he noted:

I saw a gang of prisoners taken along by the state soldiers. War has been waged all through the district of Equateur and thousands of people have been killed and homes destroyed ... Native life is considered of no value by the Belgians. Often the mission stations are applied to for succour but, as a rule, when the carriers present themselves they are thoroughly overcome by the exertion of carrying a load while ill, and they generally die ... The missionaries are so much at the mercy of the state that they do not report these barbaric happenings to the people at home.[167]

Quoting from Glave's diaries in 1903 Bourne added his own observation.

There was too much truth in the statement that 'the missionaries are so much at the mercy of the state'. Though a good deal of information tardily leaked out it was generally in such cautious language designed to conceal the identity of the informants that it was too vague and incomplete to be in any way authoritative. Fuller and more trustworthy information was, in some cases, communicated to the central organisations by missionaries in their employ ... These authentic details however were, as far as possible, withheld from outsiders. They were not allowed to reach the public ear or to arouse public opinion in favour of changes that, in bringing incalculable benefit to millions of Congo natives, might have been prejudicial to the missionary organisations ... I make this statement deliberately as the result of the admissions made to me by several Congo missionaries and by managers of Protestant and Catholic missionary organisations both in London and in Brussels.[168]

There was some truth in Glave's criticisms of the missionaries and Fox Bourne's endorsement, but it was not the whole truth.

In July 1890 George W. Williams, an African American Baptist pastor and lawyer, published an open letter to King Leopold at the conclusion of a visit to the Congo. "Your Majesty's government has sequestered their land, burned their towns, stolen their property, enslaved their women and children, and committed other crimes too numerous to mention in detail ... All the crimes perpetrated in the Congo have been done in your name and you must answer at the Bar of Public sentiment for the misgovernment of a people whose lives and fortunes were entrusted to you by the Conference of Berlin."[169] Six months later the Aborigines' Protection Society reported a debate during which "Dr Grattan Guinness said that, from his experience of sending missionaries to Africa, he could confirm what had been said about the cruelties practised upon natives in the Congo Free State".[170] From this it is evident that Guinness was aware of events occurring within just two years of the arrival of the first CBM missionaries. In May 1891 the Regions Beyond mentioned the burning of African towns by State officials[171], an accusation that was repeated in November 1893. However, Guinness also sought to

Fig 16 Rev George Washington Williams.

reassure mission supporters by saying "On the whole the picture is not so black as Colonel Williams would paint it".[172] From the Lower River, Swedish and American Baptist missionaries were also reporting ill-treatment of people.[173]

The first recorded mention of problems affecting the CBM missionaries was not until five years later, in a letter from Dr Guinness to the CBM missionaries on behalf of the Home Council, dated 4th June 1895. The staff in Congo were requested to "send a report on the attitude of our council at home with regard to publishing any details as to the action of the Rubber company on the Lolanga and Lopori". The missionaries were surprised to receive this request because they replied that individual brethren had already submitted witness statements to the Home Council concerning abuses. Furthermore, "reports are constantly reaching us which confirm all that our brethren had said. With the facts you have had from our brethren we feel most strongly there ought to be something done." Their suggestion was that the Home Council should make a "a direct appeal to the King of the Belgians who controls the laws that bring about such desolation and wholesale slaughter of human lives for the purpose of procuring rubber".[174] From this it is clear that the CBM missionaries had been sending reports of atrocities to

Guinness and his Council in London for several years before the stirrings of the Aborigines' Protection Society and Morel, public meetings in London or representations in the British Parliament.

That the behaviour of the State officials and the ABIR would affect CBM staff directly became increasingly evident during the months that followed. Armstrong recorded "It is only right to testify to the cordial relations which existed between the representatives of the company and the missionaries in those days. These neighbourly acts made it all the more difficult to protest." However, "the missionaries had, at length, to raise their voices against acts of cruelty".[175] Despite sending reports of abuses to London, relationships between the missionaries and ABIR personnel had, indeed, remained generally cordial and, as a way to thank the ABIR for their kindness on occasions, CBM staff had agreed to carry loads of rubber for them on the mission vessel *Pioneer*. However, as a consequence "some of the natives of Bongandanga insist upon identifying us with the traders and their interests ... it was believed we should wisely refrain from giving any such possible occasion for hindering the work of Grace ... we should carry no more rubber with our vessels."[176]

Building and other work on the mission stations required local men, but when only those permitted were men who had been imprisoned illegally by the ABIR a letter to the Home Council informed them of the missionaries' opinion: "We have determined to be as independent as possible of the traders so as to give them no chance of accusing us of benefitting by the evil system which obtains in the Congo Free State."[177,178,179] In future the construction of mission buildings and running the steamer would be more difficult, but the missionaries felt they had to make their opposition to every aspect of the Leopold regime quite clear. Other aspects of mission life were also made increasingly difficult by the ABIR. Timber was the prime construction material. The ABIR decreed that no tree could be felled until the ABIR had given permission.[180] The company also tried to levy a charge for any wood cut for the mission's steamers.[181]

Communication between mission stations depended on mail being carried on the ABIR riverboats[182]; the ABIR forbade the carrying of CBM correspondence, thereby hindering CBM work and endangering the lives of missionaries.[183] Transport by hired canoe was similarly prohibited.[184] Another act by the ABIR was to introduce the compulsory attendance of all village children at mission schools. This was probably thought to be a convenient way to cater for children while their parents were away as forced labourers growing food, repairing roads and collecting rubber, or the women were in prison as hostages. The missionaries, however, found that compulsory school attendance was counterproductive and associated the mission with the slave state. Although it would interfere with their desire to educate the children and would prevent their introduction to Christianity it was decided not to accept them into their schools under these conditions. Also, the missionaries took another decision that would make their personal lives more difficult. Although they imported tinned food from England the purchase of native-grown food was essential.[185] When missionaries could only purchase food from the ABIR grown by forced labour it was decided to eat only imported tinned food.[186] Vice Consul Roger Casement, during his visit to CBM stations in 1903, was so concerned by this illegal act that he wrote to the Governor General in Boma and the Foreign Office in London[187] that the missionaries were "completely at the mercy of the ABIR officials". The following year CBM missionaries were still being threatened with physical danger requiring state protection against threats to murder missionaries.[188]

In addition to all this information sent by CBM staff to the Home Council, J. B. Murphy, an ABMU missionary speaking at a public meeting in London, gave first-hand testimony of the scenes he and his colleagues had witnessed in the course of their work. He also confirmed in a report to *The Times* newspaper that he had raised his concerns with the Leopold administration as early as 1888 and 1889.

> When I left in August the people were in a very unsettled condition and most unfriendly to the State. Two of the most flourishing towns in Stanley's time, Kintama and Kinshasa, are no more and the people have gone over to the French Congo. Several Christians were arrested. The rubber question is accountable for most of the horrors perpetrated in the Congo. It has reduced the people to despair ... the soldiers drive the people into the bush ... if they will not go they are shot down ... hands being cut off ... men, women and children. Some radical change in government must take place before there can be any hope of prosperity. I have seen these things done and have remonstrated with the State in the years 1888, 1889 and 1894 but never got satisfaction.[189,190]

From the foregoing it will be evident that the missionaries were "not inclined to be silent". Rather, the behaviour of the ABIR and the difficulties experienced by missionaries were communicated frequently to the Home Council in London in the form of Field Council meeting minutes, personal letters and personal conversations. The members of the Council were, therefore, well aware from the outset of the nature of Leopold's rule, the enslavement of the Congolese, many of the atrocities committed and the effect that this had on their missionaries. What was the response of the mission executive? The minutes of the CBM Home Council meetings tell their own narrative: of the eighty-five meetings held between June 1892 and December 1903 the subject of maladministration and abuse of the Congolese was mentioned on only nine occasions.

Edvard Vilhelm Sjoblom, a Swedish colleague of Murphy with the ABMU, informed Guinness and the CBM committee of a particular incident involving a woman carrying a basket of severed human hands. The explanation was that "I have to prove to the white man that I have been diligent in pushing the rubber business, and who would punish me if I did not... bring in sufficient quantity [of rubber]". Reporting the event in the mission magazine Regions Beyond, Guinness stated it to be the first serious atrocity witnessed by missionaries. As we have seen this was not true, unless one can draw a distinction between atrocities and "serious" atrocities[191]. Nonetheless, the Home Committee agreed that the Congo Secretary in Brussels should be informed, "making a clear statement as to the facts of Congo atrocities at all of the varied mission stations".[192] Guinness travelled immediately to Brussels, where he obtained a personal interview with King Leopold.[193] The outcome was a reassurance from Leopold that he was equally concerned and agreed with suggestions made by Guinness for the improvement in the working conditions of Congolese employees.

On other occasions when Leopold was challenged with accounts of similar brutality his response was that they were isolated incidents. However, following publicity about Sjoblom's report in the Swedish press, Leopold responded by establishing a Commission for the Protection of the Natives to investigate "any cases of oppression or cruelty of the natives by Free State officials reported to them". From the outset it was evident that the commission would be ineffective, but it appeared to satisfy English public concern. In September 1896 the Home Council agreed to forward to Belgium copies of Mr Sjoblom's communications with regard to Congo abuses.[194] Others who submitted further evidence were accused of lying and threatened with charges similar to those to be brought against Sjoblom by the State.[195,196] The following year, after complaints had been lodged by missionaries, permission to establish a new station on the Juapa River was refused. This stimulated Guinness to visit Brussels again to argue the mission's cause with the Chief Secretary of State and the head of the Congo Railway. Once more Guinness was impressed by the welcome he received; the meeting concluded with an offer that CBM staff could travel free of charge in the cataract region and benefit from a 40% discount on boat travel on the upper river. It was also suggested that if a formal application was submitted for a new station at Baringa on the Lopori River it would be received sympathetically.[197] Dr Guinness then made two further visits to Brussels concerning specifically the Juapa River but despite promises given previously no permission was ever granted.[198,199] Concerning Baringa, however, permission was granted the following year[228].

Before long a new threat to missions arose: in 1901 the Congo Free State proposed to tax missionary societies. The Home Council consulted with the BMS and agreed to support their approach, judging the time was not opportune to protest and to await private interviews with officials.[200]

Throughout this period of more than seven years, during which the Home Council had received many witness reports of brutality by the ABIR from their own missionaries and elsewhere, the Council made no further attempt to draw this to the attention of the Belgian authorities. Nor does it appear that they sought any occasion to publicise these happenings or seek to draw them to the attention of any government body. Guinness knew well of Edmund Morel and Fox Bourne and their determination to expose the injustice of Leopold's regime. He also, apparently, shared their concern to achieve reform in Congo, but his motivation for doing so was not the same. Their correspondence reveals some of the difficulties.

Holt to Morel: "We have plenty of people trying to get to Heaven by looking after men's souls in Africa, but very few who take a living interest in their bodily or material welfare."[201]

Guinness to Morel: "I am interested to see that you have undertaken the self-appointed task of exposing any cruelties sufficient evidence of which present themselves. We have a great deal of information on the subject, but precisely what we do with it is a point that I am hoping to bring before our next Congo Council … The difficulty is to do good without doing harm."[202]

Guinness to Morel: "May I ask what you think can well be the practical issue of the continued expose which you propose to make?"[203]

Morel to Stead: "The position of missionaries in the Congo State is peculiar. If they speak openly against the State, what is their existence likely to be on the Congo?"[204]

Morel to Guinness: "I would like to cooperate with the missionary societies …"[205]

Guinness to Morel: "We do not want to incur the restriction of the benevolent operations of the mission except for the promulgation of facts more serious than what we have to complain of now."[206]

Guinness to Bourne: "I have several painful instances on the working of the ABIR … but we do not want to make them public and risk crippling our work on the Congo unless will be of real value."[207]

Guinness to Morel: "I have illustrations of a dreadful character I can use, showing horrible cruelties not only in the past but actually inside the last few months. I possess three terrible pictures of mutilation … what seems to me the most dastardly outrage that civilised Europeans could possible perpetrate on defenceless Africans. Please regard this letter as strictly confidential."[208]

Bourne to Morel: "It seems to me his CBM is all-important to him, and the Congo atrocities of small importance except in so far as they may bring in funds for his society."[209]

Morel to Guinness: "The consciousness of the civilised world is aroused now … the missionary societies have a sacred duty to perform to humanity."[210]

And, in the Regions Beyond in November 1903: "We ourselves have just received from one of our own missionaries fresh evidence with regard to recent atrocities. For the time being we forbear to publish these statements ... Meanwhile we ask the earnest, sympathetic prayers of all our readers, HGG."[211]

From an official standpoint the Congo Balolo Mission remained silent. However, in November 1903, that silence was broken, albeit not by the Council or its members but by one of their own missionaries.

Oli Jacobsen lives in Torshavn, the principal town of the Faroe Islands. When walking in the town's old cemetery in 2007, his attention was caught by a gravestone the inscription of which read

Daniel Jacob Danielsen
1871-1916
Virkaði í Congo 1901-1903.

Ein óræddur hermaður Harrans
("Served in the Congo 1901-1903 A fearless soldier of the Lord")

Jacobsen was intrigued. What was one of his fellow countrymen doing so far from home in Central Africa a century ago? He decided to investigate. The crucial information that he uncovered lay in the archived reports of the Congo Balolo Mission.[212]

Daniel J. Danielsen was born in Copenhagen of a Faroese mother in June 1871. Aged eighteen he went to Scotland, became a shipping engineer and travelled extensively. At the age of twenty-seven he was converted unexpectedly to Christianity, was appointed to work in the Engineering Department of the Congo Balolo Mission and sailed for the Congo in 1901. Stationed at Bonginda, the first upstream station after Leopoldville, he was both engineer and captain of the mission's riverboat, the PS *Pioneer*, sailing with the all-Congolese crew. After just two months, correspondence from his senior colleagues reported him to be a most capable man ... a real acquisition ... we are very thankful for him. His skills were then put to good use with the arrival from England of a second steamer for the mission, the PS *Livingstone*, which he re-assembled and commissioned. All the riverboats were wood-fired and, therefore, required a constant supply of wood that was cut from the forest by the forty-five crew on a daily basis. As already noted,

Fig 17 Daniel J Danielsen.

regular hard manual labour was not the norm for Congolese men and journeys were delayed by constant palavers over wood cutting.

Although engaged as an engineer Danielsen was keen to engage in missionary work. He also took active responsibility for the welfare of his crew and on one occasion confronted a witch doctor and reported his illegal activities to the Belgian authorities. However, Danielsen's management of his African crew was called into question in November 1902 when a previous colleague accused him before the London executive of abusing workers. This complaint posed significant difficulties for the mission Board. There was, also, the problem of the long delays in communication between London and Congo. Other returning missionaries and staff were questioned, the complaints were corroborated, and admissions made that some of the other missionaries had administered corporal punishment to Congolese; the conclusions reached by the Home Council concerning Danielsen were ambivalent. Given the widespread use of corporal punishment by all colonial countries the official position of the mission had been set out in its 'Principles and Practice'. However, the Council concluded that there had been "no serious abuse of power on the part of any of the missionaries (with the sole exception of Mr Danielsen) and that it was evidently necessary ... to exercise discipline – from a parental standpoint which was altogether different from the course adopted from the traders and the state". Letters were sent to the Field Committee and to Danielsen.[213]

Despite reaching this conclusion the decision was reversed at a subsequent meeting and it was decided that Danielsen should be recalled, although the Field Committee disagreed. It was clear that Danielsen's colleagues wanted him to stay. The London Council changed their minds for the second time and Danielsen's recall was withdrawn.[214] However, the tardiness of communication between London and Congo once again ensured an unexpected outcome. Believing that he should return to London Danielsen said goodbye to his colleagues and started on his journey home.

On his way downriver he stopped at the BMS station Bolobo, on the main river about 200 miles short of Leopoldville. Here he was introduced to Roger Casement, the British Consul in Boma, who had been directed by the British government to undertake an independent investigation of the growing public and media allegations against the Congo Free State. As it was important to Casement that he remain independent of the Belgian administration he obtained a passage upriver as far as ABMU Chumbiri, where he encountered Henry Billington, who had built the steamer *Henry Reed*. Billington undertook some necessary repairs for the old riverboat but was not available to travel further; another skipper was required. It was at this point that Casement was introduced to Danielsen, who could delay his return to England and happily agreed to convey Casement wherever he desired to undertake his investigation. Together the two men left Bolobo on 20th July 1903. Casement had intended to travel as far as Stanley Falls to ensure that he reviewed the whole of the accessible Congo Free State activities but by the time he visited CBM Bongandanga, where he met with the missionaries and interviewed many Congolese witnesses, he had acquired sufficient information. They returned downstream to Leopoldville, which they reached on 17th September. As the pair were the only two white men on board throughout the journey Danielsen acted as ship's captain and engineer, negotiator for wood, food and provisions, interpreter, companion and photographer for Casement.[215]

Casement's subsequent report to the British Foreign Office[216] would prove to be a turning point in the campaign against Leopold. In a letter to the Foreign Secretary Casement acknowledged his debt to Danielsen: "Mr Danielson's services were of the very greatest value: indeed, without his help I could not have proceeded very far on my journey. Had it not been for the help thus afforded me by the ABMU and by the Congo Balolo Mission my journey to the upper Congo could scarcely have been carried out."[217] Having delivered Casement back to

Fig 18 Sir Roger Casement.

Leopoldville Danielsen took the first available ship to England, where he arrived early in October 1903.[218] Meanwhile Casement took a different route and did not reach London until 1st December.

Back in England, Danielsen's immediate task was to meet with the mission's Home Council. Giving an account of his experiences with the CBM and his observations while travelling with Casement, he expressed his concern for the plight of the Congolese, eager that the mission should embark without delay on a public campaign against the Leopold regime. In addition, he presented copies of several photographs that appear to have been taken by him during the voyage with Casement. Morel was aware of Danielsen's return to London as well and wrote to Guinness within two days of his arrival. He received the following reply: "The question is whether we shall publish this matter in the next issue of the Regions Beyond."[207] Writing a few weeks later Guinness revealed, unambiguously, the policy of the mission: "We have just received from one of our own missionaries fresh evidence with regard to recent atrocities. For the time being we forbear to publish these statements ... Meanwhile we ask the earnest, sympathetic prayers of all our readers."[211] The evidence was the photographs taken by Danielsen while accompanying Casement and his own diary notes that were known to Guinness.[219] When the Home Council discussed the matter their response was disappointing. The meeting agreed unanimously "to await the arrival of Mr. Casement before using the information brought home by Mr. Danielsen of recent atrocities and the continued maladministration of the Congo State".[220] Guinness and his colleagues would follow their previous path and procrastinate.[211] The Foreign Office concurred and so did the Aborigines' Protection Society.[255] Danielsen, on the other hand, was impatient and had other ideas.

Without further delay Danielsen returned to Scotland to renew acquaintance with old Christian friends in Glasgow. News from returning missionaries was always greeted with enthusiasm by home-land churches; hearing his stories of mission life and the atrocities in Congo his friends encouraged him to address two public meetings. These were held in Edinburgh on the 7th and 8th November 1903 and were attended by several thousand people. No reporters from the press were present but Morel contacted him asking if he could publish a report in the *West African Mail*. "I have had conversation with Dr Grattan Guinness about your information. My feeling is that Government or no Government, we should lose no further time in publishing the information. I think the delay weakens our case. I have told Dr Guinness so, but each man must judge for himself. You mention that you were speaking before 4 or 5000 people in Edinburgh. I wish it were possible to infuse into your missionaries some notion of how to get at the ear of the public in connection with a matter of this kind."[221] The outcome was an article as Morel had suggested.[222] On the 7th December Casement read on the front page of the *Daily Mirror* "HORRORS OF THE CONGO. British Official Finds Terrible Slavery in the Belgian State". Meanwhile Danielsen had received a letter from Casement: "He is glad to see the Congo article in your paper ... I will be speaking at Edinburgh on the 19th and 20th ... we have slides of the boys with hands cut off. They will be shown then."[223] The week following, Danielsen spoke at an annual missionary conference in Glasgow. This time an interview appeared in the Glasgow *Daily Record* and *Mail* and the *Falkirk Herald* but, of greater significance, the previous CBM strategy of silence had been challenged at a major missionary gathering. It would have to change. Guinness and the Home Council could remain silent no longer.

The minutes of the Board next meeting read "Suggested that we publish a booklet containing missionary evidence regarding Congo mal-administration and also that a series of mass meetings be held in the main cities in the United Kingdom. The council very heartily agreed to this programme being carried out."[224] Harry Guinness conducted the first of these meetings in Bristol a few days before Casement's return to England and an article was published in the next issue of the magazine *Regions Beyond*. Employing his eloquence and evangelical skills throughout the country Guinness proceeded to make a significant contribution to the public debate in the United Kingdom that, building on the indisputable evidence contained in Casement's damning report, eventually led to Leopold's downfall five years later. Casement's report changed the politicians and the international diplomats; it was his companion, Danielsen, who first galvanised public opinion and changed the missionary society's silence.

Danielsen resigned from the mission, there was no further contact with Casement or Morel and he became a revered evangelist in his home Islands, the first Faroese speaking full-time evangelist for the Christian Brethren, whose influence is evident today. In 1904 the Faroe Islands honoured Danielsen with a postage stamp that depicted him with Casement and the *Henry Reed* against a map of Africa and the Congo. Elsewhere, until Jacobsen's research, Danielsen had remained largely forgotten.[225]

Fig 19 Stamp to commemorate Daniel J Danielsen.

Danielsen's colleagues remaining in Congo, together with the missionaries of the BMS and ABMU, continued to speak out. When, in response to Casement, Leopold set up a Commission of Enquiry in 1904 it was the missionaries from the three missions who corroborated the testimony of the many Congolese witnesses.[226] When Morel set up the Congo Reform Association it was Mr and Mrs Harris from the CBM who joined him in this work. The Commission collected evidence from villages and stations along the Congo as far as Stanley Falls between October 1904 and February 1905, including five CBM stations. When it became known that the conclusions of the enquiry would be critical of Leopold the king succeeded in delaying its publication for more than eight months.[227] However, when Morel obtained and publicised much of the evidence it contained, Leopold countered by offering inducements to Guinness that would benefit his mission directly. Preserved correspondence shows that it was considered by Guinness to be an attractive, innovative change in the State's practice. Morel disagreed and did his best to dissuade the CBM leadership, pointing out the duplicity underlying the proposals.[228] The CBM made public their rejection in December 1905.[229] The BMS leadership also changed its stance and urged the British Government to demand reform[230]; Bentley disowned his award of Chevalier de l'Ordre de Leopold II and the BMS leader in Congo, George

Grenfell, changed his approach having "long since abandoned any belief in the policy of King Leopold".[231] Eventually, the king's proposition was rejected and the details were publicised[232] but change did not follow. On January 11th 1906 representatives of the Protestant missions at the Congo Protestant Council sent their protest to King Leopold signed by fifty-three missionaries.[233]

New missionaries, Alice Seeley and her husband John Harris, established the CBM station at Baringa in 1898. Both were critics of the state administration and John gave evidence to the Commission of Enquiry. Prior to this, following the publication of Casement's uncompromising report to the British Parliament, he became increasingly vocal, pressing the Home Council to greater action. "A friend has urged us to come to terms with the Rubber Agents ... but I can only answer 'No, not for an hour, if it means selling the bodies and souls of these people. We sincerely hope that you at home will fight on with this cause."[234] Mrs Harris, whose story has been told elsewhere,[235] had a camera with which she took photographs of the mutilated victims, the first of which were carried by a missionary colleague to London in the summer of 1904. We do not know the make of camera Danielsen used when travelling with Casement but Mrs Harris' photographs were taken with a C P Goerz Anschütz press-type camera[236,237] of a much more professional standard, and it was her iconic image of a grieving father sitting before his daughter's severed hand and foot that had such an influence on public opinion.[189,238,239] Published first in the Regions Beyond, then in a pamphlet written by Mrs Guinness and one of Morel's books, this, and Mrs Harris' other photographs, were seen at public magic lantern shows throughout Britain and North America. In 1905 the Harrises retired from the CBM to work full-time with Morel and the Congo Reform Association. In this capacity they organised numerous support groups throughout Britain and spoke tirelessly at hundreds of public meetings on both sides of the Atlantic using Alice's photographs to considerable effect. The public at large in North America and Great Britain could not remain uninformed. Mark Twain, supporter of the American Congo Reform Association, joined the protest by publishing "King Leopold's Soliloquy" in which he recognised the crucial role the photographs played in turning international opinion against Leopold. The King's influential contacts could supress written criticism in the press but the horrific scene portrayed by a photograph direct from the Heart of Africa could not be denied. "Ten thousand pulpits and ten thousand

Mrs Harris photographing in the forest.

Fig 20 Mrs Alice Seeley Harris with her camera.

presses are saying the good word for me ... then that trivial little Kodak, that a child can carry in its pocket, gets up, uttering never a word, and knocks them dumb! The only witness I couldn't bribe."[240] The camera was not a Kodak but the point was made.

The foregoing paragraphs have considered only the involvement of the CBM in these events. For an account of the role of the Congo Reform Association, the relentless contribution of Morel and that of other individuals, readers should turn to Slade's meticulous reviews[241,242], Dean Pavlakis'[243] and David Lagergren's[244] thorough analyses.

Throughout this account there has, also, been no mention of the Roman Catholic missionaries working in the rubber concessions or the Catholic church's relationship with the Leopold administration. A recent report concludes that Leopold's choice of missionaries was determined by their respective attitudes towards the rubber regime. "What is difficult is the fact that they have accepted to settle on the condition that they observe silence on the atrocities committed ... The installation of missionaries in the Crown Estate was therefore to stem the exodus of natives fleeing the terrible caoutchouc [rubber] regime ... The logs of the missions attested to how frequent and widespread the atrocities were."[245] It was only after the report of the Commission of Enquiry had been published that Catholic missionary voices of opposition were heard and significant legal and political opposition in Belgium arose.[246]

In Britain many individuals, organisations and churches played their part in bringing about reform of the Congo administration. All the Protestant denominations eventually contributed, brought together through the British National Free Church Council, with the BMS as the major participant, together with leadership from the Anglican church. In North America the Presbyterian missionaries William M. Morrison and William H. Sheppard were influential through individual representations together with presidential advisor Booker T. Washington, sociologist Robert E. Park and others in the American Congo Reform association.[247]

In a letter to the CBM Home Council Harris wrote, "Remember the despairing words of the Chief: 'Inglihsa come and save us, if you don't soon come we shall all be killed for rubber.'"[234] On another occasion a village chief said to CBM missionary Padfield "Sit down, white man. Sit down and listen to me. You have come to tell us of salvation from sin but have you no word of salvation from rubber?"[248] Padfield's reply is not known but history has provided the answer. The missionary's God did not save them; the opportunity to do so was in the hands of the missionary societies and they chose not to use it for several years. Readers may wonder why.

As we have seen, the Home Council was aware of the deteriorating situation from the outset. What may not be so apparent was the pivotal role played by Guinness, as the director of the mission. Reading the minutes of Home Council meetings it is noticeable that significant decisions were never taken in his absence; such matters were deferred until his return. As co-founder of the mission and its driving force for twenty-seven years he had but one objective, the evangelisation of the Balolo people. The success of the early years was encouraging but there were still thousands who remained unreached; every opportunity for expansion should be sought, every potential threat to progress outmanoeuvred. From Leopold's perspective Protestant missions played no part in his long-term plans but in the short term they were useful. An inducement from the King of a site for a new station, tax concessions and other advantages would serve the mission's plans and were attractive. By opposing the King hundreds of Congolese could be spared untold suffering and death but, by challenging Leopold, the opportunity to evangelise the Congo might be put in jeopardy and the millions "living in darkness" would have remained unaware of the Gospel and God's Love. For Guinness the latter was the greater concern and an overriding principle that was endorsed by the fellow members of his Home Council. For Morel, the supporters of the Congo Reform Association and his missionaries Guinness was a valuable asset but he could also be authoritarian, fickle and not to be trusted.[249,250] In the opinion of one recent commentator Guinness was a disruptive force.[246] In his own words Guinness's priorities were unambiguous: "We have been indignant, but have we prayed? Could anything be more imperative, more effective, than this Providential call to prayer?"[251] In the feverish atmosphere of the post-revival Protestant evangelical world, and in the interests of the Vatican to gain religious control of emerging countries, the souls of Congolese men, women and children were deemed more important than their bodies. In the language of the 21st century, Black souls mattered but Black lives did not.

It is unfortunate that Conley and Grant confused the word "missionary" with the term "missionary society". Did the missionaries keep silent? No. It was the leaders of the missionary societies who chose to believe Leopold rather than the testimony of their own missionaries. It was the societies that withheld critical information for so long, deciding that it was in the best interests of their missions' objectives to remain silent.

The CBM Home Council was not alone in this. The leaders of the BMS were equally concerned to maintain good relations with the Leopold administration, choosing to suppress their missionaries' reports and prevent them from reaching the ears of church supporters at home as well as the general public.[252] From the outset the BMS had profited from a close relationship with Stanley and Leopold.[253] The BMS was the only non-Catholic mission to receive State subsidies. Grenfell spent many months on behalf of the State exploring the tributaries of the Upper Congo and was appointed a British Pro Consul Grenfell was also the secretary of the 'Committee for the Protection of the Natives' set up by Leopold to divert criticism from his regime. His position and that of the BMS administration did not represent that of the other BMS missionaries[254,255] and John Harris, writing from Baringa, was frustrated by his stance: "I cannot make Mr

Grenfell out. I know he is sick of the Administration and yet he keeps silent. A few words from him would do more than volumes from us".[256] Both Grenfell and pioneer colleague Bentley were decorated personally by Leopold. In the opinion of Slade, the BMS "had almost acquired a vested interest in supporting the State".[257] Eventually Grenfell expressed his regret: "I really believed the King's first purpose was to establish law and order and to promise the well-being of the people ... I regretfully, most regretfully, admit that those who have so long maintained the contrary are to all intents and purposes justified, and that I have been blinded by my wish to believe 'the best'. The recent revelations have saddened me more than I can say."[258]

The whole of this chapter has concerned itself with the actions, words, attitudes and reflections of Europeans and Americans on the colonial history of a country that was not their own. What of the Congolese memory?

In 1954 Catholic Father Buelaert organised a writing competition for Congolese people to "remember" in their own Lomongo language. Many were keen to write but others begged "Please do not ask us to remember". A few alluded to "conversations with elders who pleaded against remembering" and some "who told of grandfathers who cried that the past was too awful to commit to writing".[259]

Despite the best efforts of Murphy, Sjoblom, Danielsen, John and Alice Harris and their fellow missionaries, the decade of missionary society inactivity on behalf of the Congolese people has, regrettably but inevitably, left yet another indelible, bloody stain on the pages of Christian history.

12

Congo Belge

———

Although ownership and colonial responsibility for the Congo passed to the Belgian Government on 15th November 1908 Leopold continued to exert his considerable influence, determined that the country should become wholly Roman Catholic as well as remaining a Belgian colony. Initially, he had encouraged Protestant missions, but his welcome would be no more than a means to his ends. He had seen the industry of the missionaries as they established a European presence alongside Stanley at the Pool. He had heard of the high quality of their stations and how quickly schools had been started; he had capitalised upon Bentley's explorations and used his services to map the furthest tributaries of the upper river. All of this was of benefit to the new colony and was therefore welcomed but his continued support would be conditional upon their utility.

At the outset the King had urged the Scheut Fathers (Pères de Scheut, the Congrégation du Coeur Immacule de Marie) and Jesuits in Belgium to respond to the potential opportunities presented by the opening of the Congo, but they had shown no interest. However, Cardinal Lavigerie of Algiers and founder of the French White Fathers (the Société de Notre Dame d'Afrique) was well aware of international developments and was concerned by the predominance of Protestants at the diplomatic negotiations concerning the future of the country. Following representations to Rome he was offered the possibility of work in Central Africa where he should provide orphanages for freed slave children. The expectation was that these, in turn, would establish Christian colonies "set like beacons of light in the midst of pagan surroundings".[260] His plan, like that of Protestant Arthington, was to settle missions from coast to coast across the centre of Africa. While this Catholic initiative was in Leopold's interests he was concerned by the potential political complications arising from a French, rather than Belgian, Catholic initiative.

By the time of the Berlin Agreement the Catholic government in Belgium stimulated new interest amongst their clergy. Cardinal Lavigerie recruited Belgian priests for his White Fathers, and Cardinal Goossens proposed an African Seminary to train secular priests for Congo. In 1885 the Pères de Scheut opened their first mission at Boma, expanding thereafter in the area of the Domaine de la Couronne and Kasai province. In doing so they benefited from the king's preferential oversight that granted very generous concessions.[261]

In 1886, Pope Leo XIII ruled that the Congo Free State should be reserved for Belgian missionaries.[262] Two years later an Apostolic Vicariate of the Congo was established under the Belgian Scheut Fathers and the French White Fathers withdrew. Leopold had achieved at least part of his objective. In 1893 the first Jesuits arrived followed by a variety of other Belgian Orders, always accompanied by Congregations of women as it was recognised that work among Congolese women would be essential.

In Belgium there was still little interest on the part of Protestants, who were led by the Synod of Evangelical Churches in Belgium (SECB) and the independent Eglise Chrétienne Missionnaire Belge (ECMB). Both were aware that Protestant missions in Congo were regarded with suspicion and were anxious not to disturb their own minority position.

Recognising that the exclusion of Protestant missions would jeopardise his international standing Leopold chose an alternative approach. The Catholic church was disposed to a close relationship with the State, while Protestant missions were all non-conformist. Accepting that the Protestants who had established themselves would have to remain at least for the near future, he took care to ensure that Catholic missions could settle alongside each of the Protestant stations and that no other regions would be made available to Protestants. Catholic missions were granted tax concessions, they were given large concessions of land and their goods and personnel were transported free of charge.[263] In 1906 this was formalised by a convention between the Congo Free State and the Holy See that granted the Church ownership of land in perpetuity in return for the Catholics providing education, industrial and agricultural training, teaching French as the official language and undertaking geographical tasks as required by the State.[264] The Holy Ghost Fathers returned to Katanga where they were joined by Benedictines from Bruges; Belgian Capuchin, Salesian, Dominican, and Jesuit orders started activities in northern and eastern Congo where Protestants had been prevented from acquiring land; Mill

Hill missionaries were welcomed and American Catholics were also encouraged to settle. In 1911 the Belgian government gave a total of BF 600,000 in subsidies to Congo missions of which only BF 2,500 was given to the BMS towards their medical work.[265] By 1914 the country had been divided into twenty-eight Apostolic Vicariates under whose aegis the coordinated, centralised organisation of Catholic missions throughout the Congo was assured.[266]

Despite these obvious attempts to limit Protestant missions, interest from American and British free churches had been growing. By the turn of the century the first three missions were joined by the American Presbyterians and the Plymouth Brethren and by 1911 six more missions had been started: the US Methodist Episcopal Church South, the Congo Inland Mission (American Mennonites), the Africa Inland Mission (American Methodists), the Heart of Africa Mission (British, part of the Worldwide Evangelisation Crusade), the Congo Evangelistic Mission (British Pentecostals) and the Church Missionary Society (British). Following the transfer of Congo from Leopold to Belgium it was expected that conditions for the population would change but reports from missionaries suggested there were few signs of improvement. Food taxation remained a heavy burden while the punishments inflicted if the rubber quota was short were unchanged; forced labour and the sentry system still existed. Belgium argued that change would take time and should not be expected for a few years. Guinness reported the gradual improvement to the Home Council and it was resolved not to publish any reports against the Belgian administration without Council approval[267] but assemblies of the BMS and Baptist Union sent resolutions of protest to the Foreign Office and a Free Church demonstration was held in London's Albert Hall.[268]

The following year Mr and Mrs Harris returned to see the work in which they had been involved.[269] Overall, they found many improvements were yet to be achieved. The information the Harrises were able to give to Morel suggested that further pressure should be applied, and a memorium demanding further change was delivered to the Foreign Office. Although many problems in Congo had not been resolved fully, the task of the Congo Reform Association had been completed; the last meeting was held in July 1913. Throughout the period of change since Leopold's demise the Harrises had continued to work tirelessly with Morel on behalf of the Congolese. In this they were supported enthusiastically by the BMS and the Anti-Slavery

Society but not by the CBM, which had withdrawn from any participation in the Congo Reform movement.[270,271]

In Belgium the state-subsidised church Synod proposed a single agency to combine all Protestant missions in Congo. The purpose was to ensure uniform representation to the Belgian government but would also involve the transfer of existing mission stations and property to the Belgian leadership. This was not deemed to be acceptable as it was seen to be a preliminary move towards the eventual removal of all non-Belgian Protestants from the Congo. With time, however, the British missions realised that few of their staff could speak French leading to a policy whereby all new CBM missionaries spent several months in Belgium or France for language study. Eventually, it was also recognised that having a Belgian representative in Brussels who could speak on behalf of the missions would be advantageous.

When Congo became Congo Belge, the Cong Balolo Mission had succeeded in creating five stations. The first was at Bonginda, their first place of arrival, the second at Lulonga 35 miles downriver at the confluence of the Lulonga River with the main Congo stream. Ikau, Baringa and Bongandanga were 40, 112 and 160 miles upstream on the Lopori and Maringa rivers. All was proceeding as expected from McKittrick's previous experience. Village chiefs and children alike had responded with interest. Simple schools had been started and relationships with local communities had developed well. Then, with the arrival of the ABIR rubber company all expectations of peaceful mission were disrupted. In the chapter that follows we will explore how, despite these unprecedented difficulties, the mission succeeded in establishing a functioning Christian mission that became the foundation of the Congolese church of the Balolo people.

13

Congo Balolo Mission: The Early Years

W hen the first group of missionaries arrived at Bonginda in 1889 no white person had visited the Lulonga River, so the appearance of the missionary group speaking an unknown language would have been startling. News of Stanley's aggressive descent of the main river would be remembered, but the strange craft carrying so many people was something far beyond their knowledge and caused fear in the villagers. With the enticement of bright beads the villagers overcame their fear to emerge from the forest. A great palaver was held and the reception of the missionaries thereafter was cautious but promising. What followed was a warning of the possible dangers that lay ahead.

Mata Ibenge, the chief, recognised the day's events to be something unknown to any living memory. Not only had strangers come to their village but they had not waged war and they had not gone away. These uninvited guests said they had come in peace. All they wanted was to tell the people of Bonginda of a Great Spirit of which Mata Ibenge knew nothing and, in his opinion, of which he and his people had no need. The only way of life his people had ever known was, apparently, bad but the Spirit could bring change. Why was it bad? Why should they change? His people had never changed. He was an old man respected for his wisdom and Mata Ibenge sensed that all would not be well. Had he not seen the response of his villagers to the strangers? At the end of the palaver had not Mata Lokota declared in favour of the new arrivals with the words "These words are good, white man, you shall be our father and we will be your children"? Although this was the consensus of the people it was not something a renowned chief and famous warrior would have wished to hear. The white people posed a threat to his power and authority, and to the whole way of life for the people of Bonginda.

On the whole we received a hearty welcome but there were some who set themselves against us from the first. Mata Ibenge was our inveterate enemy and vowed to kill any native who should teach us the language. He also tried to prevent the people bringing us food but as his authority was limited to his own town he could not seriously hurt us in that way. Then he formed a plot to kill us all and burn the station. As the shades of evening fell and we were quite deserted, we surmised that something was wrong. As we waited and watched one of our boys crept up to the back of the house and told us that a terrible scheme to destroy us all was to be carried out that night. Within an hour we heard the whistle of a steamer and realised with deep thankfulness that our lives were saved.[272]

This was an isolated incident. Most of the local people were disposed to be friendly, but it gave a warning of the difficulties the missionaries were likely to face. For the CBM pioneers it was a society that could not have been more different from that of Victorian England. For the people of Bonginda the new arrivals could not have been more strange and, potentially, more disturbing, but one encounter encouraged trust in the white man. A palaver had been called where the nganga, the witch doctor, was to expose the thief of some brass rods. His method was to place a blue glass bead on an iron bell. If it fell off the accused was innocent; if the bead stuck to the bell the named person was guilty. After discounting several names the nganga called Bompole, the Congolese boy who had returned from England with the missionaries. After shaking the bell the bead remained firmly stuck. This was proof that Bompole was the culprit. The missionary immediately stood by Bompole to prevent the crowd seizing him. He then requested the nganga's equipment and showed the crowd that one side was clean but the other was coated with grease. When he wanted to choose a guilty party he placed the bead on the greasy side. "There were roars of laughter – 'The white man is the biggest bonganga!'" The anger of the villagers towards the nganga was immediately evident but the missionary protected him in his own house until it was safe for him to leave the village and never return. He and his fellow ngangas continued to exercise considerable power for many years but "The witch doctors as a class seemed to know that once the people accepted our message their livelihood would be gone".[272]

Having established themselves the missionaries began to explore the country around Bonginda. "The mission stood in the middle of a long string of towns extending over two miles. At the back of these were many slave settlements dotted here and there. The first months were very much disturbed by the quarrels and fightings. Nearly every day men dashed through the station got up in their war-paint ... carrying several spears ... drums were beaten and horns blown ... at the conclusion of the fight there would be a dance in the town."[273] When sufficient progress had been made at Boginda the possibility of opening a second station was explored. One hundred kilometres up the Lopori River they came to Ikau in the Basankusu district, another very populous area easily accessible to the great but warlike Mongo tribe. They were met once again by armed men and found burned houses and human skulls. An ambitious European trader had tried to take their land and, when refused, he had burned down the village and killed six men before leaving. The name "Ikau" was said to derive from the early days of the slave trade when the place was a slaving post. Passing canoes would urge their companions to paddle faster to avoid being caught, shouting Ika-u, Ika-u, Quickly, Quickly.[274] On this occasion the news of the peaceful behaviour of the different white men at Bonginda had preceded the party and the local chiefs welcomed them. The purchase of a plot of land overlooking the river was agreed for a second station. The task was not an easy one. "Constant fighting, fears of enemies, fears of superstitious origin, cupidity, stealing, immorality, deception, cruelty to children. The nervous strain is fearful ... now commenced the first impact at Ikau of Christianity with raw heathenism ... We are the only two white men occupying this last outpost. I was haunted by the fear that I had made a mistake in coming out here at all."[275,276]

Early the following year a third station was opened 35 miles downriver from Bonginda, at Lulonga, on the north bank of the river at its confluence with the Congo. A few weeks later a fourth station was opened in March 1900 at Baringa on the Maringa River, a distance of 200 miles and three days' journey from Bonginda in the steam launch the *Evangelist*. The ABIR was already well established in the vicinity and the traders welcomed the arrival of the CBM missionaries John and Alice Harris.[277] A simple house was built, a garden planted, a school was started, simple medical care provided and a chapel constructed, attended by villagers and the bands of men who came with their quotas of rubber. The people were "somewhat wild, friendly but terribly superstitious. Some come for doctoring when they have eaten something that contains the spirit of a departed person and they are ill as a consequence." A little medicine soon dispelled the unwelcome spirit.[276]

During that first year the *Henry Reed*, borrowed from the ABMU, sailed 6,000 miles undertaking numerous trips to and from Leopoldville with supplies, and exploring the upper reaches of the Maringa and Lopori. In November 1890 the borrowed boat was replaced by CBM's own vessel the *Pioneer*, which was assembled on the Congo. Its first task was to convey an exploratory party up the Lopori to Bongandanga, where they hoped to establish another station, 100 miles from Ikau. A suitable site was chosen and purchased by McKittrick.[278] As before, the contract was signed by the Chief and witnessed by fellow villagers, none of whom could read the English in which it was written.

Bongandanga was at an elevated position on the south bank of the Lopori. To the north the Ngombe people lived in the forest that stretched to the horizon. It was, also, well populated with thousands of people who offered a warm welcome. The usual station-development practice was adopted. Men from the village were employed to help with forest clearing and the construction of accommodation. Boys and girls were invited to undertake simple tasks in the house or garden, cooking and washing clothes, as well as attending a simple school class and Bible lessons. Cannibalism and slavery were commonplace in the surrounding district and many slaves were killed on the whim of a chief, but the missionaries were able to ransom some who they then employed on the station. Although much of the missionaries' time had to be spent on exploration and the manual labour of new stations, considerable progress had also been made with language and preaching. Learning the several local languages posed a major task as they were unwritten tongues prior to the missionaries' arrival. At Bonginda Mrs McKenzie produced the first small grammar to help her colleagues.

In 1891 Harry Guinness visited Congo himself to assess the mission's achievements. After his arrival he joined the McKittricks at Bonginda. He was impressed by the size of the local population and praised the state administration for their work in suppressing inter-tribal fighting and the Arab slave trade. He moved with John McKittrick to Bongandanga and they explored the north of the region, where lived the Ngombe people. Passing beyond friendly villages they found themselves surrounded by the men of an unknown village intent on their murder from whom they escaped, firing warning shots from their rifles to deter any pursuit. Undeterred, McKittrick and Guinness set out to explore to the south a week later but both men became ill with fever. Guinness recovered but McKittrick did not. Guinness returned to England accompanied by a grieving Mrs McKittrick. News travelled to England slowly; on 29th January the following telegram arrived at Harley House: "John McKittrick died November 22nd. Dora and self returning." Later Guinness wrote, "McKittrick has gone to his eternal reward ... he has won the martyr's crown. We buried him close to the chapel in which he had so often told out the old, old story. We could not but rejoice in spite of all our grief the next day as we baptized the first five converts of the Balolo Mission."[279] Both Mrs McKittrick and Guinness were gravely ill during the journey home but both survived.

Returning in 1892 Dora McKittrick summarised the progress made during the first three years of the mission.

Generally speaking the people were anxious to please the white-man. Very seldom have we been to any town or district where we were not accorded a hearty welcome. Less than three years after our arrival in the country a great change has come over the people of the district. Fighting had practically ceased and young folk, who would not have dared to go alone beyond their own village for fear of being kidnapped and sold as slaves, moved about freely. Spear and weapons were buried ... most of them agreed that the white-man's habit of going about unarmed was the best. We invited all and sundry to come and talk their palavers on the mission station ... by this means bloodshed was avoided and frequently palavers that had lasted for more than a generation were amicably settled. Public feeling changed, too, with regard to the murder of slaves and other barbarous usages. It has become the exception and not the rule for slaves to be badly treated. It has been proved that Christianity is the great uplifting and regenerating force which can transform individual men and women and whole communities.[280]

On every station church services were conducted twice each day, children were taught from the Bible in their elementary classes and the baptism of converts was recorded. Itineration and preaching had also commenced in villages surrounding the stations.

This was undoubted progress, but it had not been achieved without a cost. When Haupt returned from furlough with his new wife in 1892 his colleague

Scammell had remained alone at Bongandanga, 100 miles from Ikau. Before the couple reached their upstream station he developed malaria, four days from help, and when help came it was too late. Then Mrs Haupt, so newly arrived, died six weeks later. Eleven days after that the Ikau station was ransacked by Mongo tribesmen, Haupt suffered a spear wound before being rescued by State troops. In the fracas, two Christian boys were carried away. A second attempt to burn the station was foiled but at the state post nearby two Belgian administrators were killed. As rumours persisted that Molongo would return, the missionaries slept for safety on a steamer provided by the State in mid-river until the unrest was resolved by a lengthy palaver. Mr Haupt then died just seven weeks after his wife, followed by Mrs Cole, Mrs Morgan, Mr Coote and Mr Todd.

Despite such grave setbacks new recruits continued to arrive. The missionaries still lived in rudimentary houses made of poles, reeds and palm thatch, and school rooms, simple churches and small hospitals of similar construction were built on all the stations. More permanent, timber and brick housing would be an advantage but this required long days of manual labour and was not completed until 1905.[281] The Congolese had not seen European tools before and had to be taught to use them. The forest had to be visited, trees selected and felled and prepared for use. Clay had to be dug and bricks moulded and burned. With time the Congolese learned these skills but initially all this work fell to the missionaries themselves.

Teaching, preaching and medical work left little time for rest. As itineration to surrounding villages developed, up to eighty miles distant on foot, bicycle or canoe, outstations were established but the travel was time consuming. Although many young people at home were offering for missionary service the numbers of suitable candidates did not match the need. A lack of human resources hampered the expansion of the mission. Church membership grew and some Congolese teachers were trained, but in Armstrong's words "For CBM it is still the day of small things as far as church membership is concerned". There were only six church members at Bonginda.[282] Nonetheless the school at Bonginda was thriving. Under the supervision of Mrs Armstrong a teacher, Bonjare, was teaching 130 children very successfully. Mrs Armstrong also held a sewing class for women to make dresses for themselves. They paid for material in brass rods and enjoyed talking together with her. A small building housed four beds and served as a basic hospital where her husband attended to the needs of the sick – some of whom walked great distances to obtain help. Everyone paid two brass rods. Many were emaciated and starving on arrival and were treated with Bovril and milk. "Some respect has been gained by the white man's medicine. Mr Gilchrist made a number of successful cures in cases of dysentery, ulcers etc. There is no doubt in my mind that we do wrong if we attempt to minister to the souls of men and leave their bodies uncared for."[283] Furthermore, as the reputation of the missionary's medical care increased the influence of witch doctors diminished.

In other respects there was good reason for encouragement. At Bongandanga Mr Bowen had translated Matthew's gospel, Acts and Corinthians into Lomongo. Mr Ruskin became known as "The man with the book": whenever he heard a new word he wrote it down, confirmed its pronunciation and origin, and made sure he understood its meaning and usage. Together with his wife he translated the gospels of Mark and John and thirteen of the New Testament Epistles into Lomongo. All of these were published by the British & Foreign Bible Society and provided the essential tools for the missionaries' prime task. By November 1901 there was a total staff of thirty-eight missionaries: twenty-one in Congo, seventeen on furlough; twenty single men, four single women and seven married couples.[284] A year later Guinness was able to report: "In the past thirteen years, ninety-six missionaries have been sent out, of whom thirty have laid down their lives. 35 remain on the staff, 6 with the home side of the work, 8 joined other missions, 9 retired through ill-health, 8 proved unsatisfactory."[285]

Reviewing the work of the mission in late 1902, veteran Charles Harvey wrote that the local work at each of the stations was self-supporting, there was a tendency towards self-government and the people were learning well. "They have only the New Testament but soon become familiar with it and can hold their own against heathenism and Romanism. There are many encounters between Catholic and Protestant but it is a very unequal contest because the native Catholic is grossly ignorant of Christian truth. There would be little to fear of the ability of the native [Protestant] Christian to carry on the work of God on the Congo"[286] At Impilenge, a village five miles from Bonginda, the villagers erected their own church and school. Three men were baptised and other candidates started to do their own evangelism, including two women. 1902 saw another important development for Protestant missions in Congo – the first meeting of a United Conference attended by representatives of the eight Protestant missions working in the country including the ABMU, BMS, Swedish Mission, American Presbyterian Mission, Christian and Missionary Alliance, and the Congo Balolo Mission. Together they reported the following activity: 211 Protestant missionaries; 283 native evangelists; 327 native teachers; 40 main stations; 192 outstations; 6,521 communicants; 1,470 catechumens; 5,641 attending Sunday Schools; 10,162 attending Day Schools. In the same year, at Ikau, a replacement church was built, the opening of which was attended by nearly 500. The school was attended by 550 children and young adults and a further 150 attended the school at an outstation. From Baringa Harris reported that they were looking forward to receiving the first member into the church in the near future.

1904 celebrated the commissioning of a printing press at Bongandanga that employed trained Congolese assistants who were capable of the whole process of composition, proofreading, printing and binding. One of the fist publications was the first issue of the Congo Balolo Mission Record, a quarterly report of the mission's work. Soon the press was printing a wide variety of scripture translations, an improved Lomongo grammar by Ruskin together with a schoolbook with translations from the Old Testament. At Lulonga Mr Gilchrist was busy with a dictionary and grammar in Eleko. It was recognised that education would be the key to success. Schools often met in the open air with several hundred children and young adults attending. School started with a hymn and prayer followed by teaching from the Bible. At the end of the day when the sun set the Congolese usually returned to their houses but, if the moon was bright, meetings were held in the evenings too. However, the CBM area was undergoing a significant population change resulting from the oppression of the rubber trade and disease. A photograph taken in 1905 by missionary Whiteside shows a large but abandoned village: "Five years ago Lulama had between 3,000 and 4,000 inhabitants; but by constant oppression and murders on the part of the ABIR sentries, the population has now decreased to less than a hundred."[287] Year on year there were numerous deaths from smallpox and sleeping sickness. The Trypanosome that causes sleeping sickness and is transmitted by the tsetse fly had been present in Africa since pre-history. It is endemic in wild animals, and humans have little resistance to the disease. Epidemics occurred in Congo following attempts to raise livestock in the 19th century. CBM's Mrs Morgan became the first European to contract the disease in Central Africa,

Fig 21 Church at Baringa.

followed by Mrs Ruskin. Fortunately, both were treated successfully with experimental treatment in Leopoldville and London, but such therapy was not available to the Congolese. One epidemic in 1903 killed thousands in the CBM area: "Towns and villages teeming with a virile population ... counted tens instead of hundreds and hundreds instead of thousands."[288]

During the years that followed interest in the missionary message ebbed and flowed. Sometimes 300 would sit into the night to hear the good news. Before going to the hunt they would sing a hymn and have prayer. In 1904 there were seventeen on the Lulonga church roll, by 1907 there were fifty-three[289] and a fine permanent church building had been completed.[290] At Bonginda there were "revivals" in 1899, 1905 and 1907 but there followed a period of lethargy with a return to pre-Christian ways, such that the church was disbanded. After two years four previous members returned and the small church began to grow again.

At the close of 1906 the CBM had a total of thirty six staff. Some time before 1908 a trial station on the Juapa River was burned down and the mission was obliged by the State to abandon it. In 1909 a new station opened at Mompono and another at Yuli to serve the Ikalemba River population of 40,000. As time passed life on the rivers changed. The start of the second decade at Bonginda saw a significant further population decrease and it was decided that the first of the mission's stations should be closed. At the other stations the rapid extension of recent years was followed by a period of consolidation. The number of staff, forty-one, remained constant. Six years later the mission considered itself to be in a sufficiently robust condition to consider expansion once again: Yoseki, nearly 100 miles north east of Mompono, would be the CBM's eighth upriver station. Isefo from Mompono and his wife, a young schoolteacher, undertook the initial work of creating a new station before the arrival of missionaries. In the same year the Congo Protestant Council allocated areas of the country to specific missions, to avoid overlap and duplication of work. To the surprise of the CBM a large territory north of the main river, between the Ubangi and Mongalla Rivers, was apportioned to them. The country was populated thickly by the Bangala (Ngombe) people and had been untouched previously by any Protestant mission, although the presence of the Roman Catholic church was well established. Despite this potential for development, a lack of resources would prevent any expansion for eight years.

For the CBM missionaries, life was very isolated in terms of European company. Visitors would, almost always, arrive unannounced and therefore be an unexpected but welcome surprise, bringing news of the 'outside world'. Back in England, there had been several significant changes in the central organisation of the mission. Students from the Institute embarked on a new venture in the state of Bihar in northern India. A new name for this expanding overseas activity was therefore needed: the "Regions Beyond

Fig 22 Yuli, Congo Balolo Mision station.

Missionary Union" convened for the first time in January 1899 under the direction of Dr Harry Guinness.[291] His mother, Mrs Fanny Guinness senior, who had been the driving force of the Institute and the Livingstone Inland Mission, had died the previous year. Her husband, Henry Grattan Guinness senior, continued for several years with his prolific writing and international evangelism until his death in 1910. Over a period of three years there was growing criticism of the leadership of the mission that caused considerable disquiet. Harry Guinness's autocratic ways had become increasingly unwelcome; letters of resignation were written but eventually withdrawn.[292,293] Guinness continued with an expanded management board, and loyalty was restored. During this time other, new foreign missions were starting up and the pattern of recruitment, and the needs of missionaries in training, changed. As a consequence, the East London Institute became no longer viable and closed in 1914. There then followed what some probably thought could be a final blow. Dr Harry Guinness, co-founder with John McKittrick and the director of the mission, died at the age of only fifty-three on 26th May 1915. The cause was, almost certainly, amoebic infection that he contracted during a second visit to Congo in 1910.

It will have become apparent to readers that, by now, the CBM was functioning during the period of the First World War. For the missionaries in Congo, remote from the scene of war, daily life continued much as ever but by the end of 1918 the workforce was struggling. Six missionaries died, two were invalided home and one resigned. With thirteen staff on furlough there were only twenty working across six stations.

The greatest difficulty we had to face was the staffing of our stations. Great have been our losses during the war, no new workers have been forthcoming ... We had most reluctantly to withdraw the missionaries from Baringa. ... Yoseki feels bereaved for the lack of missionaries ... Our greatest need is the New Testament. The Lomongo edition published in 1908 is quite exhausted, a new version is being prepared ... The need for workers is very great.[294]

In July 1919 the Home Council received a letter from Bompongo, who wrote on behalf of his fellow Yoseki church members: "To ko sumola bosala mmendo ena Yoseki bo leki ... The work here at Yoseki is very great; the children of God are increasing in the Church. Now we have reached the number of fifty-six. We are trying now to tell the people in all our region the message of Jesus. We thank God because He sent us teachers …. [but] our teachers are not sufficient because the districts are so very many."[295]

The year following there was the international influenza pandemic. Doubtless carried from Europe by travellers, the virus made its way upriver where "it raged with great virulence". Schools and churches were closed. No missionary succumbed but amongst the church members many were victims. For so many families there were many sad days and exhausting weeks but there was also encouragement. Cartwright reported that they were opening five new schools in the Yoseki district.[296] The work and commitment of the Congolese pastors, evangelists and village teachers were crucial to the survival of the mission. Bamenga carried on the work in the absence of missionaries at Baringa, Likumba at Ikau, and Yoka at Lulonga, revealed strong leadership both on the stations and in local villages. Two years previously when Mr Jeffrey had died at Yoseki an evangelist from Mompono, Isefo, who could neither read nor write had gone to the station and led the small group of Christians.

However, in the view of Joseph Conley, the future did not look promising. "For the RBMU the third decade of the new century hardly qualified as 'The Roaring Twenties'. They were more like a whimper. The mission moved into a holding pattern. No new missionaries were sent out. Furloughs were postponed, except for medical emergency. Mission finances were exhausted."[297] Betty Pritchard, from RBMU India, shared his view: "Disillusioned by post-war Britain … people were seeking to drown their depression in a frantic search for pleasure. God and his word were disregarded and interest in missions was almost dead. The finances of the Union had touched rock bottom."[298] Exhausted? Disillusioned? A Whimper? Let us consider, again, the evidence.

14

The Roaring Twenties

———

In the immediate post-war period there was a cohort of young people in British churches, some too young to serve in the wartime military effort, who were about to embark on adult working life. In England three new missionary training colleges were opened: in 1919 the Mount Vernon Ladies' College and the Ridgelands Bible College, also for women, and in 1923 the All Nations Bible College for men. The collective outcome was a significant number of young men and women intent on overseas mission. Frederick Hart, previously with the Royal Garrison Artillery, arrived in Congo in May 1920 accompanied by three young women. The mission's financial shortfall also recurred but a single large donation rescued the mission's finances and other generous funding followed. Later in the year seventeen more new staff arrived including several nurses, young men from All Nations influenced by the college Principal, Rev F. B. Meyer, who was also the Acting Director of the RBMU. Also, crucially, Dr Edgar Wide, the first qualified doctor since Dr Simms.

There were now forty staff in Congo plus nine more on furlough. Seven stations were fully functional, three of which had their own resident pastors: Bamenga at Baringa, Injmbo at Ikau and Yoka at Lulonga. On each station a church, a school and dispensary were flourishing. A decision was taken to build a hospital at Baringa but in the meanwhile Dr Wide started a much-needed medical service at the Ikau dispensary. On foot, by bicycle or motorcycle itineration to nearby districts was expanding; village schools and churches were established, evangelists and teachers busy. Two major achievements crowned the decade, both of them undertaken by Mr and Mrs Ruskin. In 1924 the first Lomongo-French English dictionary was published on the mission press at Bongandanga.

In 1928 the whole Bible translated into Lomongo was completed by the Ruskins and published by the British & Foreign Bible Society in 1930. Thirty-four years of meticulous work, every word typed by Lily Ruskin on her portable typewriter. The first Bible in a Bantu language had been the translation into Tswana by Robert Moffat in South Africa in 1857. The BMS published a Kikongo translation in 1916 for the people of the Lower River. A whole Bible in Lingala, now the common language of northwest DRC, would not be available until 1969.

Fig 23 **Mr & Mrs E A Ruskin.**

Such was the confidence of the staff at their 1925 Annual Conference that it was decided to establish a Training Institute at Mompono for advanced teaching of evangelists and village teachers. The first nine students started in January 1926 under the supervision of Mr and Mrs Carpenter. Dispensaries were busy on seven stations. During the year there were more than 80,000 attendances. Effective injection treatment for sleeping sickness and syphilis had been commenced and infant welfare and maternity services were proving popular. Conference also took the decision to explore the Bangala Territory north of the Congo River, allocated previously by the Congo Protestant Council. A journey

Fig 24 Mrs Ruskin with staff of the printing press, Bongandanga.

with several evangelist volunteers, two weeks by riverboat, canoe and trekking overland revealed a population of more than 47,000 from three different tribes living in well organised, populous villages, many of whom

CONGO FIELD CONFERENCE, 1928.

Fig 25 CBM missionary staff at annual conference 1928.

had little previous contact with foreigners. The Roman Catholics had been in the territory for some time, although with little success.[299] It was agreed that a new station should be started at Tamudjumbe without delay. Three evangelists set to work clearing land, building simple accommodation and getting to know the village people. In January 1929 the first four missionaries joined their Congolese colleagues to commence what would be the first new major project for many years.

For a relatively small mission the geographical area of the CBM was extensive. The Yoseki district alone, to the east, was a little larger than Wales. The journey cross-country from Mompono to Yoseki took seven days on foot. Given the long distances between stations and the absence of roads the mission's riverboat, the second *Livingstone*, commissioned a decade before, was the principal mode of transport and communication. Maintained by Fred Anstice, accompanied by his wife and a Christian Congolese crew of forty, the boat covered over 8,000 miles per year. As a trained nurse Olive Anstice held antenatal and baby welfare clinics on board at every stop, an unusual but effective extension to the mission's evangelism and social work. The captain, Bonkumu, was respected by government officials, traders and African passengers; the crew ran a mechanical repair business for the passing

Fig 26 PS Livingtone on the Maringa River.

riverside villages to generate income. Services were held each day on board, riverside fishing camps and villages were visited regularly and literature in five languages was sold in large quantities. Following Dr Wide's arrival in 1928 the decision was taken to build the hospital at Baringa where leprosy was particularly prevalent, instead of Ikau.

By 1929 there were nine stations; 668 sub-stations; 14,653 church members; 10,123 enquirers; 227 evangelists; 696 school teachers and 21,438 scholars. Readers may ask if all this was appreciated by the Congolese? Did they wish missionary work to continue? A letter addressed to Mr Gamman provides an answer.

Herewith the sum of 2,000 Francs. This is a gift from the Church at Ikau to help send another missionary. They have over 11,000 Francs as a Church balance and they divided it as follows:

To send a new missionary	2,000Fr.
To build a church at Basankusu	3,000Fr.
To Ikau church fittings	1,000Fr.
To Poor Fund	1,000Fr.
To Ikau Hospital	4,000Fr.

Despite Conley and Pritchard's predictions the difficulties that threatened the survival of the mission in the immediate post-war years had been overcome. The mission had become a firmly established, thriving endeavour by the end of the decade.

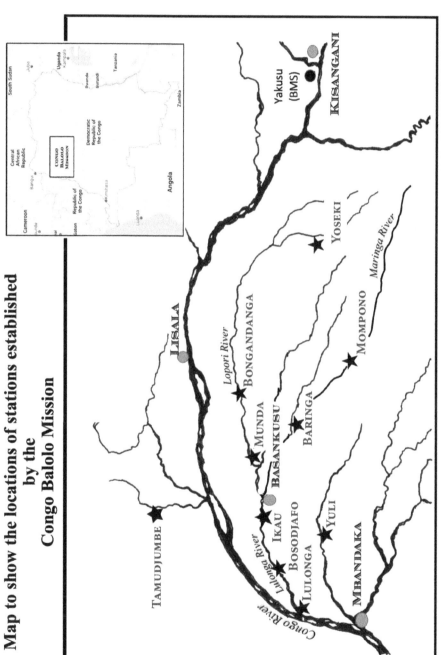

Fig 27 Maps to show the locations of stations established by the Congo Balolo Mission in the Basankusu District of Equateur Province.

15

Thirty Years: 1930-1960

Following the surge of CBM activity in the 1920s the prime objective of evangelism was well under way, although there were still many thousands of people who had not yet been contacted. All the missionaries, therefore, continued to undertake regular itineration to reach previously untouched populations. At the new station at Tamudjumbe the first converts were baptised in 1931 but by 1936 there had been significant movement of the local population. Ngbenze to the east (later known as Gwenje) was the centre of 200 villages with no Protestant presence. A fresh start was made, supported by experienced evangelists. The Ngombe people still had an aggressive reputation. Superstition and witchcraft were widespread, men carried knives and spears, and visiting government officials were sometimes attacked. In 1937 another new station was started at Munda.

On a daily basis a great many practical and administrative matters occupied the missionary's time but evangelism was the constant all-encompassing task. For the new Christian, however, conversion was just the start of a new way of life that required instruction, encouragement and sustenance. Initially that required missionary guidance and supervision but, in the long term, would have to be provided in churches by fellow Congolese Christians. In 1933 evangelist training schools were started at Mompono and Bongandanga. The carefully selected students were young men, literate and numerate, who had completed a basic education and shown promise in their personal lives and church work. The teaching concentrated on New Testament Christianity and evangelism skills. Their wives were able to attend with them and were taught to read, write and improve their domestic skills so as to be able to support their husbands and work with village women. After two years the school at Mompono was re-named the "Ecole Biblique" and extended its accommodation. Students were taught in Lingala and French so that they would be able to work in any part of the CBM area. This vital forward-thinking educational facility was led by Mr and Mrs Hanson

Fig 28 First meeting of the CBM Congolese Pastors' Conference, 1931.

and continued successfully for the following twenty-seven years, supplying the growing church with many of its future leaders.

In 1935 the CBM joined the new countrywide "Eglise du Christ au Congo" proposed by the Congo Protestant Council and a local innovation, the first Church Council for the CBM group of churches, was attended by all the pastors, evangelists and some elders. Missionaries attended ex-officio. Officers were elected, agreement was reached that ten continuous years in church membership was required to be a pastor, and women in polygamy and the young who could not read could not be baptised. Two years later the Ikau church took another lead by forming its own Church Council that met quarterly to appoint evangelists and teachers, receive donations, pay salaries, and settle palavers. In this way the Ikau church became truly indigenous, setting an example that was soon followed on the other stations. Slowly but steadily all the churches became self-supporting. In principle they were also self-governing but when problems arose it was always to the missionaries that the church leaders turned.

Although schools and medical care were considered to be secondary for an evangelical Protestant mission, they had become major concerns. If a convert was to understand his or her new religion they would need to be able

Fig 29 Students at Mompono Bible School.1939.

to read the Bible in their own language. Translation had been addressed with commendable success from the earliest days of the mission.[300] By 1930 the Bongandanga press was producing 16,000 copies a year of books and literature, with all the compilation, printing, sewing and binding done by Congolese staff. In 1935 State regulations required that the title page of all publications should be in French as well as the local language and French should be taught in all mission schools. This requirement was implemented.

Inevitably, the introduction of elementary literacy would stimulate a far greater hunger for general education, to which the mission had responded at village level.[301] The Protestant and Roman Catholic missions became the main providers of schools throughout rural Congo. In the villages the roles of evangelist and teacher were combined and given greater authority. Literacy for women was discouraged by traditional society, but many were anxious to learn and that their daughters should attend school. Baby welfare clinics and sewing groups were regularly accompanied by literacy classes. Kindergartens were started, often attended by the children of families receiving hospital treatment.

Fig 30 Girls' boarding school, Ikau. 1944.

Fig 31 Students at girls' school, Ikau 1944.

At the 1950 field conference the question of girls' education was debated vigorously. "It was generally agreed that in the past they had been neglected in favour of boys. Several ladies stressed their call to this particular work. Tribal differences, great distances, and problems of transport render central girls' schools impractical but it was suggested that every encouragement be given to run girls' schools and that ladies be set aside for this work."[302] The intention was clear, but two years later the project was abandoned for lack of the necessary personnel.[303] Again, in 1952, the need for more qualified educational missionaries was publicised but plans had to be abandoned. One factor inhibiting recruitment was the requirement of the colonial administration that all teachers should complete a one-year course in French in Belgium.[304]

By 1955 that situation had been remedied. Every station had at least one school with boarding for girls and some for boys, some of them attended by up to sixty boarders plus half as many day pupils. The children lived in dormitories, grew their own food in gardens and cooked communally, all supervised by trained 'monitors' some of whom augmented the missionary teaching staff. With the passage of time the importance of education to the development of the Congo as a country had become increasingly obvious. Recognising this, the Belgian colonial administration took an increasing interest in and greater control over education, albeit doing relatively little towards its provision. Initially, state grants were generous but when these diminished the resources of the mission were severely stretched. The 'missionary' objective, however, remained. "While the primary aim of our school work is spiritual we owe it to the Protestant community to give their children a good educational background. We long to see a literate, intelligent Church in Congo and it is to this end that our educational efforts are directed."[305]

The second major departure from evangelism was healthcare. Although not emphasised by the mission's founders, this was in keeping with most other Protestant missions. It had been the offer of medical care that challenged the use of fetishes and the power of the medicine men that impressed the Congolese first. During the 1920s several of the new recruits were nurses who quickly found themselves running a station dispensary with a few beds. Alone, with limited medicines and no doctor, seeing to hundreds of ill people, they found themselves facing injuries and problems way beyond their previous experience.

The arrival of Dr Edgar Wide in 1928 and the building of a sixty-bed hospital at Baringa transformed the acute healthcare situation for many thousands of people. The greatest demand was treatment for the endemic infectious diseases, for which the mission nurses had already been administering medicines provided by the colonial government. The second need was surgery for emergencies, trauma, Caesarean section and elective procedures. Before that was possible Wide would have to build his own hospital.

Plans were drawn, forest was cleared, bricks were made and fired in kilns, roofing timber was cut from the forest, palm thatch woven and water

Fig 32 Baringa Hospital. 1938–1944.

Fig 33 A corner of the Lifeta Leprosy Village.

pumped from a nearby stream. The new hospital was opened and dedicated by Pastor Bamenga on 27th February 1933.[306] It was a remarkable achievement for a young doctor with but a year's postgraduate experience in England and not yet thirty. The name given to Wide by the people of Baringa was appropriate: Likibi, meaning "strong foundation". A diesel generator to provide electricity arrived in 1938. In the first seven months there were 12,911 outpatient attendances by more than 2,000 people; 3,540 injections for yaws, syphilis, leprosy and sleeping sickness were given. There were 191 inpatient admissions and 146 operations performed, ninety-six of them major. The following year the numbers doubled. With help of nurses Lilian Richards and Margaret Williams a staff of sixteen Congolese nurses were trained, half of whom obtained the State "Aide-Infirmier" certificate. The nurse-led dispensaries on the other stations were all increasingly busy seeing

Fig 34 Dr E R Wide.   *Fig 35* Nursing Staff at Baringa hospital. 1964

thousands of people each year; nurses were trained at Baringa for work at these other dispensaries. Anyone needing surgery across the mission area had to travel to Baringa on foot, carried in a litter, by canoe or by riverboat. Many did not survive the journey.

Another pressing medical problem was also awaiting attention. Leprosy. It was estimated that in the Baringa district there were 1,000 people with the disease, with over 5,000 in the whole mission area. In some villages it amounted to 20% of the population. By 1939 a leprosy village, Lifeta, was created in the forest five kilometres from Baringa with sixty-five patients and their families living in individual huts with a garden to grow their own food. Clinical facilities, nurses' accommodation, a school for the children and a small church were on site. The teacher-evangelist was receiving treatment himself with chaulmoogra oil injections provided initially by local government. Twenty acres of chaulmoogra trees were planted for future home-grown supplies. Disease-free children went to the school in Baringa. Some families had travelled over 200 miles from their home villages for treatment. By 1945 there were 364 residents, of whom 232 were receiving treatment. This number would increase year on year until a peak of 1,150 was reached in 1951.[307] Over the years church membership had increased at Lifeta under the leadership of Ekwalanga Timoteo, the senior nurse who had also studied at the Mompono Bible School, but the missionaries' annual conference report noted "We wish that progress in spiritual things kept pace with the advance in medical science".[308]

Fig 36 Yoseki Hospital.

With time it became increasingly obvious that a realistic response to medical need required at least one other hospital. When Dr Arthur Wright and his wife Elizabeth, a nurse, arrived this became a possibility. A potential site at Yoseki was surveyed in 1946 and a British builder joined the mission for the construction of the hospital. Applications for state permission were processed very slowly and it was not until December 1948 that a hospital and leprosy colony were opened. A contributory factor to the delay was that state funding would contribute to the building costs, and Roman Catholic authorities made a prolonged attempt to gain access to Protestant hospitals and schools if such state funding was approved.

The new hospital was based on the design adopted at Baringa, and built by local men. Alongside the clinical facilities a cookhouse and simple accommodation was provided for patients' families.[309] The cost was significant, met partly by state funds but supplemented by generous financial support from the American Leprosy Mission and the RBMU Toronto Council. The continuing support received from the New York Medical & Surgical Relief Committee and Toronto was greatly appreciated. Within the first year the need for the hospital was confirmed with 2,857 new patients of whom 530 required admission; 49,883 outpatient attendances; 3,686 injections; 536 operations of which 183 were major; and 34 midwifery cases.[310] The leprosarium had also required a great deal of work to clear 100 hectares of forest. Those patients who were fit enough were paid to build their own houses and plant their own gardens alongside the large dispensary and church. Within a year 150 patients were receiving treatment and there had been 1,818 attendances at the outpatient leprosy clinic. Twelve people, including several children, had already returned home symptom free. A third component of the medical work at Yoseki was the provision of a visiting service to three nearby coffee and oil-palm factories which offered opportunities for Christian outreach.

Shortly after completing this medical development a third hospital was established under the direction of Dr Margaret Owen at Yuli. The new hospital was dedicated in memory of the local pastor, Bolanga Joseph, and two CBM missionaries, Trixie Broom and Margaret Brown, all of whom died in a tragic air crash en route to Leopoldville on 13th May 1948. In 1956, the local people asked that a leprosy facility should be established. Without waiting for official formalities to be completed the villagers built the necessary accommodation. Observing such enthusiastic self-help, an elderly Belgian man living in the vicinity offered financial support for the first year.

From time to time the hospitals and leprosaria were inspected by state officials. Their reports were always complimentary, ensuring grants and medical supplies were forthcoming; the Leprosy Missions on both side of the Atlantic were also generous. By 1960 leprosy had been almost eliminated from the CBM area and only a few cured people who no longer had a family or an alternative home needed to remain. It was a successful story illustrating the extent of medical need in the rural population. Although surgery was an important component, by far the greatest need was the treatment and control of infectious diseases, pre- and post-natal care, hygiene, nutritional education and public health awareness.

Another concern for any foreign organisation was the wellbeing of mission staff. For their own health it was deemed advisable that furloughs should be taken at intervals, usually one year in five. If one or other of the doctors was absent one of the hospitals was left without qualified medical personnel. This also applied to all the other activities of the mission. Because all foreign staff were so fully occupied whenever furloughs were taken evangelism, medical care and education were inevitably curtailed. Every annual conference generated an appeal for more staff. At Tamudjumbe when

Mrs Chilvers left for furlough all the girls at the school left, some to get married and others to transfer to a Roman Catholic school. On her return it took much work and patience to restart the school. At one stage Yuli was without a permanent missionary for six years, causing church members considerable distress. In 1952 the Lulonga station was closed for a year. In 1955 shortage of staff and the remoteness of Gwenge station necessitated its closure and transfer to the American Mission Evangelique en Ubengi. The lack of finance was also a recurring factor that curtailed work on several occasions. The five years following the end of the Second World War were particularly lean. While CBM churches and village schools were self-supporting, when donations in the UK fell funds for the Ecole Biblique, schools and hospitals were threatened. To limit possible restrictions of these vital activities the missionaries accepted very significant reductions in personal allowances for several years.

In 1955 a Swiss missionary society expressed interest in working with the RBMU in Congo. The outcome was that twenty-five Swiss missionaries from the Schweizerische Missions-Gemeinschaft (the Swiss Missionary Fellowship) joined the mission over the following forty-five years, a fruitful collaboration that made a very significant contribution. The first was Dorli Schwemmer in January 1956 followed by Theo and Margrit Werner-Laubli and Ruth Werner, who were amongst the longest-serving CBM staff, remaining in Congo for more than thirty years.

When reviewing the development of the Congo Balolo Mission it is relevant to reflect on the development of Christianity in Britain long before. Although there were some Christians among the Roman army of occupation in the first century, the first determinedly missionary endeavours were those of Augustine to southern England in 597, the possibly earlier settlement of missionaries from Rome in Ireland and on Iona leading to Aidan's successful commission to the people of Northumberland and the founding of a monastery at Lindisfarne in 634. Their itineration, preaching and teaching bore fruit and Christian communities grew around the focus of monasteries. As numbers increased churches were established and an organisational structure developed that would secure their continuation, self-support and self-governance. Recognising the need for copies of the Christian scriptures and devotional material, monastic scriptoria were kept busy producing these by hand. The population at large, however, was illiterate and, of necessity, mission embarked on education; the monasteries started to educate the general population and, later, the Church created universities; education at all levels was an essential extension of Christian mission. Average life expectancy in Britain was only thirty years. Disease, inter-tribal warfare and poverty were the norm. The missionaries could not stand by: monasteries added an infirmary to care for the sick and infirm. When leprosy became endemic in the 11th century it was the religious institutions that created leper houses and settlements to contain the disease and care for the dying. The provision of education and healthcare was integral to the development of Christianity in Britain for almost a millennium and proved to be so again in Africa in the twentieth century.

16

Independence

On the 30th June 1960 Congo gained its independence from Belgian colonial rule. Four days later the Congolese army mutinied. Prime Minister Lumumba dismissed all Belgian senior officers. Within weeks 25,000 Belgians had fled the country and 10,000 Belgian troops flew in to protect Belgian interests. Widespread anti-Belgian sentiment and violence erupted with many Europeans attacked, including Belgian priests who were abused and nuns raped.[311]

The CBM missionaries had been well aware of the coming of Independence. From the start of the Round Table Conference in Brussels in January they followed the daily news on the radio. There had been some preliminary discussions with church leaders about its significance, and Congolese staff were opposed to white people leaving.[312] On Independence Day itself everyone at Baringa gathered in the Foyer at Lifeta to listen to events in Leopoldville. The following day "was a quiet day ... prayer meeting in the evening".[313] Nobody predicted the social and political turmoil that ensued. The mission's Equatorial Province was described as "the quietest of the six because it is the poorest, no copper, gold, diamonds or other allurement". There was concern, however, with the attitude of the young people: "Independence for them means the taking away of all restraints and liberty for them to do just what they please."[314] School work became particularly difficult as contracts with the Belgian administration ended and all the teachers returned to their home villages as no further remuneration for Protestant schools would be forthcoming until the new contracts were arranged. Despite such problems it was agreed that the mission's schools should be restarted as soon as possible.[315]

On 10th July a Roman Catholic priest brought news that the evacuation of all European women and children had been advised.[316] CBM staff were requested to travel to Ikau for the previously planned annual conference. Two days previously Len and Mabel Hanson had been due to leave

Mompono for furlough. John Bruce took them to Boende for their plane to Kinshasa. Hardly had they left than mutinying soldiers arrived and it was reported that the resident Catholic priests "had a very bad time, not a single one escaped". The Featherstones, who were alone at Mpenzele, later recalled their journey to Ikau. As they passed through villages people stared at them silently. In the background the drums were beating and there was dancing. Their vehicle broke down at a river crossing and, at first, no Congolese would agree to help them; all other Europeans were driving in the opposite direction hoping to escape the country.

Tension was rising at Basankusu and the Congolese church elders were aware of the potential dangers but knowing that most Europeans were fleeing the country, they requested that some of the older missionaries should remain, fearing that if all the CBM staff left all the mission and church property would be endangered. Additionally, the sense of desertion their departure would create would undermine the respect and affection of the people that had been so hard won. The outcome was that Alfred Ivimey, Mr & Mrs Bajotti, Dr & Mrs Wide, Mr & Mrs Walling, Mr & Mrs Featherstone, John Bruce and Raymond Brookes would stay. If possible, the others would get to Kinshasa and possibly the UK. On the 22nd a plane landed at the Basankusu airstrip. Ex-CBM missionary Fred Anstice, working for the Belgian airline Sabena, had arranged the flight to evacuate his former colleagues. Similarly, a second plane arrived to evacuate the Swiss missionaries.[317]

The Hansons, at Boende, encountered a very different experience. Their flight had been cancelled and many other Europeans were arriving with no luggage, bloodstained from severe beatings. A plane was on the runway waiting for women and children only. Although unwilling Mabel left, leaving her husband not knowing if she would see him again. Len was arrested and imprisoned with three other men, but a senior officer identified him as a missionary and ordered his release. After United Nations paratroops secured the airstrip he and seventy-three other men were flown to Kinshasa. Much later he was to discover that the army officer was Joseph Mobutu, Army Chief of Staff and later Mobutu Sese Seko, President of the country When the Hansons returned the following year their Bible School at Mompono was no more.[318] At Ngbenze the Davey family were on the north bank of the Congo several days' journey from other CBM colleagues. Warned by a Belgian doctor of approaching danger they hurriedly dispatched their two young daughters by plane to Europe while they escaped by boat downriver to Kinshasa.

At Ikau the situation remained calm. Faced with the upsurge of nationalist feeling the Ikau pastor, Lofinda Benjamin, "exercised a calming influence over church members, teachers and adherents. Although accused of bias towards the missionary, he stood firm for what he believed was the best for the church and all concerned."[319] Sunday church services were held as usual. At Basankusu the newly appointed Congolese Administrator was determined to maintain peace and considered it safe for the missionaries who remained to return to their stations. On the 25th the Wides and Bruce returned to Baringa, where they received a tremendous welcome. "The lepers were especially glad to see us for they had doubted whether they would ever see us again so drastic had been the routing out of all the white folk from the whole region. In our territory, which is about two-thirds the size of Belgium, only three other Europeans remained."[320] A few days later the Wallings returned to Yoseki. Prior to Independence there had been over 100 European residents in the area but now there were four. "The population in general were bewildered, apprehensive and suspicious of all white intentions but the welcome from the church was overwhelming." There was, nonetheless, a determination that independence in the country meant independence for the church and all aspects of life. All church responsibilities were handed over to a superintendent pastor and a church treasurer, and the school to a Congolese teacher. "Theoretically it would seem that we now have very little to do. The medical need is of course tremendous."[321] Assessing future prospects Ivimey observed: "With the coming of Independence the nature of our missionary work has taken on an entirely different phase. For the older missionary it is difficult to adapt himself to the sudden change. To the new recruit he will have to seek for himself to know how best he can serve the Congolese church."[322]

Such negative feelings were understandable but from the Congolese perspective there was greater confidence. Pastor Lokuli Simon from Mompono wrote "Awa na Mompono mawa mingi ... At Mompono there is much sorrow ... some of the soldiers did not treat the Europeans very well and now we have no white man living with us ... if our white man is courageous he will come back to us. Although Congo is now independent that is no reason for the missionaries to leave us."[323] Similarly, Elongi Michel at Mpenzele Yuli: "Ekiso tofa la ilombe ya Nzakomba y'olotsi nye ... We have no good house of God and we remain on our own.... There is very much work and we have only one pastor."[324] And Mokalo Simon at Lulonga: "Mpo na liboso, tojali na mawa mingi mpo ... We are sad that our missionaries left us, however, we have been managing well at Lulonga. The church is well and the people have a desire to attend the meetings. Here at Lulonga all is peaceful and there are no palavers. We are praying that our missionaries may return to us."[325]

On 4th September President Kasavubu dismissed Prime Minister Lumumba and a few days later Joseph Mobutu grasped control of the government. For Europeans Leopoldville was in turmoil. United Nations army personnel advised that it was too dangerous to enter the town and arranged for military transport to the safety of Brazzaville, where flights to Europe were possible.[326]

At Baringa and Yoseki many Congolese villagers had fled into the forest for safety but began to return to their homes. More and more sick people started to arrive at the Baringa hospital. Of the 1,200 doctors in Congo before 30 June only 120 would remain; Baringa was the only functioning hospital in the whole mission area. Particularly distressing was the number of women who needed Caesarean section whose babies died in the womb as they walked through the forest in labour for several days.[327] "Folk are bewildered; most do not understand politics or the economy. What does get them is no soap, no sugar, no salt, no paraffin for their lamps. Lawlessness is everywhere apparent."[328]

Despite the warm welcome that greeted the returning missionaries, the future of missionary work seemed uncertain. Some Congolese local administrators, promoted overnight, were enthusiastic to establish their authority and encouraged anti-European sentiment. The Wallings were particularly isolated at Yoseki. Having arrived, it was deemed too dangerous to drive through hostile villages to return to Baringa. The Lumumbist Movement National Congolais (MNC) was dominant in the district, demanding evidence of "Africanisation" of all church and mission activities, seeking to infiltrate the church membership and implying that the continued presence of missionaries was possible only with their approval.[329] When Bruce drove to Mompono he found the station destroyed. Roman Catholic priests who attempted to return to Mompono were also driven away. Elsewhere, however, the missionaries were welcomed. Church–mission relationships were said in some places to be strained and some church leaders had adopted the nationalist fervour and were demanding complete relinquishment of all missionary control.[330] Despite this understandable enthusiasm to implement independence, on a few occasions when missionaries were threatened the church members and local villagers rushed to their defence and ensured their safety. "The two weeks since we returned have been pretty grim and we have had one or two rather terrifying visits but they have ended well. Our own people are absolutely grand; there is always someone near … they have succeeded in showing us such love that we did not dream they had for us."[331]

The behaviour of some members of the newly appointed civil administration certainly gave rise to tensions that were always in the background. The missionaries' concern, however, was to establish, through discussion with Congolese colleagues on each of the stations, the possible ways in which the missionaries could continue to serve the churches, the schools and hospitals if that was what the Congolese people wanted. Most of the evacuated staff were also keen to return if so wanted.

In September the first post-Independence General Council Meeting of the CBM church leaders and missionaries was held at Baringa. It was attended by twenty-three Congolese delegates and six CBM missionaries. From the missionaries' perspective the CBM had been working towards Congolese autonomy for many years with the expectation that this would be complete within a further decade. The events of July 1960 presented the meeting with the demand that complete autonomy should be recognised immediately. Although discussions were not easy there was general support for a document, prepared jointly, that set out future relationships between the mission and the new church, the Eglise Evangélique de la Lulonga. There was concern that most school directors did not fulfil government criteria. There was also concern that Congolese orderlies or nurses wished to take over the direction of the hospitals, but the long-established cordial relations between all the hospital staff avoided confrontation. The situation at Yoseki remained uneasy and the future role of missionaries uncertain. The complete loss of the Mompono station could not be reversed. At the conclusion of the Council the following decisions were agreed and ratified subsequently by the RBMU executive as the mission's future strategy.[332,333]

New church structure

The Church in the CBM area would be known henceforth as the "Communauté des Eglise Evangélique de la Lulonga" (CADELU).

- Ifole Pierre (Bongandanga) elected chairman and a missionary as secretary.
- Bofangi Daniel (Yoseki) to be Legal Representative with Bofaso Davide (Baringa).
- In place of missionaries new Congolese Pastors to superintend the church work.
- Ten School Directors approved. Payment of salaries for directors, teachers and monitors by the new administration.
- The mission to sell redundant mission vehicles to the churches.

Evangelism

The prime objective of mission had been evangelism. "Africa must be evangelised by Africans." With an established indigenous church both objectives were being fulfilled. Missionaries could continue to contribute by sharing this ministry with Congolese pastors.

Secondary education

Teaching had been a secondary objective of the mission with the intention of creating a literate church membership. Although this had been achieved at an elementary level in areas close to mission stations, an estimated 85% of church members in remote districts were still illiterate. Responsibility for village schools should pass to CADELU. Secondary education would also be essential but this was considered initially, by the missionaries, to be beyond the responsibility and resources of the mission[334] and no Congolese in the CBM area had reached a standard sufficient to be certified.

Institut Chrétien de la Maringa (ICM)

A new institute should provide comprehensive secondary education and pastoral training subsequent to the destruction of the Bible School at Mompono.

Literature

Failure to produce adequate suitable Christian literature had been a weakness of the mission. A literature expert to rectify this situation.

Printing press

The viability of the Bongandanga press was in doubt but a long-experienced Congolese printer to continue a limited range of printing.

Hospitals

There were several state hospitals within reach of the CADELU population but the likelihood of attracting Congolese medical staff to rural locations was doubted. Yoseki met an unserved need. Dr & Mrs Wright to re-open Yoseki hospital. Demand at Baringa hospital had decreased but to continue for the foreseeable future. Retention of nursing staff might prove problematic as government hospitals were paying higher salaries.

Polygamy

The only subject of disagreement. Against the missionary vote, the council agreed that the first wife in a polygamous household could be baptised and thereby be admitted to church membership.

Summarising the outcome of the Council from the mission perspective, Wide was very clear: "It is obvious that in future there is going to be a very limited scope for [European] missionary pastors; they [the Congolese] want specialists, doctors, secondary educationalists, Bible School principal. It is difficult at this stage to foresee the pattern which is likely to emerge."[332] Wright highlighted another potential concern. "While expressing full sympathy for the aspirations of the Independent Congo Republic we must keep right out of politics. The one thing which might make it impossible for us to go on working would be the insistence, on the part of the administration, that we join one political party or another."[333] Writing to update mission supporters in the UK, Walling described the future role of the CBM as misty and uncertain.[335]

Following the meeting the Wrights re-opened the Yoseki hospital. Several of the villages through which they passed were openly anti-European. When Bruce attempted to travel to Munda he encountered significant opposition and when the Wides returned to Mompono they were met by soldiers who surrounded the station. Elsewhere other missionaries returned to take up their previous tasks. Wages paid by the new government administration were doubled for some employees, including teachers, as a consequence of which people working for missionaries also wanted wage increases. Demands on mission expenditure rose considerably and budgets were strained. Adjustments to everyday relationships between Congolese leaders and the missionaries were achieved through friendly, respectful discussion but this was not an easy process for some CBM staff. With time the future role of mission in the new Congo began to take shape.[336]

From the foregoing it will be apparent that the CBM missionaries had recognised, and accepted, the implications of the profound socio-political changes subsequent to Independence. In consultation with the Congolese church leadership they proposed a programme that would introduce significant changes to the ways of missionary working. The motivation, to carry the Christian Gospel to the needy people of Central Africa, was undoubtedly the same. The Congo Balolo Mission, as an enterprise and organisation, would cease but there would be a new vision that would respond to the emerging needs of a newly independent, self-governing country. In the opinion of CADELU leaders "We are looking for mature evangelical Christians who would be willing to fit into our national church situation. We also want those who could adapt to the culture and lifestyle of Zaire. We need evangelists who can train pastors who can carry on the work in their own areas. Medical personnel are urgently required for our hospitals. Ours schools have a shortage of trained teachers. We would like to upgrade the level of teaching our pastors receive."[337] CADELU asked that forty new missionaries should be sent to support their work.[338]

17

A New Approach

———

On Independence Day there were forty-five missionaries working in nine locations in the CBM area including seven from the Swiss Missionary Fellowship, of whom thirteen had been in Congo for more than ten years. Three years later there were twenty-four. Following evacuation at Independence some had not returned; others retired shortly afterwards.

The changes in church management, agreed with the CADELU Council, were in place. Decisions were taken by the CADELU leadership. When problems arose the habit of decades whereby the advice of the senior missionary was sought was no longer so evident. Some of the older missionaries, resistant to change, were slow to acknowledge that their paternalistic role was diminished, finding it difficult to accept some of the changes introduced by Congolese colleagues and new expatriate colleagues[330] The male missionaries continued to preach on Sundays occasionally rather than regularly. When Easter was celebrated on the 'wrong' date the missionaries were very concerned, but what did it matter? During the early years of independence there were, undoubtedly, some tensions. A few church leaders openly denounced the missionaries and everything they had done, but for most there was a sense of appreciation for the past and a desire for a continuing contribution from missions, albeit by fulfilling different roles.[340]

Recognising that the days of the traditional, lifetime, evangelist missionary were over the RBMU adopted a new approach to its recruitment.[341] Two new categories of missionary were introduced. 'Associate Missionaries' would be professionals or artisans who could "fill a gap in a needful service … who by virtue of their rich Christian experience could bring most valuable help to the Churches overseas." 'Mission Partners' were people working in secular businesses or organisations "Who by their fellowship and witness are valuable evangelistic and teaching missionaries". Foreign Christian men and women could still make a contribution in Congo but their position in Congolese society would be different – something that would become fully apparent only when the most senior missionaries retired and new volunteers were forthcoming who were more attuned to the post-colonial world.

The mission had provided exemplary acute medical care for thirty years, but public health had never been addressed. Sanitation in the villages was still primitive, hygiene awareness and education were minimal, smallpox vaccination, disease prevention programmes and public clean water supplies were non-existent. Considering the original objectives of the mission acute medical care provided plentiful opportunities for personal evangelism, but addressing public health needs less so. Should a newly independent church continue or develop acute medical care and public health matters? If so, should expatriate missionaries contribute and would they be supported financially by the churches in their home countries? Similar questions needed to be asked about higher education.

The need for secondary-level education was still approached with reluctance: "Latterly we have been forced into more advanced educational work ... it is doubtful if it is a mission responsibility."[342] However, when the missionaries regrouped the first new initiative was to start a secondary school at Lifeta. The plan to use the hundred brick huts no longer needed by families with leprosy was a start but building new teaching facilities, classrooms, an assembly hall, houses for teaching staff and providing an electricity supply would be expensive. Wide expressed his reservations: "This all means considerable expenditure and it may well prove difficult to convince the home constituency of its necessity. The issues are so great that we cannot afford to make any mistakes."[342] In the event he need not have been concerned, as funding was forthcoming. Wide, who had built the hospital at Baringa and then established a large leprosy village in virgin forest, set about his final major contribution. In 1962 the buildings were complete and the first twenty-six students were enrolled; the Institut Chrétien de la Maringa (ICM) was born.[343] The first students were all men, the older ones amongst whom brought their wives and children with them. As no Congolese in the CADELU area were suitably qualified the staff had to be all missionaries. Initially, at the completion of the fourth year students graduated with a government approved certificate of education and those who continued for a further two years obtained a teaching diploma. Thereafter, the best would be able to pass on to a new Protestant university at Kisangani or the Catholic Louvain University in Kinshasa. Eventually the secondary school would be the only Protestant coeducational high school in the CADELU area.

The second component of the ICM, the replacement of the Mompono Bible School, was also addressed. Together the very experienced Ekwalanga Timoteo, the Wallings from Yoseki, the Featherstones from Yuli and Maimie McIntyre restarted Catechist and Bible schools at Lifeta.[344] To address the need for quality Christian literature Mr and Mrs Bajotti returned from Italy to start a Literature Centre at Basankusu, from which they published a regular Christian journal that soon found an eager and widespread readership.[345]

All of this was significant progress in keeping with changes that were required to ensure a sustainable long-term relationship whereby the Congolese could continue to benefit from foreign input. However, these welcome developments were interrupted suddenly and catastrophically by events that no one anticipated.

18

Simba

On 14th January 1963 when Moise Tshombe failed in his attempt to create a break-away independent state in the mineral rich province of Katanga, President Kasa-Vubu and his chief of staff Joseph Mobutu regained control of the whole country. There was, nonetheless, dissatisfaction and disillusionment with the chaotic social infrastructure that prevailed. For many people independence had not fulfilled their expectations. There were also followers of the previous president, assassinated Patrice Lumumba, who had inspired the elimination of the persistent Belgian presence and American interference. Under the leadership of charismatic individuals from across the country, Antoine Gizenga, Christophe Gbenye and Pierre Mulele, the Comité Nationale de Liberation and a rebel force, the Armée Populaire de Liberation (APL) were created. There are no lions in Congo, but the eventual insurrection broke out in the eastern provinces where Swahili was the common language and 'Simba' means lion. The Simba-Mulele rebellion adopted guerrilla tactics aimed at defeating Mobutu's Armée Nationale Congolaise (ANC).

The Simba recruits comprised ANC mutineers, tribesmen and les jeunesses – numerous militants who were mainly teenagers susceptible to traditional fetishes and magic, armed only with machetes and spears. Initially they were trained in strict military discipline but also believed that the féticheur would render them immune to their opponent's bullets. With the connivance of the neighbouring Burundi government thousands of these fanatical 'soldiers' advanced from the Burundi–Congo border. The local ANC garrisons reacted brutally but failed to defeat the Simbas, alienating the population in the process. The rebels succeeded in intimidating ANC troops, many of whom also believed in the power of fetishes.[346] In a humiliating defeat for Mobutu, the Simbas took over discarded arms and vehicles. Not only were the rebels set on political ends they were determined to eliminate those associated with colonialism: the evolués, intellectuals, the wealthy, a man wearing a white shirt or a tie, church leaders, missionaries Catholic and Protestant alike. As critical towns fell into rebel hands what followed was a massacre.

On the evening of 5th August 1964 the missionaries at Baringa were together with their colleagues at Lifeta when they heard the unexpected sound of a diesel Land Rover approaching in the darkness along the forest road from Baringa. Colleagues Arthur and Elizabeth Wright, 250 kilometres away at Yoseki in the direction of Stanleyville, used a Land Rover but there was no particular reason for them to be to be visiting; the only other such vehicles were in the hands of Simba rebel forces in the east of the country but they, too, were believed to be a safe distance away. It was with a mixture of relief and mounting anxiety that they saw Arthur and Elizbeth step down, exhausted by a sixteen-hour journey.

Late the previous night the elders at Yoseki had come to tell the Wrights that Simba forces were advancing much more rapidly than expected and if they did not leave immediately they would be in grave danger. Wright had treated some men wounded by the Simbas and knew that danger was approaching but had decided to remain. This time there could be no hesitation, the next morning might be too late. The vehicle was packed hurriedly with essentials and in the early hours they said their goodbyes. As they left the station the headlights shone on a woman blocking their path. "You gave me two children by opening my belly. My new child is coming. If you go I will die." Back at the hospital the electricity generator was started, instruments were boiled and a healthy babe was born by Caesarean section. Much later in the night the Wrights set out for the second time.

At Baringa all was well for several weeks until Congolese colleagues warned of approaching Simbas. Regretfully, evacuation to Basankusu was advised. This time the journey was different; as the missionaries passed through villages "they stood and sadly waved to us". News was received from the British embassy that all expatriates should leave, but the information was confused. When a small plane landed there was insufficient space for everybody. Women and children first. A return flight the following day for the rest.[347] By 5th September all the CBM missionaries were in Leopoldville.

The capital was crowded with evacuees, some telling terrible tales of beatings and murder at Stanleyville, including some survivors who were quite remarkable in their courageous trust and the comfort they gained from their Christian faith. A whole missionary family, including young children, who had evacuated after Independence and then returned had been killed, their bodies thrown into the river.[326] At the BMS Yakusu hospital, twenty-five kilometres from Stanleyville, the Congolese hospital administrator was beaten and killed. Six-year-old Linda Taylor, her little brother, her parents and their missionary colleagues escaped thanks only to the action of mercenaries led by the controversial South African Major 'Mad' Mike Hoare.[348] Later it would become known that in Stanleyville thousands of Congolese had been arrested and numerous Western hostages taken. A military rescue mission was organised. Called Operation Red Dragon, the raid involved a Belgian battalion of paratroopers, a surgical team from the Military Hospital, Antwerp and US Air Force planes. At great personal risk they performed above expectations in their line of duty. Some 2,000 foreigners were saved in two days[349] but many more Congolese had been executed[350] and 300 foreigners, including thirty-four Protestant missionaries, were killed.[351] Within a few days the CBM colleagues found employment in local schools, a Christian printing press and an American mission hospital. The Hansons continued with their translation work. Towards the end of October information suggested that it might be safe to return upstream; Bruce and Wright would attempt a return to Baringa.

The two men were able to take a flight to Basankusu, where all was calm. To reach Baringa they took a small outboard aluminium boat. Proceeding cautiously upstream they stepped ashore at the Baringa beach long after dark, not knowing what awaited them. Their shouts elicited a welcome reply and some sentries appeared together with Setefano Engondo, the director of the school, who had stayed despite the dangers. The following morning they were able to cycle to Lifeta, where they were welcomed enthusiastically by the school staff and leprosy residents.

Although the situation was relatively safe no useful work would be possible while the military presence continued. Bruce and Wright returned to Ikau, where they were joined by colleagues from Leopoldville while others remained downriver. Wright worked at the government hospital at Basankusu alongside the young Christian director, Manga Manasse, educated at Ikau school and previously director of the Bongandanga government hospital. He, too, with wife and children, had escaped the Simba advance by abandoning their possessions and taking the last riverboat down the Lopori River. Mercenaries and government troops cleared pockets of Simbas in the CBM area and a second visit to Baringa was possible. On this occasion they found Engondo, Belengo Timoteo, the senior nurse, and Ekwalanga Timoteo at Lifeta. These colleagues advised caution but hoped that it should be possible for missionaries to return after a few more weeks.

When the Simbas overran Baringa they arrested Belengo Timoteo and carried him off to kill him, but their commander released him. They had asked where the road through the forest led but when they heard that it went to a leprosy village they were frightened and proceeded no further. Apart from the debris, dirt and chaos left behind by the military, nobody had been hurt; the village, the hospital buildings, the church, the school and mission property were as they had left it. At the hospital the nurses had hidden all the medicines and other essential supplies in the roof. The maternity nurses Laele Mbonda and Laele Mboyo had continued working and had delivered twenty-five babies.[352] Elsewhere the news was not good. The months of Simba occupation had taken its toll. The Simbas had overrun half the CADELU area causing widespread damage. Bolombo Simon was the director of the Bongandanga school. When the Simbas had approached he dismissed the school and, with his wife, went into hiding in the forest where they remained for six months. Moving constantly, building fifteen forest shelters, catching fish in forest streams and fetching food in the night from village plantations they eventually found their way to the Congo River and safety at Lulonga.

Eventually the twelve overseas staff were able to re-establish work at Baringa, Ikau, Basankusu and Lulonga.[347,326] It was not until March the following year that visits to Mompono, Bongandanga and Yoseki were possible. On the way the missionaries were stopped frequently, sometimes to be greeted by church members but mainly by ill people desperate for help. Mompono was a sad sight.[353] An elderly pastor, Lokale Joseph had been tied to a tree and shot. Another was killed on his way to preach, together with other church members.[326,354] Everywhere, people had hidden in the forest for months. The Christians had tried to clear some roads and cut the grass but, unattended, the station became almost completely overgrown. The church had been damaged by rocket fire, the school, students' and teachers' houses and dispensary were largely derelict. Pastor Lokuli Joseph was in the forest for months before returning and doing his best to hold church services. Nurse Jele Marc had restarted the dispensary. Along the 200-kilometre road to Yoseki burned villages and deserted gardens told their own story but as news of the vehicles spread villagers came running to welcome the return.

Approaching Yoseki, ten kilometres from Lumumbist territory, the villages were clean and undamaged.

The reception at Yoseki was warm but muted. Medical assistant Ikombe Jacques had returned from hiding in the forest to help head nurse Nkoi Marc. The operating room was wrecked, although Jacques had managed to hide the operating lamp at the leprosy camp together with anaesthetic equipment and surgical instruments. Hospital buildings were still standing but had been stripped of all equipment and the electrical system torn out. The school was standing but entirely bare, and the students' dormitory had been destroyed. Facing the church a shrine to Lumumba had been built of material taken from the hospital. The Wrights' house had also been ransacked and all their possessions stolen. Jacques was beaten several times, forced to pay large sums to the Simbas and then taken 100 kilometres where he was tied up and threatened with death. Hearing of his arrest, an elderly administrator who had received treatment at Yoseki negotiated his release. Returned to Yoseki he was again arrested and threatened with death, but managed to escape with his wife and child to the forest, where they remained until mercenaries arrived. Chief Botshuna, an elderly and much respected chief, had been killed. By contrast the leprosy village was peaceful, the nurse and ninety patients undisturbed, probably due to the rebels' fear of the disease.

At a crowded meeting it was apparent that many of the population supported the rebel administration; a vocal minority were insisting that the hospital and school should be taken from foreign and CADELU ownership. In reply it was explained that all the facilities at Yoseki had been provided by the missionaries for the whole of the Bongando tribe. If the local people took control the mission would withdraw completely. The outcome of the palaver that followed was that the mission should continue. Urgent medical problems were dealt with, old friendships renewed, overdue salaries paid and plans agreed for damage to be repaired.

On the return journey via Bongandanga the missionaries learned that a senior pastor, Losala Samuel, had been murdered by retreating rebels. Mission houses had been burned down and the Ruskin Memorial Church had been damaged during an aerial bombardment. Along the road elders had been killed, numerous villages burned and churches destroyed. At Munda property had been destroyed and lay unrepaired. Despite this, 200 boys were attending the school in a temporary structure built by church members and villagers. Some villages were still entirely empty. Calling out and singing a hymn, people in hiding realised the missionaries had returned. Faces began to appear amongst the trees then people came streaming out. Embracing the missionaries and crying, many were emaciated, hungry, still fearful, some of them ill. Everywhere there were requests, oft repeated, that missionaries should return. There were many tales of bravery and remarkable resilience. The missionaries had been safe but their Congolese friends, colleagues and neighbours had suffered.

In Congo it was customary if one met an elderly man for the first time in the day one should ask him for his proverb, his "losako". When Wright met an old friend from Yoseki he replied, "Suffering has taught us".

19

Working in Partnership

———

Over the four decades that followed Independence sixty-seven new foreign workers were recruited to work with CADELU. Coming from Canada, France, Germany, Holland, Switzerland, the UK and the USA with fresh post-colonial ideas many undertook new roles as described previously by Oliver as "associate missionaries".

During the Mobutu years Congolese life became increasingly difficult in villages far from major conurbations. The deterioration of road and river transport made attendance at CADELU stations difficult and postal services were almost non-existent. A new approach to Christian education was required: Elsa Morgan and colleague Jennifer McKendrick prepared a comprehensive syllabus and literature for correspondence courses. For initial tuition they visited students at home and, when completed, students' work reached Baringa on foot, by bicycle, canoe or a passing vehicle. In this way a successful Emmaus Bible course was established.[352] Within a short time fifty students were benefiting through distance learning.

After Independence the first of the new recruits was Joyce Fergusson, a teacher from Canada. Initially she taught at the inter-mission Institut Chrétien Congolais (ICC) at Bolenge, near Mbandaka, founded in 1958 as a joint mission effort. In 1965 Fergusson transferred to the ICM secondary school. The new academic year started with ninety students aged between fifteen and twenty-five including three girls, all recovering from the traumas of the rebellion. Teaching was in Lingala, the common language for students who came from several different tribes. During her first furlough in Canada Fergusson worked as a teacher the proceeds of which would help fund her work in Congo.

In 1970 she took over the supervision of the girls' boarding school at Ikau where with colleague Mai Williams and two Congolese teachers she taught seventy-five teenage girls between grades 5 and 8. At that time no girl in the area had completed grade eight to obtain the government educational certificate. Income from her furlough bought food for the students and improved classrooms. Subsequently when establishing a new girls' school with a different mission in the Central African Republic she continued to subsidise food and supplies for students from her earnings in Canada. "My goal was to make myself dispensable and train the Congolese to take over their own schools rather than depend forever on outside help."[355]

Brian Battye, a Cambridge science graduate, joined the ICM in 1963 and became head of the secondary school. His wife Pat worked as ICM administrative secretary alongside a Congolese colleague. With their young family their relationship with Congolese colleagues was refreshing; CADELU appointed Battye co-secretary to work alongside Kole Philippe who had completed three years of study in Switzerland. In 1980 the Ecole Biblique became the Institut Théologique de Baringa (ITB), providing CADELU with a full pastoral training course to college diploma level. Teaching included the history and geography of the Bible, studies of the Old and New Testaments, Greek, Hebrew, church development and preaching skills. As with secondary education social factors limited access by young women to the ITB, but male students' wives were enrolled and expected to attend. For those with limited previous education separate teaching was provided in the vernacular by the principal's wife.

In 1966 a Swiss accountant, Danillo Gay, assisted CADELU with the accounts and legal affairs consequent upon the changing governmental administration. Mr & Mrs Bajotti established a new Literature Centre at Basankusu joined by Eugene and Stella Holland from the USA, who commenced offset printing of a wide range of new literature. Later a coffee bar was opened by local church women. In this busy town with large police and military camps in the neighbourhood hundreds of people every day visited the innovative centre, bought Christian books and attended literacy classes and Bible studies.

Over the next three years five new teachers and a nurse arrived. Eva Redmond and Richard Martin, both experienced teachers with Bible training in England and French studies in Belgium, contributed seven valuable years to the ICM, where Richard served as director. Bob Hunt was a teacher and pastor of an English village church, his wife a teacher. For three years at ICM they taught pedagogy, English, history and religious education. During this time primary education in village schools was mainly in French. Secondary education was also in French, but there were very few textbooks.

Everything was written on the blackboard, copied by the students and memorised which, in a society rich in oral tradition, the students were good at doing. The course comprised a general Cycle d'Orientation of two years followed by four years of specific subjects. The ICM concentrated on pedagogy to meet the urgent need for teachers in village schools. Graduates could then proceed to Kinshasa to complete training as secondary level teachers. The costs of living and learning materials were met by fees paid by students. Buildings, boarding accommodation, maintenance and administration relied on government salaries for the approved missionary teachers who donated their salaries to the school and lived on their meagre mission allowances. Afternoons were spent by the students fishing, hunting and growing their food but the affordability of fees was dependent on their extended families. Marriage at a young age was still the highest priority for girls and families gave preference to boys when paying for school fees.

Each six-year course concluded with a state examination held at regional centres, and high achievers were then considered suitable for university entry.[356,357] ICM entered its first students for the state examinations in June 1971. Fourteen travelled 240 kilometres to the examination centre in the school's Toyota truck. All but one of the students passed, and the ability of CADELU to train its own primary teachers had begun. Among these students was Marie Iyema, a ground-breaking success as Marie went on to be the director of the primary school in her home village.

In 1975 the Mobutu government decreed there would be no more separate Catholic or Protestant schools. All schools would be mixed faith or have no faith staff at all. However, in 1977 it was recognised that state schools could not meet the demand for nationwide education; single-faith missionary schools would be needed but should teach agreed syllabuses and conform to new standards set by the government. All schools had to be overseen by inspectors who also acted as financial managers (Conseillères Pédagogique). CADELU had fifteen schools but no one suitable for the task. At their request Elsa Morgan filled this role, followed by Robert Dear, thereby enabling the CADELU schools to be recognised officially.[352] The first Congolese Prefet (head of school) at ICM was Elangi, followed by Samuel Menga who is still co-ordinator of all the schools and a senior member of CADELU. The fulfilment of the combined missionary and CADELU development of secondary education, commenced in 1962 after many years of missionary resistance, came after more than a decade when the first ICM graduates returned from taking their secondary teaching qualifications in Kinshasa. One of these graduates, Bessau Bernard, started the CADELU Cycle d'Orientation at Yoseki, fully staffed by Congolese teachers.

At the Baringa hospital, nurses Rosemarie Jordi and Esther von Siebenthal from the Swiss mission joined the team where the nurse director was Lokela, and senior nurse Boonga Samwele was employed by the Leprosy mission. The absence of a permanent doctor at any of the CADELU hospitals meant that students wishing to study nursing had to transfer to the ex-BMS hospital at Pimu to become qualified nurses. Dr and Mrs Owen were funded by the Leprosy Mission for Yoseki hospital for one year only but as they left nurse Ida Baarsen from Holland arrived to replace them, also sponsored by the Leprosy mission. Since Dr Owen's retirement there had been no doctor at Yoseki or Baringa, although both hospitals were staffed by mission-trained Congolese nurses, some of whom were able to undertake a limited range of surgery.[358,359] After thirty years of innovative medical care leprosy had been almost eliminated, but there had been a resurgence of the disease. Wright's leprosy village at Tanga was redeveloped with funds from the Leprosy Mission to treat more than thirty people with leprosy who were not suitable for care in their home villages. Baarsen was in sole charge of this initiative and undertook week-long tours with Congolese colleagues to treat patients in their home villages. Importantly, she learned to speak the local tribal language, Longando, as well as Lingala. This was a significant contribution to the success of her work as many of the women and children in remote villages did not speak Lingala. The sponsorship by the Leprosy Mission that funded this nurse-led specialist work at both Yoseki and Baringa was a lifeline. The resurgence of leprosy was a great disappointment as well as a serious concern which, with diminishing central funds, the RBMU would not have been able to address.

Cath Ingram, an occupational therapist, arrived at Yoseki in 1978 with the intention of working with leprosy patients. However, when she discussed her possible role with the Committee de Poste the reply was that Baarsen was doing good work and they did not want another contribution to leprosy work. Instead, they needed someone to organise and run the hospital pharmacy, teach English in the school, do children's clinics in the surrounding villages, and teach women sewing. Accordingly, she became the storekeeper at the pharmacy, taught English and Health Education at the secondary school and started sewing classes for the local women. Her first term of service was worthwhile but not easy. Not what she had anticipated but what was needed. Furthermore, compared with the lifestyle of CBM missionaries in previous years life was very basic. The missionary allowance was £34 per person per month with no access to additional funds from the UK. "We ate Congolese village food: yoko, pondu, occasional chicken, bush meat, eggs, smoked fish and fruit – I lost more than two stone in the first three years ... we ate no imported food for many months."[358]

As previously noted, the mission had concentrated on acute medical care while village healthcare had not been addressed. Ingram's furlough, therefore, was spent at the London and Liverpool Schools for Tropical Medicine followed by two months at Nyankunde in northeast Congo learning about a nationwide programme to establish children's village health clinics in strategic locations. In the Yoseki area the project would be funded by Tearfund, who would provide a vehicle and a supply of medicines.

Working with CADELU colleagues village health committees were set up. Local men were recruited to build village health centres, Tearfund providing the roofing. Tearfund paid for the first year of a trained Congolese nurse. The key factor was that health centres would be the focus for health education and training village health workers to raise hygiene, water and toilet standards. Messages were sent out on the village drums as the team cycled through the forest inviting women with young children to attend. Children were weighed, mothers given hygiene and nutritional advice, sick children advised to go to hospital. The clinics commenced with brief Christian teaching and a prayer and were always well attended. Prophylactic treatment for malaria and simple medicines like aspirin were purchased from the Catholic priests, who received generous quantities from Kinshasa and were happy to share their supplies. Vaccines against diphtheria, tetanus, pertussis and polio, BCG for tuberculosis, and measles vaccine were obtained from the United Nations. In time Ingram was able to undertake weekly four-day tours of the village health centres as a member of a team with two Congolese nurses and a trained technician who gave some of the injections. When away from the relative comfort of her Yoseki mission bungalow she stayed in the village pastor's home or with local village health workers. During her absence on furlough Bowela and Bondonga continued this work, 900 children and 200 pregnant mothers attending the clinics regularly. For the following eleven years in Congo the village health programme was Ingram's main role.

In 1988 Drs David and Sue Pouncey arrived at the Yoseki Hospital, recruited and funded by Tearfund. The policy of Tearfund was to fund expatriate Christian workers for four years, during which time they were expected to develop a service and to train indigenous staff to sustain it for the long-term future. Neither David nor Sue had formal surgical experience but within days of arrival a woman presented with an undoubted surgical emergency. With his wife administering a makeshift anaesthetic Pouncey performed a successful operation. Thereafter he spent most of his time in the operating room while Sue was fully occupied in the outpatient clinic as well as caring for their newborn daughter. It also soon became apparent that the new head nurse Bolika Nsimba was a gifted surgeon so that by the time the Pounceys left Yoseki they could be confident the hospital would remain in capable hands.[360] With no support for running costs from overseas the CADELU hospital depended entirely on funds generated by charging patients for their treatment. Rampant inflation in Mobutu's Zaire necessitated the review of fees and nurses' salaries every month and made the purchase of medicines almost impossible. It was only thanks to the generosity of Catholic lay missionaries nearby and the Catholic hospital at Djolu, who willingly shared their supplies, that the Yoseki hospital survived. The sponsorship from Tearfund was, almost certainly, thanks to the continuing interest of Ernest Oliver, one-time Executive Secretary of the RBMU. Following retirement Oliver became an associate director of Tearfund[361] and, in this position, was able to stimulate joint working between the two organisations.

Shirley Marks had arrived in 1977 to commence children's work, previously done only where missionaries had been available and were interested in doing so. The intention was, therefore, to work with CADELU colleagues to develop child evangelism in such a way that it could be done by local people. Initially, Basankusu was the ideal location for such a project given its position as an administrative centre. With a small team of Congolese co-workers her main purpose was to travel throughout most of the CADELU area training village pastors and their wives the skills of child evangelism and Sunday school teaching. Sometimes, in the remotest villages, even in the late 1970s, she was the first white woman ever seen. Travel was by cycle, motorcycle, canoe or the infrequent public riverboats. The longest trips took her away from Ikau for more than two months at a time, during which she lived and ate with her Congolese colleagues in whatever village accommodation was available. Back at Ikau there were the syllabuses to prepare for the CADELU schools and the church accounts to audit. Eventually, in 1999, when no other suitably qualified missionary remained to oversee the theological institute at Lifeta CADELU appointed Marks as Principal of the ITB. Over twenty years Marks' contribution was unique. Not since the days of the Stannards and Armstrongs had a CBM missionary spent so much time living in the villages immersing themselves so deeply in Congolese daily life.

In 1981 Robert Dear and Dorothy Hider, both ICM teachers, were married and embarked on a series of tours training and equipping Sunday school teachers in village churches. Dorothy also acted as schools' inspector and taught students' wives while Robert undertook translation and prepared Christian literature. The post-independence development of secondary education and theological training paid rich dividends for the Congolese church. The ITB had played a crucial role and would continue to do so for many years. The benefits of sponsorship of three pastors for degree-level theological studies in Europe and Cote d'Ivoire soon became apparent. The maturity and wisdom of men such as Ekwalanga Timoteo, Kole Philippe, Bofaso Davide, Lofinda Benjamin and others ensured the successful transition from mission to indigenous leadership of the church.

Between 1968 and 1988 thirty-four other recruits joined the missionary team bringing skills that included electrical installation, garage mechanics,

Fig 37 Ekwalanga Timoteo. Pastor Bofaso Davide. Pastor Lofinda Benjamin.

carpentry, agriculture, accountancy, administration, teachers, nurses and doctors and the construction of an airstrip at Baringa.[362,363]

It will be very apparent that June 30th 1960 marked the beginning of a new and different period in the story of the Congo Balolo Mission. Like the Belgian government and other foreign missions the CBM had anticipated that independence would come, but little serious thought had been given to what that would mean, and very little preparation had been made for the country as a whole or for its rural communities. Given the precipitous nature of Independence and the little collective preparatory thinking it is not surprising that some of the missionaries struggled to face the dramatic change that would ensue, and decided that their days in Congo were at an end. Furthermore, seeing the extent and success of the Protestant church amongst the Balolo people some may have thought that the original aim of the mission had been achieved, and the CBM was no longer needed. However, as we have seen, that was not the view of the CADELU leadership. The mutual affection and interdependence that had grown over decades could not be jettisoned in a day. By common agreement a period of transition was needed during which the two parties worked together to ensure a fruitful future for CADELU and its people. How the RBMU would adapt to that challenge was not immediately apparent but as we have seen, together with the continued involvement of the Swiss Missionary Fellowship, new input from Tearfund, the Leprosy Mission and recruits from several countries, RBMU UK was able to help shape the development of both the Christian church and local society for a significant number of people in central Congo. As we have also seen, this achievement required a willingness to change on the part of long-experienced colleagues, a new approach to interpersonal relationships brought by new recruits, and a preparedness to address social as well as spiritual needs. Despite the forebodings of some in 1960 a significant contribution by foreign workers was not only possible but welcomed. The deficiencies recognised by that first CADELU Assembly had been addressed. Under Congolese leadership the new approach to partnership working had been successful.

Over the thirty-one years that Elsa Morgan served her beloved Congo her latter roles were very different from those of her predecessors. The contribution of new missionaries following Independence was different in two respects. First, there was a shift from the primarily evangelical role of the missionary to recruits with specific professional skills that supported and complemented the broad range of activities that had devolved to the Congolese-led church. Secondly, the contribution of most foreign workers was of much shorter duration. In the 1960s the nature of professional training and postgraduate education in the United Kingdom and Europe changed to become more specialised and programmed; entry to careers became more structured. For young people expectations of family life, their children's education and the needs of aging relatives featured more prominently compared with previous decades. Young married couples were no longer prepared to be separated from their children for years at a time. By the 1970s evangelical church members were still interested in overseas mission but the likelihood of committing themselves to tens of years of foreign missionary service became increasingly remote. It was thanks to the long-term commitment of Theo and Margrit Werner, Richard and Eva Martin, Robert and Dorothy Dear, Elsa Morgan, Shirley Marks, Ida Baarsen and Cath Ingram that continuity was provided.

How long the RBMU would be able to sustain this support for the Congolese church we will learn in the chapter that follows.

20

Closure

———

In 1897 Harry Guinness decided to support work in South America that had been started by East London Institute students in Peru. In 1899 other students commenced schools, orphanages and missionary activity in north India.[364] By 1901 it was obvious that these developments alongside the CBM would benefit from a coordinated approach. A new organisation would be needed: the Regions Beyond Missionary Union. The "Regions Beyond" defined the mission's horizons and "Union" brought together distant continents with supporting churches in the home land. Over the years that followed other new ventures followed in Borneo, Irian Jaya and Nepal. The CBM had become part of a larger missionary society. In 1942 the charismatic Ebenezer Vine was appointed General Secretary, and he succeeded in building such support for the RBMU in North America that offices were opened in Philadelphia and Toronto.[365] Choosing to lead the mission in the USA, Vine did not return to London.

Over the next three decades new ideas about overseas mission and the greater financial resources of North American churches led to a divergence between the British leadership and RBMU's other offices. When Ernest Oliver became Executive Secretary in 1961, having played a crucial role in India and Nepal, he made a determined effort to consolidate the mission's work and to unite the international leadership under a centralised administration. This initiative was rejected. From Philadelphia Vine wrote:

> With respect to the newer fields ... the London Board of Directors have lacked all sense of the Lord calling them to this responsibility. To imagine that it has been merely an absence of finance ... would be a fatal mistake. There has been almost a complete absence of interest and initiative ... It is with sorrow that this has to be declared ... this statement is made in all Christian grace, kindness and courtesy, but it is essential that it be understood.[366]

There would be no going back. In 1977 the North American office became autonomous and in 1990 the American, Canadian and Australian offices separated from the RBMU in Britain to form "RBMU International". By this time there were nearly 1,000 different overseas missionary enterprises in North America, mostly operating in isolation, and merger was the talk of the day.[367] In 1995 RBMU International joined with the American mission Worldteam to form "World Team", a global mission with 400 workers in twenty-six fields in five continents.[368]

It has to be admitted that the London-based RBMU had become a rather old-fashioned mission, although Oliver had given considerable thought to its future development. He worked to establish the Evangelical Missionary Alliance that brought British missionary societies together and forged bonds with indigenous national churches. He then united three independent missionary training colleges to create the single All Nations Christian College that continues to educate young people in world mission today.

In 1976 Oliver left the RBMU and Geoffrey Larcombe assumed the mission's direction. At that time the mission was working in Congo, Nepal, Peru, North India and Indonesia. Larcombe and his wife had worked previously in Bihar for five years, an experience that proved invaluable when approaching the mission's future. Like some other British missionary societies, the RBMU was on the margin financially. More importantly, however, there were several new recruits preparing for Indonesia and Congo. The mission had an innovative youth project, "Project Timothy", that sent young people on assignments overseas that were particularly successful in Peru.[369] Contrary to the North American view RBMU UK was continuing to develop and, in Congo, new recruits continued to join the CBM workforce. It is true that the work in Congo was smaller than in previous years. The church in Congo was self-supporting and self-governing. The principal objective of mission had been achieved. The roles that could be filled usefully by missionaries were limited. However, CADELU had an expectation that the mission would continue to maintain financial support for their hospitals, schools and property, which was not within its resources. This was illustrated vividly when Larcombe visited Yoseki. During a meeting in a packed church he sensed that although the CADELU membership still regarded the mission with respect there was a feeling that it was beginning to desert them. An elderly man posed a question in the Congo tradition of telling a parable. "There was a father who brought up his children but he was very unkind to them. He kept all that they needed in cupboards but kept them locked; he did not give to his children what he should have given them." What did Larcombe think of the father? Clearly the mission was the father. Larcombe replied that the father might seem to be unkind but he had grown ill and was not able to look after his children adequately, the children had grown up and become adults needing to take their own responsibility. He also explained that in the RBMU office in London the cupboards were not full; throughout the history of the CBM supporters had been ordinary church members just like them, who gave gifts voluntarily for the church in Congo. Back in England, bearing in mind that Congolese parable and the tension between the international branches,[370] it was time to review the mission's future direction.

The objective of Christian missions to evangelise the world had been achieved in large measure. British churches could still contribute, but what that contribution should be was not fully understood. Attitudes towards countries that had been colonies were changing. The paternalism of previous years had become an embarrassment for many and condemned by others. Support in Britain for overseas missions was in decline and other independent missionary societies were facing similar issues. The RBMU was still focused in Britain at a time when the national churches which the mission had helped to establish, had become fully functional and it was they, rather than the British mission, who should determine their future. If the RBMU was still needed it should be led by the national churches. Financial support from British churches was declining. The mission had been able to continue paying missionary personnel allowances, but those allowances were much lower than those of their American colleagues. Furthermore, the costs of the home organisation had risen, and management costs amounted to over 30% of income. Compared with other charitable organisations this was not high, but the leadership considered it too expensive to justify to devoted supporters. Ideas about the most effective, workforce-efficient ways of conducting overseas mission had also been changing. Oliver had suggested the principle of "Inter-continentalisation": rather than individual societies working in several different places across a continent the different agencies should combine to work in a more focused way. Given the uncertainties facing the mission this concept seemed attractive. There was clearly still a desire on the part of CADELU for external assistance; perhaps a collaborative approach with another mission could meet that request. Many years before, the leaders of the Livingstone Inland Mission had reached the unwelcome but inevitable conclusion that they could no longer sustain the endeavour they had initiated, and they had passed it on to others. On several occasions the lack of financial support and a shortage of personnel had threatened the viability of the CBM[371] but on each occasion funding and personnel were forthcoming and the work continued unchanged.

In 1988, after a century of undoubtedly successful endeavour, it appeared that the Congo Balolo Mission had arrived at a critical position. Was it, perhaps, time to "pass the baton" to others better able to continue the work it had started? Approval for radical change was by no means enthusiastic. Some board members were reluctant and so, too, were RBMU-supporting churches, especially in Scotland. For decades the mission had been a big family whose ties were strong. The following year Larcombe visited all the RBMU staff in Congo, Peru, Nepal and Irian Jaya to learn their views. In doing so he would talk with colleagues who had dedicated themselves to long years of mission work, sometimes in very difficult situations. The proposal would change the infrastructure of everything they were doing but would ensure continuation of their work by linking them with an alternative missionary organisation.

The staff in Peru had started new work with an indigenous Peruvian church and were working alongside the Evangelical Union of South America. Collaborating as a new continent-focused mission was attractive and it was agreed that RBMU missionaries should combine with their EUSA colleagues to form a new combined mission that would be called "Latin Link". In Nepal the staff were sad to close their long association with the RBMU but agreed to transfer their work to Interserve, a mission that had worked in the Indo-Pakistan sub-continent for many years (now Interserve International). In Irian Jaya colleagues could not agree to the proposal but eventually transferred to the Unevangelised Fields Mission (UFM), now United For Mission Worldwide.

Prior to Larcombe's visit to Congo there had been discussions with Action Partners (previously the Sudan United Mission) about the possibility of collaboration in Africa. The SUM was started in 1904 by Karl Kumm and his wife Lucy, who was Harry Guinness's sister. The principal objective had been to evangelise Muslim countries and the mission was working in Chad, Egypt, Ghana and the Horn of Africa. In 1989 agreement was reached that the RBMU staff, property and an appropriate proportion of RBMU funds would transfer to Action Partners. The German Vereinte Evangelische Mission (VEM) had offered CADELU funding and personnel in recent years; an alternative collaboration with VEM was, therefore, considered but was rejected on the grounds that they were not considered to be sufficiently evangelical and there was concern that their involvement would diminish CADELU's theological focus.

Throughout the discussions one crucial criterion was central: none of the RBMU staff should be disadvantaged and their ministry should not be impeded. Thanks to the deep, loving concern of Larcombe and his colleagues for all the mission's workers and the national churches they served this criterion was secured. There was, nonetheless, disappointment and a great sadness. Larcombe had visited Congo on three occasions, and Cath Ingram had accompanied him to translate in all the CADLEU posts; he had established a very close attachment with the staff and churches of all the mission's fields of work. His feeling that he had let them down was very strong.

When senior members of CADELU were informed of the proposed change they expressed mixed reactions. The historical link through the Guinness family and the SUM was welcomed as it offered a sense of continuity, but the CADELU leaders did not know anyone at Action Partners. Larcombe's personal visit was a great help but the news was not well received and many felt abandoned by the RBMU. However, the visit by Action Partners' David Carling, accompanied by Bob Hunt, proved to be a turning point. Hunt was well remembered and trusted from his time teaching at the ICM and recalls the discussion at Baringa. "Kole Phillipe was General Secretary of CADELU. Summing up the situation he used his skills of oratory so typical of village palavers: 'Our Inglese friends are like our parents, they are looking for a bride for CADELU. It will be good if we marry Action Partners.'"[346]

CADELU leaders appreciated having expatriate colleagues working alongside them and spent much time considering how foreign missionaries could contribute. CADELU would take over all responsibility, not just for their churches, but all the other medical and educational functions supported previously by the mission. Although the schools were nominally state schools they were staffed and run by CADELU. How would Action Partners respond? Would new foreign staff be forthcoming? The hospitals depended on mission funding which was expected to continue. Looking to the future CADELU wanted to be able to send people outside the immediate area for university-level training. Some CADELU members did not understand that the RBMU, unlike some other missions, was not a rich organisation and could no longer sustain the level of support that had been available in previous years. It was inevitable that some felt bitter and betrayed.

When the eighteen expatriate staff heard that the RBMU might come to an end there was sadness but also a sense of hope that the new mission would be able to do more than the RBMU could do at that time. Colleagues understood that the mission was spread too wide logistically and it made sense to look at each field separately. They were aware, also, of the funding problem; limited funds were forthcoming for individual missionaries but not for the mission as a whole. Provided Action Partners would enable them to continue their ministry the change could be an opportunity rather than closure.

The proposal was difficult for the missionaries at a personal level too. As Ingram explained "My initial interest had been through the RBMU. I felt part of the mission family ... When the change did occur the relationship was entirely different."[358] Judith Hymer was personal assistant to Larcombe in London. In April 1991 the London Board met for the last time. Judith recalls, "In my head I knew the RBMU had to close but in my heart I did not want it to happen. None of us did. Anyone you talk to will speak of the 'RBMU Family'. Borne out of the 'regions beyond' almost a century before we had become too small a mission to be so widely spread. It was no longer feasible economically."[372] Some other missions had the resources of denominational churches behind them but the RBMU did not. "The last two years have been exceptionally difficult. Happily, most folk now understand."[373] "When Henry Grattan Guinness founded Harley College he didn't have RBMU in mind. The passing of RBMU represents the end of an era. There is a lot of pain around. Former missionaries and some of us closest to the mission are going through a profound grief process. But the overarching objectives of mission remain. The priority is still for British Christians to participate in mission with brothers and sisters overseas."[373]

Larcombe, who bore the burden of those final months, has no recollection of the final meeting. Residual funds were divided proportionally between the future partnership organisations. To fulfil financial and legal requirements the mission continued as a registered charitable company for another seventeen years.[374] However, the Regions Beyond Missionary Union became history on 19th April 1991 although the work in Congo, developed by the

CBM, the RBMU and CADELU, continued. Fifteen missionaries remained: six RBMU, four from Tearfund, one from the Leprosy Mission, four from the Swiss Missionary Fellowship. In terms of everyday life and work there was no immediate change. CADELU, the church structure and teaching programme remained the same. The missionary staff continued as before.

The first two years that followed were relatively peaceful but in 1991 there was political unrest and social disturbance elsewhere in the country. There was no river transport; outside the CADELU area the missionaries depended on the small planes of the Missionary Aviation Fellowship. For communication with the outside world the missionaries depended on a two-way radio. This enabled regular contact between CADELU stations and BMS staff in Kinshasa and stations upriver towards Kisangani. Contact could be made twice a day but was not available overnight after 6pm. Ingram continues the story.

One day in July 1991 I heard there was unrest in Kinshasa which was confirmed by our BMS colleagues. Several MAF plans had been damaged. That evening it seemed things had settled down but next morning we received a message from the MAF that there were serious problems in the north east and we needed to be evacuated the same day. Most of the other Action Partner staff had left Congo by then and Shirley Marks, alone at Baringa, was on furlough in the UK. It was just five of us and two children at Yoseki who remained. Everybody else in the region, BMS and Americans, had already been evacuated. A plane would be at Djolu at 12 noon, two-hours away by road.

At Yoseki there was Ida Baarsen who was out on a leprosy tour of the villages, Cath Ingram, David and Sue Pouncey and their two young children and a Tearfund worker. "David Pouncey said that he was a doctor and therefore should stay but his wife pointed out that they had children and needed to go." The missionaries asked the Committee de Poste, some of whom remembered the murders of the Simba rebellion in 1964. Their opinion was unanimous: "Go, and come back when it's safe."

"On arrival at Djolu we were informed that the plane was delayed until the following day so Ida was able to return to pack and hand over her Leprosy mission work to her Congolese team. All was quiet on the road except that people were clapping and happy to see us. When the plane arrived we were too many for the small aircraft but it was the last evacuation flight. The pilot did his best and the overloaded plane managed to take off. We hit a storm and had to put down to repair the damage before flying on to reach Bangui in the Central African Republic where we were the last people to arrive. Action Partners confirmed that we should return to the UK."[358]

The hurried exit from Congo had not been good. Ingram and her colleagues felt that their work at Yoseki was unfinished. Before the year end they returned. The next eighteen months were spent developing the village health programme in such a way that it would be self-sustaining without expatriate input. Baarsen did the same for the leprosy programme and the Pounceys at the hospital. They would all leave Yoseki, but with the assurance that the work they had started would continue. In October 1993 one Action Partners missionary remained: Shirley Marks, Principal of the Institute Théologique de Baringa.

1994 the Hutu uprising and subsequent genocide in Rwanda caused the displacement of an estimated two million Rwandan refugees into eastern Congo. Nearly nine years of constant fighting followed, causing more than three million deaths across the country. Everyday life throughout the CADELU area was devastated. Twenty-nine of the thirty-two churches together with schools and hospitals were damaged or destroyed.[375] Roads were frequently impassable and all functional vehicles were commandeered by the opposing militias. The only means of travel was on foot or a pillion ride on a passing motorcycle. Riverboats had ceased to serve the waterways and traditional dugout canoes were the sole means of river transport. Soldiers raided the forest gardens and stole the villagers' crops, thereby depriving communities of their food and income from markets that no longer functioned; people died of starvation and disease. The soldiers also confiscated any radios they found so that communication between Marks at Baringa and the Catholic priests at Basankusu became impossible. News of the outside world was non-existent.

During this time a new missionary couple was recruited by Action Partners. Brian Beakhouse and his wife Anna came to Baringa but their contribution was cut short by the unremitting anxiety of the civil unrest. At Basankusu VEM sent two short-term couples in succession from Germany to provide vocational training and to build a large, new church. Apart from this, Shirley Marks remained as the only expatriate missionary with CADELU. She depended on her Congolese colleagues and neighbours at Lifeta and grew food in her garden but for most of the decade that she remained her situation was precarious and sometimes dangerous.

In April 2001 Marks took a much-needed furlough. The journey home was not easy. After four days on foot, including four hours walking through dense forest, she reached Basankusu. Travel to Kinshasa was not possible but Médecins Sans Frontières provided a flight to Gbadolite on the border between the DRC and Central African Republic. From there a flight to Europe was available.[359] Before leaving Baringa Marks had organised student courses for the following term and had cut and planted a new garden. During her absence she kept in regular telephone and email contact with CADELU and ITB staff. Arriving in England she found that there had been changes at Action Partners and a different approach to work in Congo.

When she returned to Congo in January 2002 she found the condition of the people to be devastatingly poor, although the political situation had improved. Of greater concern, Marks carried a letter from Action Partners explaining that their support for CADELU was likely to be terminated. "2002 was a watershed year. Action Partners faced a severe financial crisis … it was time for taking stock …. Projects with our partner churches would be increasingly focused on funding projects at the interface with Islam."[376] There were also logistic difficulties in supporting a solitary missionary and a church in central Congo, and concern over CADELU's growing relationship with the German VEM mission that was providing significant funding. Marks returned to continue in her role at Lifeta, carrying essential educational supplies. The journey upstream by canoe accompanied by two pastors took a week. Food was scarce, just manioc and dried fish bought from riverside villages where the party slept at night.

Arriving at Lifeta several major problems awaited her. Because one of the three lecturers had been away in Kinshasa the ITB courses were behind. In her absence state funds for staff salaries and Action Partners' funding from the UK had not been forwarded from Kinshasa. As a consequence the Institute had run out of paper, chalk, pens and books. Staff and students had been unable to pay their children's school fees or medical bills at the Lifeta Health Centre, which had run out of medicines. In May there was a measles epidemic that affected over 200 children. Despite these unwelcome setbacks the ITB students worked well and six final-year students graduated.

In August 2002 the international Roman Catholic Jesuit Refugee Service (JRS) responded to the call of the Bishop of Basankusu to open a health project in Baringa because the local population had no access to medical care.[377,378] A team, led by nursing nun Sister Chantal, refurbished and re-equipped the CBM hospital and MSF provided some medicines. In the first four days they saw 300 patients. Because Catholics working in a Protestant hospital "required careful handling" and CADELU were unable to recruit additional nurses, the nurse at Lifeta, Basomba Philippe, joined the new Jesuit work.[359] Dr Yves Bagale was appointed and the revitalised hospital, built by CBM's Dr Wide in 1932, provided desperately needed medical care once again.

On October 4th Gerard Pontier, Director of Action Partners, visited for brief discussions with the CADELU Administrative Council, during which it was made clear that Action Partners could not continue sponsorship of CADELU and Marks. The financial support for CADELU would be terminated, Marks could remain until the end of the academic year. The future of ITB would be a matter for CADELU Council to decide.

Marks was in no mind to leave in a hurry. Returning once more to Lifeta, she spent the next seven months preparing extensive new course notes to ensure that future students would have comprehensive study material after her departure. She worked with the student-librarian to organise and catalogue the 1,400-book library, and with Pastor Bokuta who would be the future Principal of the Institute. On the last Sunday in June 2003 she witnessed her final graduation ceremony for sixteen student couples who would move on to contribute to the witness of the Church in Congo. The occasion was a joyful one but "The overwhelming feeling was one of sadness. No one wanted me to leave and in my heart I did not want to go." Congolese people have a wonderful way of creating special songs to mark special occasions. It must have been very hard for Marks to listen as the children sang "We will be looking for Mam'Esongo, asking each other when she will come back, only to realize anew that she will not be back."

Over the following days she handed over the Institute Théologique de Baringa to her trusted colleague Pastor Bokuta; final documents were sorted and goodbyes were said. In Kinshasa she had the encouragement of meeting some of her old students: three were studying for degrees at the Mennonite Faculty in the capital, Pastor Imbelenga, previously Principal of ITB, was a Community Evangelist, and student Bonyoko was ordained Pastor of a Kinshasa church before a congregation of a thousand. On Friday 18th July 2003 Shirley Marks, the last of the CBM missionaries, left Congo for the last time.

21

Failure?

The education of girls and young women were Joan Sledmere's priority during her thirty-one years in Congo. In retirement after the events of 1960, her resume was perceptive and realistic. "In the realm which we as a mission consider the most important we have achieved much. We have planted churches with 40,000 in full membership, mostly self-supporting and self-governing, and to a certain extent self-propagating, but we had left the church ill equipped educationally and theologically to meet the new dangers of the day ... unable to cope with the rising demand for better education ... and Christ's commands to heal the sick."[379] Joseph Conley interpreted this as "the Achilles heel of the RBMU's great work in Congo".[7] The term "Achilles heel" has come to mean a weakness which can lead to downfall in spite of overall strength. In his opinion the inability of the CBM to secure high-level education and to future-proof the provision of healthcare were fatal flaws after nearly a century of mission. By contrast, John Ellery defined success as "the prosperous termination of anything attempted. For foreign missions that was the salvation of souls".

While it is true that many missionaries did not return after Independence the church was not left to face its future alone. A significant proportion of CBM staff remained and over the following twenty years they were joined by many more. Evangelism continued. Within months CADELU was established. In 1961 there were over 38,000 adults in CADELU church membership. With large numbers of enquirers and children of Christian parents, "the number of those within or associated with the church must be at least 100,000". Taking the situation at Ikau as an example Lily Shield wrote "From the early days the indigenous principle has been followed. There are records of elder's meetings as far back as 1906. The women have played a large part in the activities of the church. For years they have had their own evangelistic work, carried on quite independently of the men. During the last year Pastor Benjamin Lofinda has been engaged in building a new primary school, a house for the new girls' school in addition to all his pastoral work. The local church is administered by a group of elders and the pastor; some of the elders are women." Considering the situation across the country as a whole evangelism had been successful. Compared with the single church at Palaballa in 1881, at Independence there were 45 different Protestant missions, 345 mission stations, 2,608 missionaries, 645 pastors, 20,128 village evangelists and 821,025 church members.[380]

These figures may impress, but with the Protestant Christian community accounting for only 2.25% of the Congolese population after eighty-two years, could the influence of Protestant missions have been greater? The answer is, almost certainly, yes. There was, however, another significant factor. "The white men are strangers and they are ignorant. He does not understand our customs, just as we do not understand his. We say he is foolish because he does not know our ways, and perhaps he says we are foolish because we do not know his."[381] As Botele Bo-Ekwela Kelly observed in his review of the CBM, "Culturally, the missionaries were fantastically intolerant of African culture and asked the converts to renounce all old beliefs and practices. The convert had to become a completely new man. The Protestants introduced a Christian morality among the evangelists. The latter must have suffered from a type of evangelism that caused a deep alienation. It was a necessity for the Balolo to restructure their society in order to find a new balance."[382] In practical terms this meant a total rejection of polygamy, the wearing of charms, smoking tobacco and hemp, drinking alcohol, lying, cheating and stealing – nothing unusual for a British Protestant evangelical at home a century ago but a demand that would alienate a new Congo Christian from his family, friends and fellow villagers. Catherine Guinness recognised that all missionaries were not the same: "There are those who trample on dreams and those who respect them ... "they cannot escape the reality of the power they wield as members of the colonising class, but they can wield that power with compassion and understanding."[383] Such insight was held by a minority and did not change the CBM approach. As the years passed there were reports in correspondence that the church had been closed or that church members had been dismissed because they had "fallen into sin". The greatest sin and the one that caused a significant limitation to church membership was polygamy.

Polygyny, the purchase of wives and the inheritance of wives from a deceased father or brother, was the backbone of Congolese family structure. Polygyny addressed the problems of high infant mortality, female sterility and the tradition of female sexual abstinence for two years following the birth of a child.[384] As we have noted previously John Harris was empathetic towards his Congolese neighbours:

There is no country whose women are so continuously industrious. In the purely pagan areas the woman regards polygamy as a desirable condition. The position of the husband is gauged by his possessions ... she prefers being the wife of a man who can afford to keep more than one. In one or two cases Christian men have put away wives inherited from a deceased relative. But the women concerned have always felt the shadow of disgrace as if they are outcasts from the social life of the tribe.[41]

The reverse situation was also problematic; for a wife in a polygamous marriage who became a Christian it was required of her to leave her husband. This would necessitate the repayment of dowry money by the woman's family, sometimes paid by the husband over many years, causing severe financial difficulties as well as great emotional and social distress. In the opinion of the Congolese evangelists "These women are keen to become Christians and comprise the greater number of our enquiries and provide a good part of our church gifts. If we refuse to baptise these women the seekers will disappear, the gifts will decrease with the inevitable result that fewer evangelists will be sent out." In the mind of these men the church would die altogether, but the missionaries noted at their annual conference "We are thankful happy to report that such a catastrophe has not occurred".[385] The principle that any person who wished to become a church member should renounce their polygamous marriage remained mission policy until the first General Assembly of CADELU in 1960, when the missionaries were overruled. At the present time polygamy is, officially, illegal in the Democratic Republic of Congo but is tolerated without prosecution. Within the CADELU church the existence of polygamy is acknowledged and men who take more than one wife may attend services but they may not partake of communion or become church members. The first wife, only, of a polygamous marriage may become a church member. The Catholic church also opposes polygamy; those who attend mass but practise it are refused the sacraments.

These crucial issues and their limiting influence on the growth of the Protestant church were summarised by Ruth Slade: "Both Catholic and

Protestant missionaries were unconscious of the real dilemma which faced them ... they broke into a static tribal society which could never accept these ideas and this way of life without being torn apart in the process. Their problem – although they were not even aware of it – was how to adapt the new life which acceptance of their message involved to the particular Bantu Society of the Congo interior."[386]

How the Protestants and Catholics proceeded with their mission is now clear to see and with hindsight it is possible to understand the difference in outcome that followed the very different approaches adopted. The Protestant missions agreed not to overlap their areas of activity, but worked entirely independently. By contrast, the pattern of Catholic development was directed centrally, fulfilling Leopold's intentions and, following 1886, utilising only Belgian missionary priests.[387] While the Protestant missionaries concentrated on evangelism, focusing on individuals and individual towns and villages, the Catholics gathered refugee slaves and orphaned children around them, creating new "chrétianité", communities that were glad to abide by the priests' rules in exchange for a home, food and safety from the officers of Leopold's state. Such communities sometimes counted more than 1,000. The process was facilitated by the fact that many of the new Catholic adherents were orphaned children who became separated from traditional village life. The social structure was thereby altered; the family unit was promoted, girls and women were no longer sold into a marriage they did not want; men shared the manual labour of food production, polygamy lost its significance. Seeking to extend the Catholic influence the early Jesuits established "fermes-chapelles". Under the supervision of a catechist small groups settled close to villages, planted gardens, sold their produce, taught the catechism and enjoyed the benefits of simple education. In this way Christian villages grew up, separate from the mission colonies but close to, and protected from, the temptations of traditional tribal society. Supported by Leopold's preferential generosity they had large areas of land at their disposal permitting a self-supporting agricultural economy to develop. By comparison the Protestant missionaries spent their days itinerating, travelling from village to village preaching their gospel. Their mission stations were far smaller and offered material advantages to many fewer potential adherents. One feature common to both Catholics and Protestants was the provision of elementary education. The ability to read and the acquisition of new knowledge gave rise to increasing social separation of mission followers from their childhood contemporaries. For the Protestant converts, still living in their villages rather than a chrétianité, this posed additional difficulties as they were reminded constantly of the traditional customs from which they were expected to withdraw. The temptation to revert to former ways was considerable.

From an organisational perspective the Catholic missions also held a strong advantage from the outset. Compared with the fragmented approach of the Protestants, with a growing number of independent, disconnected, multinational societies largely dependent upon charitable financial support, the Catholics' arrival was overseen by a centralised structure guided and supported financially by Rome. It is said that the adoption of Lingala as the first of four national languages for the country was stimulated by the need for Catholic priests to learn a single language that would serve them wherever they were posted. Given that Lingala is considered to be one of the easiest tongues for Europeans to acquire, this was an additional advantage. While Protestant missionaries spent months learning individual tribal languages and years working on multiple translations of the scriptures the priests were able to press on with their education and other work. The Catholic Basankusu diocese, which was equivalent to the CBM area of work, had twenty-four stations compared with CBM's eleven.

When Independence came followed by the Simba uprising the problem to be addressed by foreign missions was no longer primarily evangelism: "We should ask the questions. Does God want foreign missionaries in the Congo? Does the church need them at this stage of its development? How can we plan so that missionaries do not retard the growth of the church? Do we need to cooperate more to provide higher education that is thoroughly Christian or should this be left to the government and secular organisations? What should be the mission's attitude to the Congo's need for increased medical help?"[388] The answers lay in exploring the three problems identified by Sledmere: theological teaching, education at secondary and university level, and the provision of medical care.

Theological training of future pastors at university level had been discussed by CBM missionaries in 1942. "Conference considered the proposal of a university for Congo under the auspices of Protestant missions. It was agreed that whilst such facilities for education might not be undesirable in themselves, the provision of them is outside the scope of our responsibility as a mission; such higher education would unfit graduates for useful service in our mission area."[389]

The need for secondary education was debated at the missionaries' annual conference year after year but the problem had proved insoluble. "Every year we lose hundreds of the children of Protestant parents to the Roman Catholics because we are unable to cater for all who come to us."[390] When this issue was discussed in 1953 the hindrance was found to be limited funds and the lack of suitably qualified staff. This was not for want of trying. Almost every issue of the mission's promotional magazine highlighted the need, but the necessary funding and recruits were not forthcoming. The CBM was not alone in failing to provide secondary education. At the time of Independence, among the forty-five Protestant missions there were only two six-year secondary schools in Congo.[391] By contrast there were numerous Roman Catholic secondary schools and two universities. Louvanium University in Kinshasa (1954) founded by the Jesuit University of Leuven, and the Université Officielle du Congo et du Ruanda-Urundi, in Lubumbashi (1956) founded by the University of Liège.

The Roman Catholic dominance in education was not in the least surprising. It had been Leopold's intention that his domain should be a Catholic country. From the earliest days Catholic missionaries were granted a variety of special concessions that were not made available to Protestants, and the subsequent Belgian colonial administration pursued a similar path. Internal Belgian memoranda emphasised that "No obligation existed to subsidise the Protestant missions ... If we were to yield ... such a policy could seriously compromise the Belgian influence on the Congo."[392] In 1931, looking for ways to limit Protestant education, the Inspector-General for Education suggested introducing a condition for obtaining subsidies in teaching French and in French from the third year. The colonial government should affirm its right to reserve government subsidies only for those schools committed to teaching subjects that were loyal and faithful to Belgium.[393] The gentleman in question underestimated the CBM's response: henceforth all new recruits spent up to a year in Belgium to become fluent in French, thus enabling teaching in French and allowing the mission to access government subsidies but in 1960 it was estimated that 75% of all students in Congo were within the "réseaux Catholique".

In view of the pivotal role of education for a developing nation, the failure to provide secondary schools could be ignored no longer by the Protestant missions. Within three years the number of secondary schools grew from two to over fifty. As we have seen, the response of the RBMU was the creation of the Institut Chrétien de Maringa followed by the Institut Théologique de Baringa which, together, provided a necessary resource for CADELU's future. Several gifted students were sponsored to receive higher education in Europe. One of these was Kole Philippe who was sponsored by the Schweizerische Missions-Gemeinschaft to study at the Emmaus Bible College in Lausanne, following which he returned to fulfil an important leadership role in CADELU.

At a national level the Congo Protestant Council also decided that the absence of a Protestant university could no longer be countenanced. In November 1963 the Free University at Kisangani, the Université Libre du Congo, opened with the first fifty students and six full-time professors. A small group of American missions, together with the governments of West Germany and the Netherlands, financed the venture. John Carrington, a long-serving missionary with the BMS, made a notable contribution as Professor, Vice-Chancellor and Dean of Faculties.[394]

The third issue raised by Sledmere was the provision of healthcare. At Independence there was a medical faculty at Louvanium, but not a single qualified Congolese doctor. The scattered state hospitals staffed previously by mainly Belgian doctors lay deserted save for a few short-term United Nations personnel. The new medical schools would produce home-grown doctors in due course, but until that time the country would depend upon missions. The achievements of CBM's three hospitals and station dispensaries over forty years were remarkable but the continued provision of healthcare for the population of an area almost the size of England was not feasible for CADELU. So long as the RBMU could recruit doctors and subsidise the costs the hospitals could continue, but that was possible only until the mid-1980s.

For a mission looking to the future it was important to understand the nature of the healthcare the country needed. Surgery and emergency obstetric treatment had offered a high profile that attracted support from caring Christians in Britain and North America, but was only a small component of the overall medical need. In 1963 of the 60,000 attendances by 4,345 new patients at Yoseki hospital only 739 needed admission, 123 Caesarean sections were performed and 433 underwent other surgery.[395] Seventy percent of the patients accounting for 97% of attendances suffered from endemic diseases for which nationwide immunisation programmes, nutritional and sanitation education, baby and child welfare advice, and clean water supplies were by far the greatest need. Thanks to assistance from the Leprosy Mission and Tearfund, innovative community-based healthcare programmes were commenced successfully by Ingram and Baarsen at Yoseki and Boonga Samwele at Baringa. These admirable initiatives were invaluable but, being beyond the capacity of CADELU, they could only continue as long as charitable foreign funding was forthcoming. Other missions engaged in contracts with the new government administration but, like the RBMU, struggled to recruit medical staff and survived for only a few more years.[396]

If there was an Achilles heel it was not the paucity of secondary education, nor the absence of a Protestant university and medical school when Congo became independent. It was present at the birth of the mission.

The success of a century's work by the CBM depended on the same organisational model as had been adopted by all evangelical Christian missions in the late 19th and early 20th centuries: the vision and enthusiasm of the founders, the willingness of young Christian people to devote their lives to years of living and working in far-flung places, and the generous financial backing of individuals and churches in the home country. The Livingstone Inland Mission, the Congo Balolo Mission and the Regions Beyond Missionary Union were "faith missions". That is, they relied 100% on the voluntary financial and practical support of like-minded Christian people to enable the endeavour. They set no annual budget, took no loans, indulged in no crowd-funding or fundraising campaigns. If God called, if God sent, God would provide. In practical terms that provision came from a support base among the members of independent evangelical chapels and tabernacles, some Baptists, Plymouth Brethren and other non-conformist churches. During the decades when these congregations were multiplying in Britain the missions were well supported but as church attendance declined in the twentieth century so, too, did commitment to overseas mission. The steep decline of 50 to 60% between 1930 and 1980 rendered the independent non-denominational faith missions particularly vulnerable.

Coupled with struggling finances there was a second, equally significant factor. Evangelism, saving the lost souls of the Dark Continent, had been the driving force of Tilly and the Guinnesses in 1878, for McKittrick and Harry Guinness in 1889 and the missionaries of the CBM since. Following the success of primary evangelism there then came a need to educate and build leadership in the new church, and we have seen how that was addressed. But what the mission failed to see, or possibly, to accept, was that the Christian church at large was changing. The 1960s saw a growing tendency to associate Western missionary activity with past imperialist colonisation. As international travel and television brought the relative poverty of many people in other countries into view young people were adopting a humanitarian rather than a strictly religious response. The leaders of the World Council of Churches recognised a need for change: "The transition from a traditional understanding of mission primarily in terms of missionary-led proselytism towards a new emphasis on mission as the task of the whole Church with humanisation as its central objective ... We have seen the end of one missionary era; we are beginning a new one in which the idea of world mission will be fundamental."[397] Some missions, however, including the RBMU, were not comfortable with this change in emphasis, preferring to maintain an adherence to conservative, evangelical theological principles. "The overriding priority and concern of the RBMU remains the ongoing life of the church and, in particular, the training of leaders. You can have superb medical care, well taught children and nutritious food, but unless that practical service is built on a solid biblical foundation it accounts for little."[398] Robert Dear, also, was concerned that the priority given to evangelism had declined: "It is embarrassing to admit that as an evangelical missionary society we are not really engaged in specific evangelism as such, and we are standing by while evangelism as an activity in our daughter churches dies out."[399] The RBMU, together with some other faith missions, could not share the new vision for mission of the future. By rejecting ecumenism and diminishing the value of humanitarian aid for its own sake, the RBMU's conservative principles no longer chimed with an increasing number of British churches and individual young Christians. "The partnership approach to global mission does not arouse the same intensity of popular enthusiasm as the heroic mood of the nineteenth century pioneers, on whose efforts the eternal destiny of the heathen was believed to depend."[400] After 125 years where were the volunteers? There were none. And funds? They were not sufficient. What, then, has happened since the departure of the RBMU from Congo?

The seven years of Congo's wars following more than three decades of misrule by former President Mobutu Sese Seko left violated, disoriented, untaught and diseased populations, especially in the villages and small towns of the eastern provinces. Basankusu, the administrative centre for the previous CBM area, now has a population of nearly 25,000. Most houses are without electricity although some with a solar panel have a single electric light. Several communal borehole wells supply water, for three of which CADELU is responsible. About a third of residents have basic mobile telephones but are dependent on Facebook and Messenger for the free communication they offer. A factory fifteen kilometres from the town producing palm oil, soap and coffee offers some employment but there is little else.[401] Very few roads outside the towns and through the forest are passable by motor vehicles, even by motorcycle. Travel has reverted to the rivers mainly by motorised canoe as the riverboats of previous years, carrying goods and people, are rare. Many people work their forest gardens, the boys go to fish and the men to hunt but many do not. Impoverished diet, inadequate sanitation and supplies of clean water, ignorance, sparse medical facilities and endemic diseases such as malaria and worm infestation have all taken their toll.[401]

Since the termination of all foreign missionary support in 2003 CADELU has developed considerably and is now one of sixty-two Protestant denominations federated under the umbrella of the nationwide Eglise du Christ du Congo (ECC). The headquarters are at Ikau with a subsidiary office in Kinshasa. Basankusu now has five churches. In recent years CADELU has developed a collaborative association with the Communauté des Disciples du Christ au Congo (CDCC) and the German Vereinte Evangelische Mission that the RBMU declined to partner in 1990. The church community organises a sustainable agriculture programme producing food crops and raising cattle and chickens.[402] To stimulate the role of women in the community the CDCC Department of Women and Family has introduced a local branch of its Microcredit Union that enables women to work to improve themselves financially. HIV/AIDS and domestic violence are both major problems for which the church runs an educational prevention team that raises awareness of these issues in surrounding villages. Responding to the high mortality rate from malaria and other diseases, especially in children, the CADELU pastors help families through a church-led bereavement support service. The Catholic cathedral was rebuilt recently and CADELU engages with the Catholic diocese in ecumenical activities, holding joint celebration services at New Year.

Elsewhere throughout the CADELU area there 312 parishes, 26 postes and 26 ecclesiastical districts overseen by 267 pastors and 45 village catechists. At Lifeta the ITB has 29 students and ICM 293 pupils, despite struggling for several years with financial difficulties. To augment the capacity for theological education a new Institut Supérieur de Théologie et de Development has been opened in Basankusu funded from student fees. Overall CADELU is now responsible for 237 primary schools, 61 secondary schools, 31 health centres and four hospitals, the latter with nursing staff who perform surgery but rarely have a doctor. All struggle with inadequate pharmaceutical supplies.[402] Leprosy treatment has been taken over by the government. Since the departure of the missionaries CADELU has grown well beyond the expectations of some. Despite the trauma and social disruption of wars and the consequent poverty the Christian contribution is strong. The hopes and plans of 1878 for an indigenous church have been realised. How then is the Congo Balolo Mission and the contribution of the other Christian missions in the Congo to be judged?

Edgar Wallace, like this author, was no Christian. He was an international journalist, war correspondent, prolific writer and frequent exponent of provocative opinion. In 1907 he visited Congo to investigate the behaviour of the Congo Free State under Leopold's leadership. After months of exhausting travel he spent a few days at CBM Bongandanga to recuperate and observe Christian missionaries at first hand.

What the missionaries have done, I can see with my eyes, and seeing, I am prouder of my country and my countrymen and women, than ever I have been before. No battle I have witnessed, no prowess of arms ... has inspired me as the work of these outposts of Christianity. I am no more of a Christian than the average man of the world ... my sense of proportion allows me to rightly judge the value of the work ... As a rank outsider, I would not be a missionary on the Congo for £5,000 a year. All that is best in this sad land is the work of the missionaries. And all this has not been accomplished by sitting tight and waiting for miracles. It has not been done by lazy prayerfulness ... They made me ashamed of my futile life by the side of their great achievements. In England I met a smug Christian and told him of the missionaries. 'We owe them our prayers' he said, sententiously. I laughed. 'Write your prayers on the back of a five-pound note and send the note to the Congo Balolo Mission.[403]

Roger Casement, also, had no doubts: "The more I see of Mission work here in Central Africa the more convinced I am of the vital need for such agencies of human love and brotherhood."[404]

Dr Onesimus Ngundu of the Harare Theological College, Zimbabwe, writes of the DRC: "That country will never be the same as a result of missionary efforts and service. As an African I am very grateful to God for the sacrificial work of missionaries whom God used to transform Africa."[405] Micky Mbonda lives in the northeast of England but was born in Basankusu. When I ask for his opinion of life in his hometown in the modern-day DRC he replies "Thank God for the missions."

Since the departure of foreign missions there have been shining examples of local innovation and self-help. Malnutrition and its severe form, kwashiorkor, are widespread in rural districts. Thousands of Congolese children die annually as a result. At Basankusu Judith Bondjembo, Francis Hannaway and twelve local volunteers run a programme to rescue malnourished children. Brought by their impoverished mothers, children stay at the project for one to two months. Children who arrive in extremis are admitted to the small Catholic hospital next door and given intensive treatment under their supervision. Following recovery parents are taught how to provide an affordable, locally sourced nutritional diet for their children before they return to their home village. Funded initially by British Mill Hill Missionaries, running costs of the project are met by online charitable donations. In the past seven years the centre has treated over 3,000 malnourished children and has saved many young lives.[401]

When foreign staff evacuated Vanga Evangelical Hospital, east of Kinshasa, in 1960 it was expected to close but when missionaries returned after eighteen months they found a functioning hospital led by head nurse, Musti, and his colleagues, supported remotely by specialists in the USA. Vanga hospital is now a 500-bedded teaching hospital.[406] At Nyankunde, near the border with Rwanda, under the auspices of the Christian Health Service Corps a 150 bed hospital is staffed by five Congolese general practitioners and four American specialists.[407] Although supported by foreign financial sources local Congolese initiative has borne fruit.

The most remarkable has been the work of Congolese gynaecologist, pastor of a local church and Nobel Peace Laureate, Dr Denis Mukwege. Unable to ignore the desperate plight of the thousands of women who have suffered rape and extreme sexual violence during and since the two Congo

Wars of 1996-2003 Mukwege has built two hospitals in the eastern Kivu province of the DRC, saved the lives of many thousands of women and taken their cause to the United Nations. Having survived assassination attempts and escaped to the USA, he has returned, at the request of Congolese women, to his hometown of Bukavu where he continues to work and live with his family at great personal risk, guarded continuously by United Nations peacekeeping forces.[408]

While acknowledging the contribution made by such initiatives Jean-René Lingofe is concerned that they are, nonetheless, dependent upon continuing foreign charitable support.

> Congo does not need charity. The legacy view instilled by the Catholic missionaries of the missionary as the 'white man who brings money' is not helpful. Most charitable organisation does not seem to be interested in funding education of the local, but is rather concerned with fixing short-term issues, enhancing spiritual celebrations and protecting animals such as bonobo. Projects that meet immediate needs that depend on charitable funding from abroad, although well intentioned and appreciated, are not sustainable for the long-term future. When foreign financial support ceases the projects fail. What is the point of saving children's lives now if there will be nothing for them as adults?

Lingofe was born near Basankusu, the son of a school head teacher. He now lives in London where he leads his own successful company developing case management software. As a fifteen-year-old he joined the CADELU vocational training course at Ikau to learn the practical skills of mechanics, carpentry and commerce and then continued at the Baringa Catholic school to train for the priesthood. Aged twenty-five he moved to England to study as a Catholic missionary and obtained a masters degree in theology, but his life took a different direction.

Recalling his own education he concluded that learning about the mysteries of the Catholic church and becoming a priest would do nothing to meet the needs of the Congo people. Catholicism offered nothing that would build an African country. The prime purpose of Protestant missions was also to instil their religion but, in addition, they taught vocational skills. It has been Protestant trained bricklayers and carpenters who have built properties for the Catholic church, nurses trained by Protestant mission hospitals that continued to staff the country's hospitals. CADELU, having inherited a hospital from the missionaries but with so few qualified doctors available, arranged the training of two nurses and the university education of a doctor who returned to the Baringa hospital. The church's resources, however, could not meet the considerable cost which was met by funding from European sources.

Despite the rapid rise of heavily populated cities in the DRC a large proportion of the population still live in remote towns and villages with poor access to centralised facilities. The urgent need, therefore, is for the people of rural Congo to provide their own young people with the skills that will address local problems. For the immediate future this will depend on the growth of local economies using local resources to generate income. One major locally available resource is land. Families use this for their own food supply but on a collective scale it can be used for the benefit of the wider community. Palm oil is a basic ingredient of Congolese cooking, a daily necessity as well as a source for a variety of products. Lingofe's family has established a palm plantation generating an income that will make it self-sustainable; a local solution for the local people with no external dependency. Most importantly, the profits will be invested in the education of young people from Basankusu and the surrounding district. Many other similar initiatives are not only possible but necessary. "We must realise our own potential to build a self-sustaining future."[409]

22

Missionary Children:

Third Culture Kids

———

The foregoing chapters have presented a foreign missionary society from inception to closure, but there has been an important omission. Many of the missionaries were married. What of their children, growing up in Africa remote from other European children?

The first mention of children in the mission writings was a chapter by Harry Guinness in 1910 entitled "The white baby":

> The child problem is one of the most serious difficulties. On the Congo the white baby cannot live for more than two years ... the evils of surrounding corruption tend to soil the pure minds of the little ones, and leave an almost ineffaceable mark on childhood and youth ... Then missionaries have no business to be married, answers some thoughtless critic. In reply one need only say that ... The celibate missionary has a sadly restricted sphere of service. Women are needed to reach the women and family life above all is needed to show what such life should be. What then is to become of the children?[410]

The Guinnesses were admirers of Hudson Taylor's China Inland Mission, where women missionaries were not expected to marry until they could read at least one of the gospels in colloquial Chinese, a fluency that could take three or four years. Missionary wives were expected to undertake full-time evangelistic work alongside their husbands, allowing little opportunity for the needs of their children. Taylor set a precedent; his children were left in England in the care of others. In South Africa David Livingstone's family remained with him but they lost one child, scarcely saved another and his wife suffered serious illness. When he was determined to explore the centre of the continent his mother-in-law prayed that God would stop him: "Will you again expose her and them in those sickly regions? All the world will condemn the cruelty of the thing." Livingstone was torn.[411] Mary and the children returned to Scotland.

By 1895 "the problem" of the white missionary baby could not be ignored by the RBMU. A home for missionary children was opened by Mrs Guinness.[412] The four children placed under her care were from Congo, but numbers grew and children came from many different countries. During the first five years forty-two children were cared for and a much larger home was purchased. Everything was provided "that will conduce to the comfort and health of the children". Everything, that is, except the presence, love and care of their parents. The children's ages varied from six months to eighteen years. Some stayed only a few months, others nine years; three to six years was the average.

Separation from their children was by no means easy for the parents but childhood malaria could be very serious and the missionaries were grateful for a solution to their problem: "Please accept our best thanks ... I can assure you that the prospect of their being left under your superintendence makes the task much easier. It will be hard to leave them, especially for the mother ... We left our children behind in your care with a very restful heart ... confident all will be well with them ... By welcoming our daughter you have lifted the only cross of our missionary life."[410]

How long the children's home lasted is not clear. In 1921 there were ten married couples working with the CBM who had twenty-seven children between them, none of whom were with their parents in Congo. The addresses for the children included private homes and schools scattered across Britain.[411] In 1924 Mrs Harry Guinness donated the lease of her own home in South London to provide a new home for missionary children, which provided care for thirty-eight children over the following decade.[413,414,415] In December 1935 a larger property, in South Norwood, "Homelands", was purchased to accommodate the growing number of children.[416] Many were accommodated there until the bombing of London in 1940, when they were dispersed.

The situation faced by young families living overseas was by no means new. Throughout the history of empire young military men, diplomats, administrators and entrepreneurs have travelled to far corners of the world and, when married, have faced decisions concerning the upbringing of their children. In her account *Children of the Raj*[417] Vyvyen Brendon illustrated the difficulties encountered by expatriate families in choosing what they thought would be best for their offspring. As Guinness had also indicated, keeping one's children in India was considered to pose two overriding risks. The first was the risk of disease, the second the deleterious effect that mixing with the native population would have on the children's young minds. In due course many British schools were set up in India, initially by missionaries. For other missionaries, keeping their children in India but sending them a thousand miles away to a boarding school was not without its worries. In England well-intentioned Christian men and women established boarding schools for returning children whose parents wanted to ensure a specifically Christian education. Much later, during the Second World War, when British cities were being bombed and the Atlantic was not considered safe for passenger vessels, the risks of sending children to the home country were considered too great and the British schools in India experienced a resurgence.

So much for the parents' concerns, but what of the children? The central issue was, of course, separation. Troubled children seldom expressed their true feelings to parents in their letters. Similarly, parents were seldom made aware by schools of behavioural problems that arose in the children. Some families educated their children in their mission home. A Baptist couple in Bengal taught the girls at home. When it came to secondary education mother decided to be a 'good mother' but a 'poor wife': she came to England and remained with them. Looking back, some children consider that their mothers suffered more than they did. Some have said that the separation taught them resilience and independence that served them well in later life. Others never came to terms with the separation. For one boy, "Christianity to me means that parents were in one place and you in another."[418] No matter how loving and caring relatives or family friends could be, few could replace the presence of parents.

For those who remained with their parents and moved to their parents' country of origin when teenagers, the wide range of potential psychological and developmental issues that could arise have been described as "reverse culture shock".[419] They first received academic attention in the 1960s through the work of Dr Ruth Hill Useem who coined the acronym TCKs, 'Third Culture Kids'.[420] They have also been discussed by the American sociologist David Pollock.[421] Few missionary children have published personal accounts of their childhood experiences. Linda Taylor has made her experience in Congo the subject of a doctoral thesis.[348] For Margaret Newbigin Beetham her feelings concerning her missionary upbringing in India and the UK merited only brief mention in an autobiography.[422] The memoirs published by Marylin Gardner, whose parents were missionaries in Pakistan, and Faith Cook whose parents worked for the China Inland Mission, make disturbing reading.[423,424] In recent years, pioneered by Pollock, a number of North American colleges and universities have established courses recognising missionary parents' concern, but nothing of this nature was available to the children of the CBM. This book has been concerned with the history and outcomes of a unique missionary enterprise. If we are to complete that picture it is appropriate that we should ask how CBM children fared.

Living in London my parents agreed to care for the children of some of their colleagues who were still working in Congo; I was joined by seven new 'siblings' aged between five and fourteen years who would not see their parents for four years. So far as I recall, we lived as one large happy family. How true that was I cannot be sure. Letters to distant parents were written regularly but would have been checked. Letters from Congo were subject to the uncertainties of river transport on the Congo. We did, indeed, have many happy times together but there can be no doubt that many tears were shed. When my mother became ill alternative arrangements had to be made; one mother returned urgently from Congo. Talking of that day many years later her child Barbara said with considerable emotion, "Your mother becoming ill was the best thing that happened to us – it brought our mother home". In the pages that follow CBM children tell their stories.

Evie

"Ngai nazali mwana ya Africa mpo nabotami na Congo". "I am a child of Africa because I was born in Congo". This I sang in Lingala with sister Dorothy marching around the mission school quad with our Congolese classmates. As we were the only white family at Ngbenze we were very involved with our parents' activities with the Congolese. When I was seven I went away to Sakeji, a Christian boarding school in Northern Rhodesia. My name was Luti but at school it was Evelyn, a name I could neither pronounce nor spell. Sakeji was very different but a fun place where we were looked after lovingly and received a good education. It was not possible to go home for the Christmas holidays but we were always welcomed by other missionaries in Angola or Zambia, which added to the adventure. Our birthdays were in June and July which was a special family holiday time.

The violent uprising of Congo Independence was unexpected and, for my sister and me, it was exceedingly sad. We had to be separated from our parents and the only home that we knew. We were enjoying family breakfast together on the veranda when a dirty old car suddenly raced towards the house. The Belgian doctor leapt out and gestured excitedly while speaking in French. We did not understand but noticed a look of horror on our parents' faces. Our father said "Children, you must go with the doctor and his madam now. Leave your porridge! You must go at once!" After a quick prayer and a long hug we climbed into the back of the car. Our distressed parents hoped the guns under the floor mat would not be needed.

After crossing the Congo River by canoe and ferry we arrived at a dusty air strip. We asked why there were lots of holes in the walls. The soldiers could not speak English so could not explain the recent gunfire. More Belgians arrived and the doctor's wife cried as she shepherded us into the small, cramped aeroplane. We felt dazed but calm and brave. We were sure that God was with us. After the emergency flight from Lisala to Brussels and then to London we were delivered to elderly grandparents in suburban England. Meanwhile our parents had escaped down the Congo River and were able to return when the danger had passed. In England, we knew nothing of their whereabouts for nearly four months but, one day, the front doorbell rang and I saw a familiar sunburned bald head. Mum and Dad were home!

Life was so very different in England. Dorothy was eleven and I was fourteen. Water not only came out of a tap but we could actually swallow it immediately. In Africa it was bailed from a stream, boiled and filtered first. Instead of comfortable African sarongs were dressed in layers of vests, jumpers and coats. Beautiful silent snowfall replaced angry frightening tropical storms. Unlike my sister, I failed the grammar school entrance test. I felt a failure and went to a rough secondary school where I was the object of great curiosity as our story had been on the front page of the local newspaper. I was totally innocent of the youth culture in the 1960s. Most fourteen-year-old teenagers flounced around in skirts which flowed over crinoline underskirts; I wore the pleated skirts which the Women's Voluntary Service had provided. Instead of winkle-pickers and stiletto heels I wore round-toed Clarke's buckled shoes. I had long hair in plaits, not short bouffant hairstyles and spraying. The other girls wanted to know all about Marilyn Monroe. The only Marilyn I wanted to know about was my school friend in Northern Rhodesia whose whereabouts were unknown to me. I yearned to play bongo drums with my Congolese playmates, not the "Beatle mania" music. I felt so lonely and homesick as I stood alone in the corner of the playground. I closed my eyes tightly and prayed for a friend who understood me. A gentle voice called my name. "Hello Evie. Don't worry, I can be your friend." The voice was not from an angel, but it was another schoolgirl. Her name was Shirley and she is still my friend to this day.

After Independence our parents did not return to Congo. Dad became the pastor of a church, Dorothy a teacher and I trained as a nurse and midwife. Married to John, a doctor, we worked in Thailand as missionaries with the Overseas Missionary Fellowship for fourteen years during which time our son enjoyed two years at the Chefoo boarding school in Malaysia. When the time came for our children's further education we returned to England. I have happy memories of Congo and childhood family life. We are so "Grateful for all that is past and we trust Him for all that is to come".

The Hanson Family

Len Hanson was one of seven new recruits in 1924. After his first wife died because the nearest doctor was three days' journey away it became apparent that he was a gifted linguist. He married fellow missionary Mabel Smith and together they established the Bible School at Mompono. It was a great success, and the Hansons spent twenty-three years training the future leaders of the Congo Church. Following the upheaval of Independence they returned to Congo. Mabel compiled a new book of over 270 hymns and Len embarked on the revision of the Lomongo Bible, first translated by Ruskin thirty years previously, working with two Congolese colleagues and Mr Hobgood of the Disciples of Christ Mission. The task took six years and was competed in England after retirement, the culmination of forty-two years of missionary service. Len and Mabel Hanson had three children. Paul was born in 1933 during furlough in the UK, and Beryl and Frances later in Congo.

Paul was left at the Homelands children's home when he was seventeen months and saw his parents during their year-long furloughs only when he was six, thirteen and seventeen. For many years he wondered if they really were his parents. Even now he cannot recall ever being hugged and held by them in a loving way. On the other hand an aunt visited him regularly at boarding school, took him to concerts and museums and showered him with love and affection. A wonderful surrogate mother. Unsurprisingly, he often thought that she was his real mother. Another person who showed him affection as a young boy was an elderly, widowed neighbour whom he visited secretly during the first year of the war. One night a bomb destroyed her home. "Hot tears streaked my cheeks. Nobody will ever hug me again."

Not yet seven, he had been living with "horrid missionaries" in the Midlands but arrangements were made for him to attend a Christian boarding school. Arriving at Liverpool station he had no idea where he should go, but when Auntie Winnie appeared all was well. Despite the Christian background to the school, fagging and bullying were an everyday reality and homosexuality was rife between boys and staff. Recalling his school days Paul concluded, "I was extremely naive for my age, I didn't understand, which was a saving grace." The wife of the Headmaster was very kind, taking a personal interest in him and encouraging his talent for painting. Subsequently he moved to another boarding school which he left at sixteen to coincide with his parents' return on furlough.

Living together as a family proved very difficult. His parents had not seen him for four years and could not comprehend the changes in their teenage son. When his desire to become an artist was dismissed out of hand he rejected his father's ideas for employment and found himself a job as an engineering draughtsman. The attempt at family life failed. A confrontation brought the end. Taking a bag with his few belongings he left his parents and sisters, walked across town and asked his aunt and uncle to take him in. Although he saw his parents on Sundays he avoided them whenever possible. Once they returned to Congo he seldom saw them again. "That furlough above all the others was devastating. Every furlough engendered that awful inability of missionary parents to treat their erstwhile-left-behind-kids in a manner appropriate for the children's age." A few years later found him in California, married with a family and working as a designer-illustrator with a Hollywood advertising agency, one of whose clients was the Billy Graham evangelistic organisation. Later he formed his own very successful design company, with most of the Christian television channels among his clients.

When Paul was still at boarding school it was decided that his sisters should remain behind for their education. They came to live with the Halls in London. Beryl was nine and Frances five. After that they, like Paul, lived with their parents only during furloughs. Spending school holidays with his sisters was a new experience. "I did not know my sisters as sisters. I only met them four times before they settled in England. They were strangers pushed into my life. As a very immature boarding school brat I didn't know them and wasn't going to enter their life. As a result, I had little to do with them after Mum and Dad went back to Congo. My behaviour from that time brings tearful remorse to this day, an enormous sorrow-of-guilt that I did not help them when they suffered so intensely during their teenage years." Frances, Paul's youngest sister, takes up her story.

Frances

I was born at Baringa in 1942. When I was four we came to England for a year for our parents' furlough. At the end of the year it was decided that my older sister and I should not go back with them but would stay in England with missionary friends of our parents. They were Mr and Mrs Hall plus their son, but another CBM child joined us and later three more children arrived. We lived as a large happy family and Beryl and I have very happy memories of that time. There were so many children we had a rota for chores to do in the mornings before school. We went to church each Sunday and I loved Sunday school.

After four years, when I was nine, Mum and Dad came home and I can remember feeling shy when they came in and I hid behind the settee. They were strangers to me! We moved to the north of England where we lived as a family in a small, dark, damp downstairs flat provided for us by a local church member. There was only one bedroom so Paul had a curtain round his bed while we girls shared a double bed and Mum and Dad used a Put-you-Up in the sitting room. The bath was in the kitchen and the toilet in the back yard. Our parents had very little money and were just glad to have a roof over our heads.

After a year Mum and Dad went back to Congo. Paul was eighteen and lodged with relatives but there was no one to look after Beryl and me. With three weeks to go before our parents were due to go, the church leaders asked for volunteers who would take the "Hanson Girls". Inevitably, the most unsuitable family offered and were accepted. They had four children of their own and money was scarce. We were with this family for about a year when the mother became pregnant with her fifth child, an appeal was made at the church and another couple came forward. This was when things went from bad to worse. They had one daughter who we had to look after from time to time and she got us into trouble frequently. Our situation must have been noticed by someone outside the family because one day a social worker visited. However, with our unofficial foster mother in the room we were unable to say anything and life continued as before. When that lady became ill with mental health problems we were bundled off to another home, this time a lovely caring family. We were very happy there.

Four more years of parents in Congo, us in England, and then Mum and Dad back again for a year during which we lived in that small downstairs flat. Paul had given up on family long ago and gone to start a new life in North America. Beryl was working, lodging with a different couple from the church. When Mum and Dad went off to Congo I was sent to a boarding school but by this time, I had had such a disrupted education that grammar school level was way beyond me. However, when it came to the first holiday I was fortunate: a lady who worked in the RBMU office knew about me and with her husband took care of me, looking after me for each of the holidays. A few weeks before I was due to leave school Independence was declared. We in England heard that trouble had arisen for many Europeans and that many missionaries were being evacuated. Beryl was getting married and to our surprise Mum arrived having escaped any harm but leaving Dad behind, hoping to follow. By now I was seventeen, went back to live with Mum and Dad and started training to be a nurse and midwife. I was an active Christian and was very much involved with church life where I met my future husband. John became the assistant Pastor in charge of youth work. We married and started a family.

It wasn't until I had my own children that I wondered how Mum and Dad could leave their children with someone else to look after them. We didn't really have any close relationship with our parents; we knew and loved people in the church much better. The consequence of this was that when Dad died and Mum was on her own, and we had moved away, I felt guilty that I could not look after her in my own home. I struggled with this for years but family relationships cannot be rebuilt in a few months.

Beryl

I am pleased Frances has written about those years. There were certainly lots of aerograms written to our parents which got thrown away and never posted because I thought better of it and didn't want to worry them. We felt as though we had been pushed from pillar to post through no fault of our own. However, I am pleased that Dad's hard work, contributing to the revised Lomongo Bible, was published and appreciated. Our last year just prior to Mum and Dad coming home was much better. That host family was extremely good to us. How many people would have been willing to turn their lounge into a bedroom for two homeless mish-kids? Not many I should think!

Morag

My older sister was almost three when I was born at Baringa in 1945. The boys came later. Our parents followed a then-fashionable child raising method of F. Truby King. As Mum explained to a close friend, "We wanted to pet and spoil Sheila but knew we must not". Ten minutes of cuddling was allowed per day. Breastfeeding was on a strict four-hour schedule and for six months only.

Growing up as a young child on a mission station in Congo was very different from the life I would have experienced if we had lived in Scotland. Missionaries were from many backgrounds and stations in life, some from privileged families and some working class. We were the latter. As children we learned from the adults around us. Margaret Williams was a fine self-effacing nurse. Once, when I was ten, a nurse came from the hospital came to say a baby had died. Margaret had been working to save this baby and started to cry. I was shocked to realise that grownups can cry. Muriel Langley taught in the girls' school and loved each girl with all her heart. Congolese people were accustomed to harshness from authority figures, but she was gentle and funny.

When our youngest brother was born I was already at Sakeji School with several other CBM children and had no idea we were expecting another baby brother. I started at Sakeji just before my seventh birthday. It was almost a thousand miles away and the journey could take up to two weeks. Travelling with older girls somewhere new I went off happily and was never homesick. Although we were gone for ten months at a time we received newsy letters every week from our parents which were wonderful to have. The school was quite isolated and there was great freedom to enjoy the outdoors, up trees and swimming in the river. I was very happy there. We were unsophisticated and untouched by any outside culture but the principal had a violent temper and was abusive towards the naughty children. The rules were very strict. We were mostly compliant but few escaped his vicious punishments. Our weekly letters home were all read before mailing so we were careful not to include anything negative. One girl did write that she hated the place and was soundly thrashed. My older sister was a natural rebel and Sakeji destroyed her. Not so much the separation from our parents but the abusive treatment. Her adult life was sad and chaotic.

When I was fourteen we went to Britain. I loved Congo and when I left Baringa and knew it was my last time I knelt down on the grass and dug my fingers into the soil to get the luscious fragrance for the last time. Back in Scotland, living together as a family was particularly hard. I was living with my parents for an extended time, the first since I had gone away to boarding school. They thought they could waltz into my life and I would let them in. My father didn't seem to care, but my mother really tried hard and I hated it. Of course, I had no idea why, just that she was manipulating and smothering me. I was naturally compliant and did not know how to escape the loving intervention. When it was time for our parents to return to continue their work at Baringa it had been planned that, together with my older sister, I would remain in Scotland for my secondary education. One day my parents and brothers came to take me on an 'out-day', and when they left it was goodbye for four years. I was really happy that they were going away, but Mum was very distressed. During their absence Independence had been declared and all they met was missionaries travelling in the opposite direction. They returned home. Dad became the Scottish secretary of the mission so all our family stayed in the UK.

I think by that time our parents realised how bad separation from children can be, but I was very disappointed that they were coming home to stay. On leaving school I trained as a nurse and midwife and since moving to Canada I have loved providing truly woman-led midwifery care. My first marriage was not a success but I have now been happily married for over twenty years.

Looking back, as children, we tended not to think from our parents' perspective and it was not until I was an adult that I recognised that those long months of separation must have been agony for my mother. Also, it was not until my mid-30s that I understood the effect that the separation had on my teenage behaviour and my feelings towards my parents. My subconscious conclusion was that my parents were happy I was going away and that damage was not dealt with for many years, when I spent time with a counsellor. However good intentions may be, it is how a child interprets them that the subconscious damage is done. When my mother was dying I spent some weeks with her. I did not broach the topic of separation as that was water under the bridge. She was so excited at the prospect of seeing the Lord's face that our conversations revolved around that. Those were rich days for me.

Gibbie

I am one of Morag's younger brothers. My early years at Baringa were happy. I learned the Lomongo language, loved the sound of tropical rain and when Sheila and Morag returned in "summer" from Sakeji we had rare times playing together. I always felt safe and had no issues with my relationships with our parents during those years. Mum would be at home, teaching at the school or helping at the hospital and Dad would be building something, working in the carpentry shop or travelling and preaching.

When I reached my seventh birthday I went to Sakeji school with the others. Dispatched to our dormitories for the first night's sleep children cried. I was beside a boy who was very homesick. For many years he bore a resentment of his parents because it looked to him as if his parents loved the Africans more than him; they were prepared to send him away so that they could stay with the African people. Later in life he took a senior position in the school, reconciling these feelings with his parents before he adopted the post. His parents had no idea they had left this mark on their son.

I was happy at Sakeji although along with many others, often the girls, I suffered the wrath of the headmaster. When a reunion was held to celebrate the school's 75th anniversary a public apology was made for the abuses of the early years, although those who needed to hear it most were not there of course. Despite this, I loved going back for the reunion. It was cathartic, memorable and emotional. The years rolled back and memories of people, places, games, smells, tastes and customs were a delightful eclectic mixture. It ended all too soon, before I could properly process it. In the 1950s, no thought was given to the psychology of abandoning young children for nine months a year without parental love and care. There was no one to talk to, other than teachers. They were dutiful and kind but had no close relationship. Many children suffered the effects of this in later life and resented their experiences blaming God and their parents for their treatment. For some, their visit to Sakeji for the reunion lanced the boil.

When our parents were unable to return to Congo the missionary theme continued through the rest of my teenage years. Dad travelled around the country to promote support for the mission and the mission prospered in Scotland under his care. One of the downsides of the missionary life persisted, however; we were rarely together as a family. Instead, our home in Glasgow was often full of visitors, for the monthly prayer meeting or visiting missionary folk staying. My younger brother and I were secure due to our ages but our sisters were passed from pillar to post and "sacrificed" for the "sake of the Gospel". Who would have thought that parents could leave two of their children in the care of aunts for a possible 4 years, in order to fulfil the call of the mission field thousands of miles away in another continent? It took the uprising of Independence to cut that short, but in many ways the damage had been done. One of the upsides was that we mish-kids shared a sense of adventure, open spaces and travel and enjoyed experiences which stood us in good stead for our futures. Personally, I did not suffer any spiritual fallout as a result of what might have been potentially catastrophic. My commitment to God as a boy of seven in Baringa developed. I joined actively in our local mission-based church and I was involved for a decade in a Christian rock band. I'm not sure what my parents thought of it but it was "for the sake of the Gospel" so they couldn't say much!

Barbara

I was born in 1940 at Baringa, followed by sister Julia, Arthur and Martin. When Julia was born there was no CBM nurse or doctor but there were Roman Catholic sisters nearby and they helped with Mum's delivery; they let Dad be at the birth and he admired them very much. Arthur was a twin but there were problems with the birth and his brother could not be saved. When Martin was due Mum travelled with us children back to Glasgow to have the baby at the hospital and to be near her parents. Dad supervised the Bongandanga printing press and did preaching work while Mum was a nurse running the small hospital. She taught us at home in the afternoons when she had finished work. While she was busy in the mornings each of us was looked after by a "boy", a trusted Congolese teenage lad.

Life as children in Congo was wonderful. Apart from Martin getting malaria none of us were ill. We have very happy memories. We lived in a brick house not far from the river and played together as a family, but not with any of the Congolese children. We lived very differently from the other Europeans on their plantations nearby. They seemed well off and posh but friendly. They had Congolese wives, sometimes two, and we loved visiting them for tea.

When I was seven we all came to Scotland on furlough for a year. Towards the end of 1948 we moved to London to live with Mr and Mrs Hall. I do not remember our parents saying goodbye and I don't remember crying. I don't think we actually went to say goodbye. That's probably why Arthur was so upset. He was only six when Mum and Dad went away. I think he suffered the most. He would cry on the way to school and I would hold his hand to comfort him. Julia and I had each other, but he was on his own and he missed his mum. We were very close as children and have remained very close since.

Living in London without parents was totally different. Mrs Hall could never be our mother but I do remember feeling sorry for her, looking after all these children. We wrote letters to Mum and Dad. I think most times they were read before they were posted but I didn't mind that because we always wanted something nice to arrive for them. I know my mother found it very hard to be without her children. I think she was glad to come home. When she did come home we had a real mother. We went to Scotland, to start again, to be on the path for what was going to be right for our lives. Dad stayed in Congo for another two years. They had decided to leave the mission because they had made a contribution but were not receiving sufficient financial support to be able to care for their family properly. Mum worked as a nurse and Dad became a minister in the Church of Scotland. I became a teacher and my husband was a minister.

Looking back I am amazed how I accepted the separation from our parents. I'm almost blank about the things that happened when we were all together. I think I was so focused on looking after my wee brother who cried for his mum every morning. Writing this has brought a lot of feelings back to me. It was a very big thing but children are resilient and I got over it. I never thought we were treated differently. I have no grudge but I would always be against women doing mission work abroad if it meant they would be separated from their children: there's plenty of mission work to be done in our own country, and always has been.

Jo

When I was born I was given the African name of Amba. In 1949 we moved as a family to Yoseki where Father established a hospital and what was then called a Leper Colony. I had early home-schooling from my mother and a fellow missionary. At the age of seven I was the first of the CBM children to go to Sakeji School. My father took me the first time on that week-long trip. The day he left was like a black tunnel and, of course, I was homesick but the overriding memories are happy ones. Like the others I only got back to Yoseki once a year as the journey took so but I remember happy times spent with kind families who lived nearer the school.

When I was thirteen and my sister Ruth was nine we were sent to Clarendon School, the boarding school in North Wales. We called it "The Evangelical Nunnery" and it was a bit of a culture shock: a girl's school as opposed to the co-ed school we had enjoyed in Africa with the freedom of the river and the surrounding bush. The weather was a huge contrast and swimming in an out-door pool filled by sea water was grim. We were happy enough and had our wonderful Aunty Ethel and Grandpa Wright as our official guardians. We saw our parents every two years. For me the important thing was that I was confident that my parents loved us and loved each other. They involved me in decisions about schooling. Ruth and I knew that they were where they felt God wanted them to be and we were at school with friends who were in much the same situation.

Going to university was different. I missed the parents, I wished they were in the UK, at home, to discuss matters. University was harder because, for the first time, I was exposed to the secular world the "Big Wide World". Hitherto I had been sheltered in a school for missionaries' children and then in a school for "daughters of the clergy". University was a great time but I felt different from my peers: there was not the shared experience of having parents hundreds of miles away. It was, also, a shock to find that my fellow medics were good people with a desire to work for others despite not being Christians. That sounds naive in the extreme. I was "green as grass". The Christian Union kept me on the straight and narrow and provided me with friends outside the medical group of students.

The day I started year two at university our parents returned to Yoseki despite the potential dangers following Independence. Four years later, they were caught up in the Simba uprising. Mercifully we were unaware of the danger they were in. We received little news and I do not recall being anxious about their safety.

We owe much to the uncles, aunts and cousins who had us for visits during the holidays. Happy times, happy memories. On reflection I think it must have been worse for Mother and Father, especially Mother. Now that I have had my own children and am enjoying the grandchildren I cannot imagine how they felt. I thank God for them and for Aunty Ethel who did so much for us both.

Ruth

My first proper recollections of Congo are as a six-year-old at Yoseki where our parents worked at the mission hospital. My sister Jo was already at Sakeji school and our friend Val had been sent to school back in England. I was therefore a home-schooled "only child" but I have only happy memories with so many adults and Congolese staff around. We had very few toys but I loved the freedom and all our pets. African food was delicious. Banganju, a palm nut curry, and nsau cooked and dipped in sugar.

When I turned seven it was off to Sakeji which was enormous fun. I was fortunate in having my big sister with me so I never felt the homesickness that I know others felt but the general feeling was of great companionship and fascinating experiences. When I was nine we came to Clarendon school which I enjoyed. Life was more restricted and cold but we were happy. Aunt Ethel and Grandpa cared for us wonderfully at speech days, half terms and holidays. Two years later we went back to Yoseki for the summer holiday. What a welcome we received! Drums beating, villages adorned with flowers and gifts at every stop. That was to be my last visit to Congo.

We saw our parents every two years and these times became progressively more uncomfortable, coping with getting to know each other again and me now a teenager. Although I never doubted being loved I began to feel, no doubt incorrectly, that they didn't 'know' me. They missed my entire nursing career. Equally I had missed their Simba rebellion experience. Aunt Ethel, and Jo, were my constant.

Only when I left school did I begin to realise what an unusual upbringing I had. I had no idea how to 'do life'. The hot-house Christian experience of mission left me unprepared for the secular world and I struggled to correlate the two. Thankfully I met another Christian and in the end it was okay for me. After qualification as a nurse and health visitor I worked in Zambia and Rhodesia. My Christian life deteriorated somewhat but faithful prayers of family and friends brought me through and I eventually began to work out how to "do life" better.

Married with a family, in tune spiritually and living close to our parents after their retirement I was able to make up for lost time which was a joy. I will never know how agonising it must have been for them to see me go 'off the rails' in spite of their best efforts. It was not something I recall discussing. I often defend my parents. I do believe it must have been really difficult for them, worse for them than us, to send us off when we were so young, but it was the 'done thing' and they had absolute faith that God would look after us. As He indeed has, for which I constantly thank Him.

The Manning Family

The Librairie Evangélique du Congo (LECO) was set up by the Congo Protestant Council in 1935 as a publisher, printer, bookshop, and distributer of bibles, Christian literature and educational material. Situated in Kinshasa it was an invaluable, focal service that supplied the needs of Protestant churches and missions throughout Congo. The information, advice, and friendship it offered for missionaries passing though Kinshasa was greatly appreciated. In 1952 Ross and Chris Manning, who had worked previously with the CBM, took over its management.

Ross came from Adelaide but there was no Australian mission working in

Congo, the country of his calling. Accordingly, aged twenty-two, he travelled to London, joined the RBMU and arrived at Ikau in 1932. Ross had no prior trade or profession but a humble personality with an aptitude for languages won the confidence of colleagues. He undertook building projects, taught at the school and preached fluently to large crowds. He married CBM nurse Christine Attwood and together they worked at Ikau and Bongandanga for fourteen years.

It is said of Ross that it was the personal contact with individuals that he appreciated most, especially in isolated villages distant from the mission station. There he sat listening to understand their culture and their needs, and he learned to beat their talking drums. When it was time to leave for a welcome furlough, having said goodbye to the people on the station, he and Chris decided, late on their last evening, that they should see their friends in the leprosy village away in the forest. They might not see some again. Taking their leave someone suggested they should sing. Standing by the roadside in the moonlight they sang a farewell hymn together with croaking leprosy-affected voices.

The decision to leave the CBM and move to LECO was not easy but the move also helped to resolve a family need. Their children, Beverly and Edwin, had reached school age and a Kinshasa school met that need until senior education was required. After six years of happy family life in Kinshasa the children were settled at a boarding school in the UK, spending holidays with their parents' friends and previous colleagues. Aged twelve and ten they became Third Culture Kids. After Independence the parents were unable to return to Kinshasa. Ross then worked with the British and Foreign Bible Society in Nigeria and became consultant for Africa for the United Bible Societies.

Beverly

My memories of Congo are pleasant, though vague. The first six years were at Bongandanga, where we were the only European children; our friends and carers were local people and our native language was Lomongo as much as English. We led a simple but happy life. In Leopoldville we attended the Belgian state school where our friends were mainly non-Congolese, Belgians and the children of various missionaries.

During that period we went as a family to Australia for a year's furlough returning via Ceylon, Dar-es-Salaam and across by train and riverboat back to Leopoldville. The fact that we were unfazed by these adventures and upheavals must have been a result of the love and security that we felt from our parents. The move from Bongandanga to Kinshasa was presented to us as a token of God's loving care; we were spared separation from our parents and being sent to the Sakeji boarding school at an early age.

When, in 1958, it was time for secondary education in England we were well prepared. We were lucky to be together at the same coeducational school, another example of "God's goodness", but an important factor. Arriving in England we stayed with the Halls, who would be our official guardians but whom we had never met. I remember being confused when I saw them in the garden at eight o'clock in the evening when it was still light, learning about the Twist and Connie Francis, and the pleasure of having acquired an older 'brother'. It was a sort of introduction to normality. I have no unhappy memories or memories of homesickness. When we went to boarding school there were, of course, some bedtime tears but I have no memory of any kind of lasting unhappiness. Those years were happy.

University was an eye opener and to some extent a time of rebellion. When we did not follow our parents' Christian beliefs I was never able to have a discussion about it with Dad. It seemed as if we spoke different languages and I don't think he ever came to terms with that. Mum was saddened as she felt we were missing out on something, but it never interfered with our relationship.

In retrospect, I am surprised that we were never bullied or ridiculed for our ignorance or naivety. Whether it was a result of being brought up in the blind faith of being cared for by an ever-loving God and therefore not worrying, or whether it was all the experiences of being Third Culture Kids, I cannot be sure, but we became contented, free-thinking individuals. The movement from one extreme social, cultural and linguistic environment to another does not seem to have done too much damage.

Edwin

When we lived at Bongandanga the Congolese children were our only playmates so we developed a degree of "colour blindness" at an early age. Moving to Leopoldville we went to a French-speaking school with mostly

European kids. We soon forgot Lomongo and picked up the French at school where we mish-kids did quite well. At home we had good access to reading material which included children's books in English that made me realise ours was not a normal situation and I became envious of a more normal, i.e. English, schoolboy environment, although it never occurred to me that this would involve separation from my parents.

Leaving Congo at the age of ten I do not remember any tearful farewells but I don't think I fully realised what was happening. Settling down in England we were fortunate to have caring guardians on the same wavelength. The Belgian school in Leopoldville left us well ahead of our English counterparts as far as education was concerned, but I do remember feeling different because of my ignorance of things that were important to normal English boys. When our parents were back in England on furlough, I began to feel homesick; saying goodbye on Sunday nights was never easy.

Following Independence our parents returned unexpectedly, their days in Congo over. They subsequently went to work in Nigeria but that included six months leave every eighteen months and we also had a trip to Lagos every two years so family separations were not protracted.

The Anglican school we attended in England was founded in 1553 for "waifs and orphans" and, on one occasion, our mother asked the headmaster how many of the students were from "broken" homes. The reply was not as expected: "Some people might say that yours was a broken home." We certainly did not feel like a broken family. We had no bitterness or resentment at all towards our parents for the periods of separation and we were constantly aware of their love, support, and prayers.

University was our first real experience of freedom, a major escape from childhood naivety and in many ways quite a shock. That was also the time when my sister and I diverged from the religious beliefs of our parents, which certainly caused them considerable stress and inevitably resulted in a barrier between us. There was no point in trying to discuss these things as it all boiled down to a matter of "faith". The subject of religion was avoided as far as possible. I would consider myself to be an agnostic, but I still appreciate the Christian values of our early years. Following graduation, I was not particularly close to my parents, but we always kept in good contact despite often being on different continents.

After graduation I spent seven years in Zambia which were a real privilege. I later returned to work in other parts of Africa but have come to despair of the pervasive corruption and no longer feel that I have "Africa in my blood". After the death of my father I lived close to my mother where I was able to provide support and repay some of the love that we had received from her throughout our lives. That was a very precious time for us both and made up, at least in part, for the many previous years of separation.

Val

My parents met and married in Congo in 1937 where they worked at Yoseki. I have happy memories of roaming with Anyesi and Aliam, my Congolese playmates, and being home-schooled by my mother. It was a happy time. Some of the other missionary children went to the Sakeji boarding school but when I was six it was decided that my mother should bring me to England to be cared for by a family who had provided a second home to my father when he was a teenager. My memories of that time are vague, apart from the day my mother and I boarded the riverboat, waving my father goodbye, then trying to comfort my mother.

The family who gave me a home were warm and loving but their children had all left home and I was cared for mostly by their housekeeper, of whom I became very fond. It could have been a lonely time but at the primary school I made a very close friend and with weekly letters from Congo I believe I always felt surrounded by love. However, it could never be the same as real family life and the few months, when I was nine, that I lived with my parents on furlough, I remember as idyllic. It was harder when they left again and I went to Clarendon boarding school. There were a good number of other missionary children at Clarendon so I think I accepted it as God's will, hard as it was. Looking back it feels as if there was a total lack of affection; certainly none was demonstrated. Staff were formal and remote. Even at the time of the trouble in Congo when my parents were in danger, I was summoned to the Headmistress to be given a message from the Red Cross to say they were safe, and that was it.

In the in the summer holidays I went to my grandparents and aunt in Scotland, which I loved. Other holidays were spent with other families but it left me feeling rootless. My choice of university, St Andrews, was, I'm sure, so that I could be near my Scottish relatives. The periods of family separation varied in length and included one period of five years without seeing my father. While desperately fond of each other my father and I became 'shy' of each other and sometimes resorted to jokes and word games to ease the tension. My parents finally left Congo in time for my graduation.

The effects of childhood separation I find difficult to assess. Of one result I am certain: I have always had a strong feeling of never really belonging anywhere, of being an 'add on' in other people's families. My choice of social work with children and families as a career stemmed, I am sure, from a strong identification with children in care. First in a local Children's Department then social work in the London followed by a year in India and Nepal helping in a TB clinic. When my father died suddenly, I could not leave my mother and became involved with a shop selling fair trade handicrafts from third world countries but travel led to teaching in India, resettlement work with Vietnamese refugees, social work with deaf/blind people in residential care and, finally, with visually impaired people in an Eye Hospital. Not a career as such, more a muddled wandering, looking for people and organisations with ideals I could relate to. These I found only in my last two years, with a voluntary organisation in a very committed team of like-minded people. It felt like 'coming home'. I never married or had children, a source of sadness, but having said that, life has been full, varied and rewarding, with many close friendships. For the last few years I have been with a partner whose family has given me the warmest of welcomes. As the poet Lemn Sissay said, reflecting on his childhood rejection by foster parents, "I am not defined by my scars, I have to live in the present". I, too, live in the present.

23

The Heart of Darkness

The description of Africa as a dark continent has been attributed to Stanley, who coined the term to promote the book recounting his epic journey down the Congo River.425 The image was repeated by him in *In Darkest Africa*426 and then continued by Joseph Conrad with his *Heart of Darkness*.154

Benighted. A comfortable-sounding word denoting nightfall: "I am like to be benighted, for the day is almost spent."[427] With darkness comes the end of a day's work, a time to eat with family and friends, to rest, to sleep. But there are, also, more sinister implications.[428] "To blind." With darkness comes the inability to see, to become lost. It is common to hear depression described as "a dark place". "Whom error doth benight". Ignorance, moral corruption, brutality, savagery. "Want of spiritual or intellectual sight." Were not the intellectual and philosophical developments of the 17th and 18th centuries known as the Age of Enlightenment? In 1877 revival London it was the perceived dark want of spiritual sight that motivated Tilly, Arthington, the Guinnesses and others to send the light of the Christian Gospel to save "benighted" souls and dispel the "darkness" of Central Africa.

Conrad has been criticised as "a thoroughgoing racist",[429] which to current readers may seem surprising in view of recent interest that seeks to show that the author's purpose was to locate the heart of darkness, not in Africa but in Europe.[430] Looking westwards up the river Thames to England's capital city the narrator's first words were "this also has been one of the dark places of the earth".[431] Conrad was a strong supporter of Roger Casement, to whom he wrote: "I form the warmest wishes for your success. It is an extraordinary thing that the conscience of Europe tolerates the Congo today. It is as if the moral clock had been put back many hours. The Belgians are worse than the seven plagues of Egypt ... England ... too busy with other things ... to take up cudgels for humanity, decency and justice."[432] Bertrand Russell considered Conrad to be "a very rigid moralist".[433] However, Chinua Achebe's masterly essay from 1977 will dispel any doubt: "Conrad saw and condemned the evil of imperial exploitation but was strangely unaware of the racism on which it sharpened its iron tooth."[429] As Daniel Podgorski has commented, "Heart of Darkness is a book well worth teaching, well worth praising, and well worth condemning".[434]

Although Britain abolished slavery throughout most of its empire in 1833, Britain had been the most successful slave trading nation in the world and a previous monarch, James II, had employed the Royal Navy to enforce his monopoly. Following the Slave Compensation Act of 1837 the equivalent of £17 billion was paid as "compensation" to slave owners and shareholders. During the American Civil War warships built in Liverpool crossed the Atlantic to support the Confederate forces. The products and profits of slavery were central to the economy of mid-19th century Britain and its empire.[435] One example is to be found at the heart of the CBM.

Catherine Guinness, granddaughter of Dr Harry, has explored the story of her maternal great-grandfather Henry Reed.[436] Reed, from Yorkshire, became an ardent evangelical supporter of the CBM and other missions. As a young man, he made his fortune in Van Diemen's Land, Tasmania. Within a few years his entrepreneurship yielded a very generous income based on shipping and farming. The latter was on extensive lands stolen from the Aboriginal Tasmanian Nations, acquired as part of determined British action that suppressed all indigenous opposition and led to the extermination of the aboriginal population. In Henry's memory his wife Margaret donated to the CBM the sum of £5,000 to provide the first riverboat for the missionaries to explore and settle on the upper Congo. The *Henry Reed*, which carried the first CBM missionaries to the Balolo people in August 1889, was paid for by the lives of the dispossessed, murdered people of Tasmania. Fourteen years later, nearing the end of its life, the *Henry Reed* also carried Roger Casement on his tour that produced the damning report of Leopold, and its captain was Daniel Danielsen whose photographs taken during that voyage were the first visual exposure of the atrocities.

Despite valiant attempts to establish the rights of freed slaves, racist attitudes continued to permeate British society. Speaking of the human rights of Africans the Liverpool businessman John Holt wrote in 1901 "Their political and other rights are least thought of by any. When shall we as a race be able to deal justly with other races?"[201] We have seen Edgar Wallace's praise for the CBM missionaries, but what of his opinion of the Congolese? "I do not regard the native as my brother or sister ... Between the native and myself there is a gulf of a thousand years and I do not wish to bridge that that gulf." In his view the missionaries were "creating a manhood from a degraded race".[403] What, then, of the CBM's founders and the missionaries themselves? Was there racism in the Evangelical churches of Britain?

When Mrs Guinness senior set out the intentions of the new mission she noted that "Men of the world mock at the attempt, and ridicule the idea that such human beings can ever be transformed into spiritually minded Christians".[437] To the founders of the mission the Congo people were "uncivilised ... benighted savages ... although they were not of a savage disposition". After several years of preaching at Palaballa Henry Richards was able to report a breakthrough: "The stolid, stupid people have waked up." And, to his surprise, he had discovered "They are exactly like us inside; the difference is only skin deep!" Reflecting on the villagers of Bonginda at the time of the missionaries' first arrival Dora McKenzie recalled that their "Dark brothers and sisters ... lived in the dark places of the earth". For a Victorian woman their behaviour was often repulsive and disgusting and "a woman's life is spent in a degradation too dark to be described ... Yet in all their Darkness and degradation [they] have much that is lovable".[438] For Fanny Guinness the explanation was obvious. "We regard them as the sin-degenerated descendants of originally purer, wiser, and happier races."[439] A Catholic missionary was able to write "The black race is certainly the race of Ham, the race cursed of God". And Bentley of the BMS: "Fiendish cruelty and heartlessness have made their home in these dark places."[386] Although the women wore no clothes the missionaries organised sewing classes which proved encouraging because "a desire to be clothed indicates an interest in much deeper things".[440] Seemingly the leaders of evangelical mission were unaware that the son of a Guadeloupe slave, Chevalier de Saint-Georges, admired by Queen Marie Antoinette, had been a champion fencer, virtuoso violinist, composer, conductor of the leading symphony orchestra in Paris, and dubbed "the most accomplished man in Europe"; that Scott Joplin, son of a former slave was changing world music with his innovative composition of ragtime in America; and in 1896 at London's Royal College of Music, Gustav Holst and Ralph Vaughan Williams were lesser musicians in the orchestra playing the premiere of a symphony composed by Samuel Coleridge Taylor, descendant of freed slaves.

Thirty years later, speaking of the people at Tamudjumbe Armstrong wrote "They are still suffering from the thraldom of darkness that has been upon their land for centuries".[441] In 1950 a CBM missionary wrote of the Congolese who worked at a nearby factory, "The crowds of young men and their families congregated in these places which are centres of gross materialism and vice".[442] By contrast the worst that Harry Guinness wrote of London's East End drunks, exploited women and the unwashed, shoe-less children that flocked to the soup kitchen in late Victorian London, was that they were poor.

"Savages" was a word commonly used by 19th century Western Christian society to describe the people of Africa. Savage: "Uncivilised; living in the lowest stage of culture. Rude, harsh, ungentle, fierce, ferocious, cruel."[443] The concept of the "noble savage"[444] sought, but failed, to disguise the intended sentiment of the word. Although the post-impressionist painter Eugene 'Paul' Gaugin would never qualify as a role model for would-be missionaries, in a more thoughtful moment he revealed an insight rare amongst his generation. As missionaries were establishing their first foothold at Bongandanga Gaugin left the French-dominated capital town of Tahiti in search of a life among the indigenous Polynesian population. After two days' travel he exhausted his provisions but, mistakenly, expected that money would buy his needs. "The food is certainly there, on the trees, on the mountain top, in the sea ... but one needs to be able to climb a high tree, to go up the mountain ... catch fish ... There I was, a civilised man, definitely inferior to the savage. I was ashamed. I caught sight of a small dark head with quiet eyes. A little child was examining me ... These black people, these cannibal teeth, brought the word 'savage' into my mouth. For them I was the savage."[445]

George Washington Williams was an African American soldier in the Civil War, who later became a Baptist preacher, lawyer and historian. In the year that the first CBM missionaries settled at Bonginda he visited Europe, met with King Leopold and travelled in the Congo Free State. When he witnessed the abuses of the Leopold regime he wrote an open letter to the king, condemning what he regarded as the inhuman treatment of the Congolese, one of the first to raise awareness of the Africans' plight in Congo. William H. Sheppard was also an African American, born in Virginia to parents who were freed slaves and probably descendants of slaves taken by the Portuguese from the Congo.[446] After university he became pastor of a church in Atlanta but was determined to go as a missionary to Africa. Despite reports that the Presbyterian Foreign Missionary Board would not send a black man without a white supervisor,[447] he was welcomed, and when sufficient funding was forthcoming he, and Samuel Lapsley, travelled to Congo in 1890 where they were to work "as co-equals" and pioneer the work of the American Presbyterian Congo Mission.[448] On their way they were welcomed by the Guinnesses at Harley College and in Kinshasa they collaborated with Sims of the ABMU. Following Lapsley's death Sheppard was joined by William M. Morrison and served for twenty years, during which he made significant contributions to exposing the Leopold regime through photographs and numerous publications in the USA.[449,450] The initial reaction of Africans towards him was ambivalent. Not understanding the combination of his African origins and American behaviour the Congolese gave him the name Mundele Ndom, "Black white man" or, literally, a black man with clothes. In 1907 Sheppard published an article critical of the rubber concession company in the mission journal. The Kasai Company sued for defamation and he, with Morrison, was found guilty. At the subsequent appeal, with the assistance of a Belgian lawyer, the two missionaries were exonerated. Of Sheppard's contribution to Congo Walter Williams concluded: "Sheppard rejected the view that soul-saving excluded earthly considerations and he worked hard to aid those Congolese in material ways. Whether giving medical aid, ransoming slaves, or protesting colonial exploitation, Sheppard tried to improve African standards of living ... Because of his influence on black Americans and his efforts on behalf of Africans, he deserves to be ranked amongst the most important of early Afro-American missionaries."[451]

George Grenfell was renowned amongst the missionaries of the BMS, but his early years were marked by racial issues. Following the death of his wife after only three years with the mission in the Cameroons, he fathered a child with his Jamaican housekeeper Rosana Edgerley which, despite marriage to Rosana, led to his immediate resignation from the mission. He found employment with a commercial company and his career as a missionary appeared to be over, but when the BMS became established at the mouth of the Congo he was invited to re-join the mission, albeit in a management capacity only and not as a missionary.[452] Together the couple contributed greatly to the progress of the BMS on the Congo, but Rose was never accepted as a missionary.[453]

The CBM did not employ any African American missionaries but in 1893 the Home Council did consider an offer from a church in Jamaica, and it was agreed that "if possible we ought to employ such labour as an experiment".[454] Within a few months it was agreed to accept a Mr James who had been a pastor in Jamaica for six years, "a man of colour eminently suited to work on the Congo", who would be joined by his fiancée after a period of medical training in London. Should the experiment fail "In the event of them being unsuitable" the mission would be responsible for the cost of their return to Jamaica. They were soon joined by Mr Sawyer, a carpenter from Jamaica, and colleagues reported that they "did excellent work and proved to the natives what they themselves might become in the service of Christ".[455]Before a few years had passed, however, the "experiment" failed. Sawyer was involved in making complaints of mistreatment of Congolese by Danielsen and other missionaries and was himself dismissed. Back at home in Jamaica he became an ordained minister in the Baptist church.[456] The other Jamaican staff also returned home. Concern was expressed by the British missionaries that because the Congolese identified themselves more closely with their Afro-Caribbean colleagues the authority and effectiveness of the superior white man's gospel teaching was undermined. Racism was endemic throughout Western society, including Western Christianity and missionaries.

Christian missions have also been the object of considerable criticism of a related nature: their association with colonial imperialism.

From the day that Paul set out from Antioch on the Orontes on the first of his missionary journeys around the eastern Mediterranean in AD 45[457,458] his purpose was, if not imperialist, certainly colonialist. Taking his new religion, uninvited, to the Jewish diaspora and the Gentiles, he established new colonies of "Christians" in Syria, Turkey and Greece. Repudiating some of the ancient tenets of Judaism and replacing the polytheistic beliefs of Graeco-Roman society would involve fundamental changes in social behaviour and long-established cultures, as well as the adoption of new religious beliefs. Christianity was also inherently imperialist. "I am the way, the truth and the life: no one comes to the Father except though me"[459] has long been considered by Christians to apply to all cultures and all races. "The missionary movement ... was at heart an imperialist cultural venture dedicated to converting people's beliefs and ways of life".[460] Christianity became imperial in the political sense following the publication of an epistula by the Emperor Theodosius throughout the Roman empire in 381: "Never before ... had there been such a sweeping imposition of a single religious belief alongside the active suppression of alternatives."[461] In the late 19th century European mind Empire would be beneficial for the conquered and the occupied; Christianity even more so. The founders of the LIM were unambiguous about their intentions: first and foremost, evangelism. However, a more far-reaching corollary was added: "It is not sufficient merely to preach the gospel ... We must endeavour to show them a better way in everything ... We must seek to introduce an entirely new order of things, and in place of ignorant, cruel degrading, heathenism, to establish social order and justice, intelligent industry and mutual goodwill."[14] Given such entrenched belief critics should not be surprised that missions acted as they did.[462,463,464,465]

Christianity usually followed on the heels of an empire's acquisition of new territory, as happened in the coastal Kingdom of Kongo when Roman Catholicism followed the Portuguese conquest in the 15th century. In Congo the Protestant missions preceded Leopold and their exploration assisted the development of the Congo Free State. For centuries Roman Catholics and Protestant churches on both sides of the Atlantic supported the concept of empire and were active in establishing Christian colonies throughout the world. Andrew Wingate, British Commissioner, Bombay, looked to Christian missions to assist British rule in India. "Armed with new weapons but not restrained by morality or fear of God these enormous populations will become a peril unless the Christian Church should sow the seed of the gospel."[466]

Over a century ago Hobson opined that imperialism was "a depraved choice ... a perilous doctrine ... imposed by self-seeking interests" including in his condemnation "any missionary society which considers it has a peculiar duty to attack the religious sentiments or observances of some savage people".[467] Equally strong opinion has been expressed much more recently by Mark Sealy, who considered the photographs taken by Alice Harris were "tainted with ingrained racist ideologies" and amounted to a "site of Western violence, myth, fantasy and disavowal".[468] Furthermore, the presence in Africa of religion and commerce "wreaked havoc in the Congo" and the Harrises "were a component of a violent penetrating phase of aggression that propagated white supremacy". If considering Sealy's premise readers should be concerned that in reaching his conclusions he has relied in considerable measure on other recent commentators, having considered none of the original evidence in the Harris correspondence and the records of the CBM and Congo Reform Association. Others have deemed overseas missions imperialist on the grounds that they were driven by British imperialism as evidenced by their growth in parallel with Victorian expansionism. To the contrary, Brian Stanley has illustrated convincingly that was not substantiated by the evidence.[39] Empire sprang not only from greed but from a belief in "an inherent natural order in the process of colonisation".[469] For the missionary that belief took the form of a deep personal Christian faith and their individual response to what they believed to be the call of God,[470] but did they consider the consequences of their contribution to that process of colonisation? Denis Mukwege writes from present-day DRC: "The arrival of Christianity resulted in a rupture with the past, even though the new faith was willingly accepted by the community. But this early form of Christianity sought not to enrich or fuse with local spiritual and social traditions but to replace and supplant them outright. It was a cultural catastrophe in many ways, in which so much of what was precious and ancient was condemned as primitive and degenerate."[471] And Chinua Achebe was uncompromising: "The white man is very clever. He came quietly and peaceably with his religion. We were amused at his foolishness and allowed him to stay. He has put a knife on the things that held us together and we have fallen apart."[472] Nonetheless, the DRC population of 85.3 million is now overwhelmingly committed to Christianity: 95.8% describe themselves as Christian of which 48.1% are Protestant and 47.3% Roman Catholic. Overall, 70% attend religious worship. The written language, the books, the schools, the hospitals, the Christian teaching and Christian communities have, indeed, transformed much of Congolese society. Were none of these for the better? Which component of the missionary message was most influential?

Inkosi Albert Luthuli was born in what is now Zimbabwe, the grandson of a Zulu chief. A teacher and politician, he became president of the South African National Congress and in 1960 was awarded the Nobel Peace Prize for his role in the non-violent struggle against apartheid. Reflecting on the arrival of Protestant missionaries in his country he concluded that the reason for their initial success was "the intimacy of the relationship between missionary and people ... Because the Christian life was being lived in the midst of the people, they had the chance to inspect and assess it over an indefinite period. An increasing number came to accept the truth of Christianity ... while even those who did not could see a part of its value and respect it".[473]

When Lily Ruskin developed sleeping sickness her husband accompanied her to Matadi and said goodbye as she sailed for England, alone. He then returned to continue his work; neither knew if the newly available treatment for her disease would be successful or if they would see each other again. At Bongandanga no action of the missionaries passed without notice. "Now we know that you love us, if you will send Mama home alone to come back to teach us. And she, too, loves us or she would not let you return."

In early 1917 the members of the RBMU Home Council were surprised to receive a letter from one of the Congo evangelists, Imolo. "To our friends in Europe – Formerly we were in darkness but you had love for us and sent teachers to us, and we return love and wishes to you. On December 25th church members and ordinary folk gave gifts to the Lord. They gave fifty francs. We send this money to you in Europe that you may give it to any man needing it, that he may go and instruct those people who are without a teacher."[474]

The following year Somerville Gilchrist at Ikau had the sad task of reporting the death of his colleague Charlie Bond after seventeen years with the CBM. "Likumba, the native pastor, informed me that through all the villages far outside Mr Bond's parish the natives felt that they had in Mr Bond one who loved them. Among white men outside mission circles there was a wholesome fear of Mr Bond on account of the insistent, unsparing and fearless way in which he demanded relief and redress in all cases of unjust treatment brought to his notice."[475] Ross Manning's approach to mission was akin to that of John Harris. As a young new missionary, committed as he was to a personal Christian mission, he was keen to stay in the villages, sharing the Congolese way of life, not criticising but trying to understand the different way of thinking and the different cultural background, prepared to learn from them as well as believing that he was able to give something of eternal value in return. With his wife, the late-night visit to their leprosy friends, singing a farewell hymn with them, will not have been forgotten. Arthur Wright's colleagues used to say of him that he lived by 1 Corinthians 13: "I may be able to speak the languages of human beings ... I may have the gift of inspired preaching ... but if I have no love I am nothing." When nurse Margaret Williams wept on hearing that a newborn child at Baringa had died every woman in the village would have heard about it and loved her for it. Leprosy is a disease acquired through repeated, frequent contact, usually over many years. A typical photograph of Maimie McIntyre shows her crouching to talk with some young Congo children; her devotion to the women and the children of Baringa knew no bounds. Finding a patch of skin that did not feel right, she returned to London to seek a medical opinion. She was probably the only European to contract leprosy in Congo.

Readers may not know the name of Albert Schweitzer, the German philosopher, theologian, organist and Nobel Peace Laureate who qualified as a medical doctor at the age of thirty-six to be able to provide healthcare for the people of French Equatorial Africa, now Gabon. In his autobiography he explained his motivation: although a renowned teacher of theology and a popular preacher, as a missionary doctor he intended not to talk about his Christianity but to put it into practice.[476] His subsequent paternalistic attitude has been criticised, with justification, but reflecting on his years at Lambaréné Hospital he concluded "It is by means of Christian sympathy and gentleness that he shows in all his everyday business that he exercises his greatest influence … due to nothing so much as to the success of Preaching without Words."[477]

The Venerable Bede recounted that when Oswald, king of Northumbria in the year 635, invited Columba, Bishop of Iona, to send someone to teach his people about Christianity, the missionary monk who was "of severe disposition" met with no success and returned complaining that the people were too obstinate and barbarous to learn the Christian faith.[478] A fellow monk, Aidan, observed "Brother, you were more severe to your unlearned hearers than you ought to have been and did not at first give them the milk of more easy doctrine, till being by degrees nourished with the word of God, they should be capable of greater perfection, and be able to practice God's sublime precepts." Accordingly, Aidan, being "endued with singular discretion, which is the mother of all virtues" was sent as his replacement. Adopting a gentle approach, travelling always on foot rather than on horseback the better to speak with everyone he met, indifferent to people's social standing, concerning himself with the detail of their everyday lives, he demonstrated his message successfully, through kindness, generosity and humility, "for he was most compassionate, a protector of the poor and a father to the wretched". To this day Aidan is considered to be the father of Christianity in northern England.

I do not know how many of the CBM missionaries read Bede but many of them did demonstrate the principle epitomised by Aidan. If we are to choose one word that accounts for the appeal of the Christian message to the Balolo people the word "compassion" comes to mind.

Postscript

Norbert Mbu-Mputu was born in 1966 in the village of Nsho, by Lake Mai-Ndombe, in the Democratic Republic of Congo. Educated at the local Catholic missionary school and a Jesuit seminary in Kinshasa, he became a journalist working also for the United Nations and the Organisation Mondiale de la Santé. Following repeated arrests for political activity he fled the DRC in 2004 to become a refugee seeking asylum in London. Here he slept on the streets, in a night shelter and police stations. Homeless and helpless he improved his English, struggled and made friends. Eventually the immigration authorities sent him to Newport, Wales, where he was welcomed and has become a historian and writer. His books include the history of the Peres de Scheut, the first Belgian Catholic missionaries to the Congo.[479]

In God's name: From home to back home.

All life is a story. Every story is a story of a lifetime. Mission. Impossible? Taking Christianity to the Congo is also a story; a long story and a true story. Because all stories become stories of our lives this story must be grafted onto the common core of human history, the history of our countries, of our humanity. Man is a community being. In Lingala, the lingua franca of the old Kingdom of Kongo, it says to itself "mutu na kati ya batu" – the human between humans. I also remember the proverb from my late father the day when, at the age of twelve, I had to leave my parents for boarding school "If you are not yet dead, never swear that you will be buried with the same head you were born with".

When writing the history of the Peres de Scheut I often visited Papa André Bong'Ilanga, one of our Mai-Ndombe patriarchs. It was he who revealed to me that, in his clan, some of their grandparents had their hands amputated by the agents of King Leopold II during the exploitation of the infamous "blood rubber", immortalised in Lontomba, my local language, by the words

"Botofe bole iwa" – "the work of rubber is equivalent to death". And of the old missionaries, the "good whites", he said we would, perhaps, still be living under the trees in our forests and many would not have survived because of the many tropical diseases eradicated by these men and women, many of whom also perished among us. Good men, men of God, exceptional men, men of open-mind and heavy-hearted. And the Sister who, every morning, the mothers going to the field came together to greet her and weeping with pity for her, because, thin, the Congolese mothers really could not understand how such a granddaughter, to their eyes, could be allowed by her parents to leave them to come so far. So many stories not often told and reported. Nothing to do with what you would call colonisation. The schools, the hospitals, the maternities, the dispensaries, the churches with architecture not to envy anything to those of Europe. I had to arrive in Europe to appreciate the depth of their sacrifice: the word of God in one hand certainly, but above all the human promotion of the Congolese at the heart of their missionary activity. I am one of the products of these men and women of good will. Mathematics, science, French, Latin and English, all studied and learned in the heart of the Congolese bush.

Independence Day 1960 was a momentous day in a tumultuous story that culminated in the assassination of Congo's first Prime Minister, Patrice Lumumba on January 17, 1961. Killed with the complicity of the CIA, Belgian and possibly British authorities,[480] sixty years later this year we will experience a historically important event: the return to Congo of some of the remains of Patrice Lumumba taken to Belgium by one of his murderers. In his last letter to his wife Pauline, Lumumba left a testament: "Africa will one day write its own history". Or as Malian Amadou Hampaté Bâ famously said "In Africa, when an old man dies, it is a burning library. It is indeed up to Africans to speak of Africa to foreigners, and not for foreigners, however learned they may be, to speak of Africa to Africans." In the words of a Malian proverb: "When a goat is present, we must not bleat in its place." Having read, as we often hear lately, of the bad works of missionaries in Africa a century ago, and in Congo in particular, and their implication in the slave trade and colonisation, *Mission Impossible?* is a story in simple writing to be read and swallowed in one gulp, above all, from a white Congolese,"mwana mboka" a son of the country.

I have lived in Wales for more than fifteen years, to the point of considering it my second homeland. Without these men and women, especially the missionaries, it would not be possible for me to consider myself a Congolese and a Welshman. Let's say there are many British-Congolese sons and daughters who often wish to return to their native Congo. Or we are those new Congo-British changemakers for a new world under the God shadow...

The Congolese themselves must have the right to speak. I will not state that the missionaries were and are little angels but considering them to be devils in person risks being a very bad re-visitation of the history of the Congo. Another proverb says that at night, do not think that all cats are grey, even if they sometimes look like it. The missionaries succeeded more than they failed; they have made a significant contribution to building Congolese communities, humans created in the image of God. The current challenges of our countries and our populations require from the baptised Congolese and Africans, courageous choices taking advantage of the foundations of yesterday and the day before yesterday.

Norbert Mbu-Mputu

References

1. Joseph F. Conley, *Drumbeats that Changed the World. A History of the Regions Beyond Missionary Union and the West Indies Mission.* William Carey Library, Pasadena, CA, 2000.
2. W. Garden Blaikie, The personal Life of David Livingstone, Student Missionary Campaign, Chicago, 1880, p. 485.
3. W. Garden Blaikie, The personal Life of David Livingstone, Student Missionary Campaign, Chicago, 1880, p. 73.
4. Mrs H. Grattan Guinness, *The First Christian Mission in the Congo: The Livingstone Inland Mission.* Fourth edition. Hodder & Stoughton, London, 1882, pp. 88/9.
5. W. Garden Blaikie, The personal Life of David Livingstone, Student Missionary Campaign, Chicago, 1880, p. 439.
6. W. Garden Blaikie, The personal Life of David Livingstone, Student Missionary Campaign, Chicago, 1880, p. 458.
7. Fanny E. Guinness, *The New World of Central Africa*, Hodder and Stoughton, 1890, pp. 175/6.
8. Fanny E. Guinness, *The New World of Central Africa*, Hodder and Stoughton 1890, p. 235.
9. Brian Stanley, *The History of the Baptist Missionary Society 1792-1992*, T&T Clark, Edinburgh, 1992, pp. 118/9.
10. Mrs H. Grattan Guinness, *The First Christian Mission in the Congo: The Livingstone Inland Mission.* Fourth edition. Hodder & Stoughton, London, 1882, p. 27.
11. Mrs H. Grattan Guinness, *The First Christian Mission in the Congo: The Livingstone Inland Mission.* Fourth edition. Hodder & Stoughton, London, 1882, pp. 6/7.
12. Fanny E. Guinness, *The New World of Central Africa*, Hodder and Stoughton 1890, p. 180.
13. Mrs H. Grattan Guinness, *The First Christian Mission in the Congo: The Livingstone Inland Mission.* Fourth edition. Hodder & Stoughton, London, 1882, p. 41.
14. Mrs H. Grattan Guinness, *The First Christian Mission in the Congo: The Livingstone Inland Mission.* Fourth edition. Hodder & Stoughton, London, 1882, p. 39.

15. Mrs H. Grattan Guinness, *The First Christian Mission in the Congo: The Livingstone Inland Mission.* Fourth edition. Hodder & Stoughton, London, 1882, p. 38.

16. Fanny E. Guinness, *The New World of Central Africa*, Hodder and Stoughton 1890, p. 177.

17. Michelle Guinness, *The Guinness Legend*, Hodder & Stoughton, 1990, pp. 67/71

18. Michelle Guinness, *The Guinness Legend*, Hodder & Stoughton, 1990, p. xviii.

19. Michelle Guinness, *The Guinness Legend*, Hodder & Stoughton, 1990, p. 27.

20. Michelle Guinness, *The Guinness Legend*, Hodder & Stoughton, 1990, p. 64.

21. Michelle Guinness, *The Guinness Legend*, Hodder & Stoughton, 1990, p. 95.

22. Fanny E. Guinness, *The New World of Central Africa*, Hodder and Stoughton 1890, pp. viii, 16.

23. The Luciads. Portuguese poem by Luís Vaz de Camões. 1572. Translation in English by William Julius Mickle, 1776.

24. Margarite Hutchinson, 'A Report of the Kingdom of Congo and of the Surrounding Countries', John Murray, London. 1881. Translation from Italian to English of the report by Filippo Pigafetta in Rome, 1591, drawn out of the writings and discourses of the Portuguese, Duarte Lopez, pp. 14/15.

25. Olfert Dapper: www.atlasofmutualheritage.nl/en/Map-south-west-Africa.6862.

26. Professor Smith, 'The Journal of Professor Smith', in Captain J. K. Tuckey, *Narrative of an expedition to explore the River Zaire, usually called The Congo in South Africa, in 1816.* Pub. John Murray, 1818, p. xi.

27. Captain J. K. Tuckey, *Narrative of an expedition to explore the River Zaire, usually called The Congo in South Africa, in 1816.* Pub. John Murray, 1818.

28. Harry H. Johnston, *A history of the Colonisation of Africa by Alien Races*, Cambridge University Press, 1913, p. 322.

29. Sir Richard Francis Burton. Reports by Consul Burton of his ascent of the Congo River, in September 1863. Confidential report for the British Foreign Office 6th September 1864.

30. Byron Farwell, *The Man who Presumed*, Longmans, Green & Co., 1958, p. 164.

31. Rev W. Holman Bentley, *Life on the Congo*, New edition. Revised. The Religious Tract Society, 1893, p. 35.

32. Herbert Ward, *Five years with the Congo Cannibals*, Chatto & Windus, Piccadilly, 1890, pp. 38/9.

33. John H. Harris, *Dawn in Darkest Africa*, E. P. Dutton & Company, New York, 1912, p. 37.
34. Herbert Ward, *Five years with the Congo Cannibals*, Chatto & Windus, Piccadilly, 1890, p. 132.
35. Herbert Ward, *Five years with the Congo Cannibals*, Chatto & Windus, Piccadilly, 1890, p. 136.
36. Herbert Ward, *Five years with the Congo Cannibals*, Chatto & Windus, Piccadilly, 1890, p. 262.
37. Herbert Ward, *Five years with the Congo Cannibals*, Chatto & Windus, Piccadilly, 1890, p. 139.
38. Herbert Ward, *Five years with the Congo Cannibals*, Chatto & Windus, Piccadilly, 1890, pp. 246/7.
39. John H, Harris, *Dawn in Darkest Africa*, E.P. Dutton & Company, New York, 1912, p. 106.
40. John H, Harris, *Dawn in Darkest Africa*, E.P. Dutton & Company, New York, 1912, p. 40.
41. John H, Harris, *Dawn in Darkest Africa*, E.P. Dutton & Company, New York, 1912, pp. 53/56.
42. John H, Harris, *Dawn in Darkest Africa*, E.P. Dutton & Company, New York, 1912, pp. 58, 71.
43. John H, Harris, *Dawn in Darkest Africa*, E.P. Dutton & Company, New York, 1912, p. 35.
44. Rev W. Holman Bentley, *Life on the Congo*, New edition. Revised. The Religious Tract Society, 1893, p. 51.
45. Rev Herbert Probert, Life and Scenes in Congo, American Baptist Publication Society, 1889, p. 57.
46. Rev W. Holman Bentley, *Life on the Congo*, New edition. Revised. The Religious Tract Society, 1893, p. 69.
47. Rev W. Holman Bentley, *Life on the Congo*, New edition. Revised. The Religious Tract Society, 1893, pp. 51/63.
48. Pew Forum, Pew Research Center: Religion and Public Life. Global Religious Landscape, December 18, 2012.
49. Sir Henry H., Johnston. The River Congo from its mouth to Bolobo. Proceedings of the Royal Geographical Society. November 12th 1883, p. 703.
50. Sir Henry H., Johnston. The River Congo from its mouth to Bolobo. Proceedings of the Royal Geographical Society. November 12th 1883, p. 698.
51. Henry W. Wack, *The Story of the Congo Free State*, by Pub. G.P Putnams, New York & London, 1905, p. 248.

52. Sir Henry H. Johnston, A visit to Mr Stanley's Stations on the River Congo. Proceedings of the Royal Geographical Society. October 1883, pp.572/3.

53. Mary H. Kingsley, *Travels in West Africa*, Macmillan & Co Ltd, 1897, p. 358.

54. Fanny E. Guinness, *The New World of Central Africa*, Hodder and Stoughton, 1890, p. 181.

55. H. Grattan Guinness, *Not Unto Us: a record of twenty-one years missionary service* – Primary Source Edition. Regions Beyond Missionary Union, 1910, pp. 48/51.

56. Mrs H. Grattan Guinness, *The First Christian Mission in the Congo: The Livingstone Inland Mission*, Fourth edition, Hodder & Stoughton, London. 1882, p. 92.

57. Adam McCall. Letter 19 November 1880. RBMU archive, University of Edinburgh.

58. Adam McCall. Letter 22 April 1880. RBMU archive, University of Edinburgh.

59. Mrs H. Grattan Guinness, *The First Christian Mission in the Congo: The Livingstone Inland Mission*, Fourth edition, Hodder & Stoughton, London. 1882, p. 86.

60. Fanny E. Guinness, *The New World of Central Africa*, Hodder and Stoughton, 1890, p. 182.

61. Brian Stanley, *The History of the Baptist Missionary Society 1792-1992*, T&T Clark, Edinburgh, 1992, p.1 22.

62. Mrs H. Grattan Guinness, *The First Christian Mission in the Congo: The Livingstone Inland Mission*, Fourth edition, Hodder & Stoughton, London. 1882, p. 71.

63. Fanny E. Guinness, *The New World of Central Africa*, Hodder and Stoughton, 1890, pp. 328/9.

64. Sir Henry H., Johnston. The River Congo from its mouth to Bolobo. Proceedings of the Royal Geographical Society. November 12th 1883, p. 702.

65. Fanny E. Guinness, *The New World of Central Africa*, Hodder and Stoughton, 1890, pp. 363/4.

66. Fanny E. Guinness, *The New World of Central Africa*, Hodder and Stoughton, 1890, pp. 367/9.

67. Fanny E. Guinness, *The New World of Central Africa*, Hodder and Stoughton, 1890, p. 378.

68. Fanny E. Guinness, *The New World of Central Africa*, Hodder and Stoughton, 1890, p. 380.

69. Mrs H. Grattan Guinness, *The First Christian Mission in the Congo: The Livingstone Inland Mission*. Fourth edition. Hodder & Stoughton, London, 1882, pp.106/7.

70. Fanny E. Guinness, *The New World of Central Africa*, Hodder and Stoughton, 1890, p. 387.

71. Fanny E. Guinness, *The New World of Central Africa*, Hodder and Stoughton, 1890, p. 385.

72. Fanny E. Guinness, *The New World of Central Africa*, Hodder and Stoughton, 1890, pp. 239/240.

73. William H. Brackley, Paul S. Fiddes & John H.Y. Briggs, Eds., *Pilgrim Pathways: Essays in Baptist History in Honour of B.R. White*, Mercer University Press, USA, 1984, p. 308.

74. Fanny E. Guinness, *The New World of Central Africa*, Hodder and Stoughton, 1890, pp. 394/6.

75. Rev E. F. Merriam, *The Congo Mission. Report of the American Baptist Missionary Union*. Third Edition, Boston, 1884, p. 9. (https://catalog.hathitrust.org › Record: The Congo Mission, HathiTrust Digital Library).

76. Fanny E. Guinness, *The New World of Central Africa*, Hodder and Stoughton, 1890, p. 398.

77. Fanny E. Guinness, *The New World of Central Africa*, Hodder and Stoughton, 1890, pp. 401/2.

78. Professor Smith, 'The Journal of Professor Smith', In Captain J.K. Tuckey, *Narrative of an expedition to explore the River Zaire, usually called The Congo in South Africa in 1816*, Pub. John Murray, 1818, p. xlv.

79. Fanny E. Guinness, *The New World of Central Africa*, Hodder and Stoughton, 1890, p. 489.

80. Fanny E. Guinness, *The New World of Central Africa*, Hodder and Stoughton, 1890, p. 493.

81. Fanny E. Guinness, *The New World of Central Africa*, Hodder and Stoughton, 1890, p.500.

82. R. Ross, 'On some peculiar pigmented cells found in two mosquitos fed on malarial blood. (1897)', *British Medical Journal* 18th December; 2 (1929): pp. 1786-1788.

83. Gachelin G., Garner P., Ferroni et al., 'Evaluating Cinchona bark and quinine for treating and preventing malaria', *Journal of the Royal Society of Medicine*. January 20th 2017.

84. Achan J., Talisuna A.O., Erhart A. et al., 'Quinine, an old anti-malaria drug in a modern world: role in the treatment of malaria', *Malaria Journal* 10;144. May 2011.

85. Robert D. Hicks. http://civilwarrx.blogspot.co.uk/2014/09/the-popular-dose-with-doctors-quinine.html.

86. E. A. Barton, *The Colonist's Medical Handbook*, Cassell & Company, Ltd, 1890, p. 115.

87. Mary H. Kingsley, *Travels in West Africa*, Macmillan & Co Ltd, 1897, pp. 681, 685,689.

88. Mary H. Kingsley, *Travels in West Africa*, Macmillan & Co Ltd, 1897, p. 685.

89. Horace Waller, FRGS, *The Last Journals of David Livingstone, in Central Africa from 1835 to his death*. vol.1. John Murray, London, 1874, p. 177.

90. W. Garden Blaikie, The personal Life of David Livingstone.1. Student Missionary Campaign, Chicago, 1880, p. 482.

91. Horace Waller, FRGS, *The Last Journals of David Livingstone, in Central Africa from 1835 to his death*. vol.1. John Murray, London, 1874, p. 177.

92. Fanny E. Guinness, *The New World of Central Africa*, Hodder and Stoughton, 1890, p. 303.

93. Fanny E. Guinness, *The New World of Central Africa*, Hodder and Stoughton, 1890, p. 339.

94. Minutes of Congo Field Committee. 17 October 1905. RBMU Archive, University of Edinburgh.

95. Joseph F. Conley, *Drumbeats that Changed the World. A History of the Regions Beyond Missionary Union and the West Indies Mission*. William Carey Library, Pasadena, CA, 2000, p. 59.

96. Brian Stanley, *The History of the Baptist Missionary Society 1792-1992*, T&T Clark, Edinburgh, 1992, p. 125.

97. Mrs H. Grattan Guinness, *Some are fallen asleep; or, The story of our Sixth Year at the East London Institute for Home and Foreign Missions*, Hodder & Stoughton, 1880, p. 9.

98. Ruth Slade, English-speaking Missions in the Congo Independent State 1878-1908, Académie Royale des Sciences Coloniales. Brussels, 1959, p. 231.

99. Fanny E. Guinness, *The New World of Central Africa*, Hodder and Stoughton, 1890, p. 351.

100. Fanny E. Guinness, *The New World of Central Africa*, Hodder and Stoughton, 1890, p. 19.

101. Fanny E. Guinness, *The New World of Central Africa*, Hodder and Stoughton, 1890, p. 191.

102. Fanny E. Guinness, *The New World of Central Africa*, Hodder and Stoughton, 1890, p. 276.

103. Fanny E. Guinness, *The New World of Central Africa*, Hodder and Stoughton, 1890, p. 331.

104. Fanny E. Guinness, *The New World of Central Africa*, Hodder and Stoughton, 1890, p. 380/1.

105. Fanny E. Guinness, *The New World of Central Africa*, Hodder and Stoughton, 1890, p. 317.

106. Fanny E. Guinness, *The New World of Central Africa*, Hodder and Stoughton, 1890, p. 378.

107. Fanny E. Guinness, *The New World of Central Africa*, Hodder and Stoughton, 1890, pp. 413/421.

108. Fanny E. Guinness, *The New World of Central Africa*, Hodder and Stoughton, 1890, p. 431.

109. Fanny E. Guinness, *The New World of Central Africa*, Hodder and Stoughton, 1890, p. 437.

110. Mrs E.A. Ruskin. Ruskin of Congo. Regions Beyond Missionary Union, London. 1948. p. 135.

111. Brian Stanley, *The History of the Baptist Missionary Society 1792-1992*, T&T Clark, Edinburgh, 1992, pp. 126/7.

112. Michelle Guinness, *The Guinness Legend*, Hodder & Stoughton, 1990, p. 216.

113. Sims, Aaron 1800s-1922. In *Dictionary of African Christian Biography*. Center for Global Christianity Mission.
https://dacb.org/stories/democratic-republic-of-congo/sims-aaron.

114. C. W. MacKintosh, *Dr Harry Guinness: The Life story of Henry Grattan Guinness, MD FRGS*. Regions Beyond Missionary Union. 1916, pp. 12/17.

115. Fanny E. Guinness, *The New World of Central Africa*, Hodder and Stoughton, 1890, p. 470.

116. Fanny E. Guinness, *The New World of Central Africa*, Hodder and Stoughton, 1890, p. 478.

117. James Stewart, Dawn in the Dark Continent, or Africa and Its Missions. The Duff Missionary Lectures. Oliphant, Anderson & Ferrier, 1903.

118. Gustav Warneck, *Outline of a History of Protestant Missions*, Authorised translation of 7th edition from the original German by George Robson. Flemming H. Revell Company, 1901.

119. Horace Mann Esq., *Census of Great Britain, 1851. Religious Worship in England and Wales*, George Routledge and Co. 1854, pp. 75/76.

120. Horace Mann Esq., *Census of Great Britain, 1851. Religious Worship in England and Wales*, George Routledge and Co. 1854, pp. 86/93; 109/142.

121. Alan Munden, *A light in a Dark Place, Jesmond Parish Church, Newcastle upon Tyne*, Clayton Publications, 2006, pp. 72/4.

122. H. Grattan Guinness, *The Approaching End of the Age viewed in the light of history, prophecy and science*, Hodder and Stoughton. Second edition, 1879.

123. Joseph F. Conley, *Drumbeats that Changed the World. A History of the Regions Beyond Missionary Union and the West Indies Mission.* William Carey Library, Pasadena, CA, 2000, p. 34.

124. Kevin Ward, 'Taking Stock: The Church Missionary Society and its Historians', in Kevin Ward & Brian Stanley, *The Church Missionary Society and World Christianity*, William B. Eerdmans Publishing Company, 2000, p. 29.

125. Fanny E. Guinness, *The New World of Central Africa*, Hodder and Stoughton, 1890, p. 483.

126. H. Grattan Guinness, *Not Unto Us: a record of twenty-one years missionary service* – Primary Source Edition. Regions Beyond Missionary Union, 1910, p. 71.

127. La patrie doit être forte, prospère, par conséquent posséder des débouchés à elle, belle et calme. – The King to the Count of Flanders The Count of Flanders's papers. January 26, 1888.

128. Rev W. Holman Bentley, *Life on the Congo*, New edition. Revised. The Religious Tract Society, 1893, pp. 104/5.

129. Herbert Ward, *Five years with the Congo Cannibals*, Chatto & Windus, Piccadilly, 1890.

130. Henry M. Stanley, *The Congo and the Founding of its Free State. A story of Work and Exploration*, Harper & Brothers, 1885, Vol. II, p.379; 195/206.

131. Tim Jeal, *Stanley. The Impossible Life of Africa's Greatest Explorer*, Faber and Faber Ltd. 2007, pp. 280/288.

132. Thomas Pakenham, *The Scramble for Africa*, George Weidenfeld & Nicolson, London, 1992.

133. David Olusoga, *Black and British. A short, essential history*, Macmillan Children's Books, 2020, p. 136.

134. Henry Phillips Jr., An account of the Congo Independent State, *Proc. Amer. Phil. Soc.* vol xxvi, 1889, p. 461.

135. Anon. A Belgian. Letter from the King-Sovereign of the Congo Free State to the State agents in The Truth about the Civilisation in Congoland. J Lebegue & Co. Brussels, 1903, pp. 3/4.

136. Byron Farwell, *The Man who Presumed*, Longmans, Green & Co., 1958, p. 200.

137. Byron Farwell, *The Man who Presumed*, Longmans, Green & Co., 1958, p. 227.

138. Henry Phillips Jr., An account of the Congo Independent State, *Proc. Amer. Phil. Soc.* vol xxvi, 1889, p. 463.

139. Robert Harms, 'The end of Red Rubber: A Reassessment', *Journal of African History*, Vol. 16(1) 1975, pp. 73–88.

140. Robert Harms, 'The World ABIR Made: The Maringa-Lopori Basin, 1885–1903', *African Economic History* (12) 1983, pp. 122–139.

141. Robert Harms, 'The end of Red Rubber: A Reassessment', *Journal of African History*, Vol. 16(1) 1975, pp. 125/139.

142. E. D. Morel, *The Congo Slave State*, John Richardson & Sons, Liverpool, 1903, p. 87.

143. E. D. Morel, *The Congo Slave State*, John Richardson & Sons, Liverpool, 1903, p. 86.

144. Regions Beyond. Jan/Feb. 1908 p.33. RBMU archive, University of Edinburgh.

145. James Ramsay, Essay on the Treatment and Conversion of African Slaves in the British Sugar Colonies, James Phillips, London, 1784.

146. Stefan Heym, *Introduction to Mark Twain. King Leopold's Soliloquy*, Seven Seas Books, New York, 1961, p. 13.

147. Viscount Mountmorres, *The Congo Independent State: A Report on a Voyage of Discovery*, Williams & Norgate, London, 1906.

148. Henry Phillips Jr., An account of the Congo Independent State, *Proc. Amer. Phil. Soc.* vol xxvi, 1889, p. 473.

149. Joseph F. Conley, *Drumbeats that Changed the World. A History of the Regions Beyond Missionary Union and the West Indies Mission.* William Carey Library, Pasadena, CA, 2000, p. 84.

150. Kevin Grant, *A Civilised Savagery. Britain and the New Slaveries in Africa, 1884-1926*, Routledge, New York & London, 2005, pp. 32,45.

151. Kevin Grant, *The Congo Free State and the New Imperialism*, Bedford/St Martins, Boston, 2017, p.1 8.

152. E. D. Morel, *Red Rubber the story of the rubber slave trade flourishing on the Congo in the year of grace 1906*, The Nassau Print, New York, 1906, p. 4.

153. H. R. Fox Bourne, *Civilisation in Congoland: a Story of International Wrong-doing*, P. S. King & Son, Westminster,1903, pp. vii-x.

154. Joseph Conrad, "Heart of Darkness", serialised in Blackwood's *Edinburgh Magazine*. Pub, William Blackwood & Sons, Edinburgh & London, 1899

155. Joseph Conrad, *Youth: A Narrative and Two Other Stories*, Typhoon, New York, 1902.

156. Mark Twain, "King Leopold's Soliloquy", PR Warren Co., Boston, 1905.

157. A. Conan Doyle, *The Crime of the Congo*, Doubleday, Page & Company, New York, 1909.

158. Frederick R. Karl & Laurence Davies, *The Collected Letters of Joseph Conrad*, Cambridge University Press, vol iii, 1903, p. 96.

159. Adam Hochschild, *King Leopold's Ghost. A story of Greed, Terror and Heroism in Colonial Africa*, Houghton Mifflin Company, 1999, pp. 169/181.

160. Adam Hochschild, *King Leopold's Ghost. A story of Greed, Terror and Heroism in Colonial Africa*, Houghton Mifflin Company, 1999, pp.169/186.

161. E. D. Morel, *The Affairs of West Africa*, William Heinemann, 1902.

162. E. D. Morel, *The Congo Slave State*, John Richardson & Sons, Liverpool, 1903.

163. E. D. Morel, *King Leopold's Rule in Africa*, Funk & Wagnalls Company, New York, 1905.

164. E. D. Morel, *Red Rubber the story of the rubber slave trade flourishing on the Congo in the year of grace 1906*, The Nassau Print, New York, 1906.

165. E. D. Morel, *Red Rubber the story of the rubber slave trade flourishing on the Congo in the year of grace 1906*, The Nassau Print, New York, 1906, p. ix.

166. E. J. Glave, 'New conditions in Central Africa. The dawn of civilization between Lake Tanganyika and the Congo', *The Century Magazine*, April 1897, pp. pp. 900/915.

167. H. R. Fox Bourne, *Civilisation in Congoland: a Story of International Wrong-doing*, P. S. King & Son, Westminster, 1903, pp. 194/198.

168. H. R. Fox Bourne, *Civilisation in Congoland: a Story of International Wrong-doing*, P. S. King & Son, Westminster, 1903, pp. 199/200.

169. George W. Williams, An open letter to His Serene Majesty Leopold II, King of the Belgians and Sovereign of the Independent State of Congo by Colonel, The Honorable Geo. W. Williams, of the United States of America. Stanley Falls, Central Africa. July 18th 1890
(https://www.blackpast.org/?s=george+washington+williams)

170. Transactions of the Aborigines Protection Society, 1890-1896 (The Aborigines' Friend). The Aborigines' Protection Society. Westminster, April 1891, p. 161.

171. Ruth Slade, English-speaking Missions in the Congo Independent State 1878-1908, Académie Royale des Sciences Coloniales. Brussels, 1959, p. 179.

172. Regions Beyond. November 1893. RBMU archive, University of Edinburgh.

173. Ruth Slade, English-speaking Missions in the Congo Independent State 1878-1908, Académie Royale des Sciences Coloniales. Brussels, 1959, p. 241 ref.3.

174. Field Committee correspondence to Home Council. December 1895. RBMU archive, University of Edinburgh.

175. W. D. Armstrong, 'Sunrise on The Congo. A record of the earlier years of the Congo Balolo Mission', p. 204. Unpublished. RBMU archive, University of Edinburgh.

176. Field Committee correspondence to Home Council. 17 October 1898. RBMU archive, University of Edinburgh.

177. Home Council Minutes. 25 September 1902. RBMU archive, University of Edinburgh.

178. Minutes of Congo Field Committee. 6/7 November 1903. RBMU Archive, University of Edinburgh.

179. Field Committee correspondence to Home Council. 8 November 1903. RBMU archive, University of Edinburgh.

180. Minutes of Congo Field Committee. 22/23 November 1904. RBMU Archive, University of Edinburgh.

181. Field Committee correspondence to Home Council. 28 May 1906. RBMU archive, University of Edinburgh.

182. Home Council Minutes. 19 April 1893. RBMU archive, University of Edinburgh.

183. Seamus O Siochain & Michael O'Sullivan, *The Eyes of Another Race. Sir Roger Casement Diary*, University College Dublin Press, 2003, p. 102.

184. Regions Beyond. 1891. p.375. RBMU archive, University of Edinburgh.

185. Minutes of Congo Field Committee. June 1903. RBMU Archive, University of Edinburgh.

186. Field Committee correspondence to Home Council. 25 November 1904. RBMU archive, University of Edinburgh.

187. Seamus O Siochain & Michael O'Sullivan, *The Eyes of Another Race. Sir Roger Casement Diary*, University College Dublin Press, 2003, p. 326 ref.115.

188. Letter to M. Schoot 27/07/1904. RBMU archive. University of Edinburgh.

189. T. Jack Thompson, 'The Camera and the Congo: Missionary Photography and Leopold's Atrocities', in *Light on Darkness*, Wm B Eerdmans Publishing Co., Michigan 2012.

190. H. R. Fox Bourne, *Civilisation in Congoland: a Story of International Wrong-doing*, P. S. King & Son, Westminster, 1903, pp. 205/210.

191. Regions Beyond. 1903. p. 133. RBMU archive, University of Edinburgh.

192. Home Council Minutes. 24 June 1896. RBMU archive, University of Edinburgh.

193. Michelle Guinness, *The Guinness Legend*, Hodder & Stoughton, 1990, pp. 273/4.

194. Home Council Minutes. 24 September 1896. RBMU archive, University of Edinburgh.

195. H. R. Fox Bourne, *Civilisation in Congoland: a Story of International Wrong-doing*, P. S. King & Son, Westminster, 1903, pp. 219/222.

196. H. R. Fox Bourne, *Civilisation in Congoland: a Story of International Wrong-doing*, P. S. King & Son, Westminster, 1903, pp. 211/218.

197. Home Council Minutes. 23 February 1899. RBMU archive, University of Edinburgh.

198. Home Council Minutes. 25 May 1899. RBMU archive, University of Edinburgh.

199. Home Council Minutes. 22 June 1899. RBMU archive, University of Edinburgh.

200. Home Council Minutes. 30 May 1901. RBMU archive, University of Edinburgh.

201. Letter from Holt to Morel 11 Jan 1901. ED Morel archive, London School of Economics.

202. Letter from Guinness to Morel 8 Nov.1902. ED Morel archive, London School of Economics.

203. Letter from Guinness to Morel 17 Nov.1902. ED Morel archive, London School of Economics.

204. Letter from Morel to Stead, 16 October 1902. ED Morel archive, London School of Economics.

205. Letter from Morel to Guinness 24 Nov 1902. ED Morel archive, London School of Economics.

206. Letter from Guinness to Morel 16 Dec 1902. ED Morel archive, London School of Economics.

207. Letter from Guinness to Fox Bourne 2 March 1903. ED Morel archive, London School of Economics.

208. Letter from Guinness to Morel 16th October 1903. ED Morel archive, London School of Economics.

209. Letter from Fox-Bourne to Morel, 24 November 1903. ED Morel archive, London School of Economics.

210. Letter from Morel to Guinness, 20 Dec 1902. ED Morel archive, London School of Economics.

211. Regions Beyond. 1903. p. 279. RBMU archive, University of Edinburgh.

212. Oli Jacobsen, *Daniel J. Danielsen and the Congo: Missionary Campaigns and Atrocity Photographs*, BAHN (Brethren Activists & Historians Network), 2014.

213. Home Council Minutes. 26 March 1903. RBMU archive, University of Edinburgh.

214. Home Council Minutes. 24 September 1903. RBMU archive, University of Edinburgh.

215. Seamus O Siochain & Michael O'Sullivan, *The Eyes of Another Race. Sir Roger Casement Diary*, University College Dublin Press, 2003, pp. 242–269.

216. Correspondence and Report from His Majesty's Consul at Boma respecting the Administration of the Independent State of the Congo. His Majesty's Stationary Office, London.1904.

217. Oli Jacobsen, *Daniel J. Danielsen and the Congo: Missionary Campaigns and Atrocity Photographs*, BAHN (Brethren Activists & Historians Network), 2014. p. 50.

218. Oli Jacobsen, Daniel J. *Danielsen and the Congo: Missionary Campaigns and Atrocity Photographs*, BAHN (Brethren Activists & Historians Network), 2014, p. 175 ref.2.

219. Oli Jacobsen, *Daniel J. Danielsen and the Congo: Missionary Campaigns and Atrocity Photographs*, BAHN (Brethren Activists & Historians Network), 2014, p. 60.

220. Home Council Minutes. 22 October 1903. RBMU archive, University of Edinburgh.

221. Oli Jacobsen, *Daniel J. Danielsen and the Congo: Missionary Campaigns and Atrocity Photographs*, BAHN (Brethren Activists & Historians Network), 2014, p. 61 ref.23.

222. Oli Jacobsen, *Daniel J. Danielsen and the Congo: Missionary Campaigns and Atrocity Photographs*, BAHN (Brethren Activists & Historians Network), 2014, p.62.

223. Oli Jacobsen, *Daniel J. Danielsen and the Congo: Missionary Campaigns and Atrocity Photographs*, BAHN (Brethren Activists & Historians Network), 2014, pp. 67/8.

224. Home Council Minutes 23 November 1903. RBMU archive, University of Edinburgh.

225. Oli Jacobsen, *Daniel J. Danielsen and the Congo: Missionary Campaigns and Atrocity Photographs*, BAHN (Brethren Activists & Historians Network), 2014, p. 154.

226. Evidence laid before the Congo Commission of Enquiry at Bwembu, Bolobo, Kulanga, Baringa, Bongdanga, Ikau, Bonginda and Monsembe. Together. Congo Reform Association. Commision Chargee de Faire Enquete Dans Les Territiores L'etat Du Congo. J Richardson and Sons, Liverpool. 1905.

227. Regions Beyond. 1905. p. 277. RBMU archive, University of Edinburgh.

228. Ruth Slade, *English-speaking Missions in the Congo Independent State 1878-1908*, Académie Royale des Sciences Coloniales. Brussels, 1959, p. 295, ref.213.

229. Regions Beyond. 1905. pp. 317/320. RBMU archive, University of Edinburgh.

230. Ruth Slade, *English-speaking Missions in the Congo Independent State 1878-1908*, Académie Royale des Sciences Coloniales. Brussels, 1959, p. 298.

231. Regions Beyond. 1905. p. 278. RBMU archive, University of Edinburgh.

232. Ruth Slade, *English-speaking Missions in the Congo Independent State 1878-1908*, Académie Royale des Sciences Coloniales. Brussels, 1959, p. 296, ref.1-5.

233. Regions Beyond. 1906. p. 62. RBMU archive, University of Edinburgh.

234. Letter from John Harris to Home Council 18 December 1904. John Hobbis Harris archive, London School of Economics.

235. Judy Pollard Smith, *Don't call me Lady. The Journey of Lady Alice Seeley Harris*, Abbott Press, 2014.

236. Jos Erkamp photographic antiquarian, Netherlands. Personal correspondence 2020.

237. Dr Michael Pritchard, personal correspondence 18 April 2020. Jos Erdkamp first suggested that the camera used by Harris was manufactured by CP Goerz Anschütz in Germany. Historian Kevin Grant found the only known photograph of Alice with her camera in the archive of the Anti-Slavery Society, Bodleian Libraries, Oxford. When a copy was submitted by the author to the Royal Photographic Society, England, Dr Michael Pritchard identified the camera as a CP Goerz Anschütz press-type, dry-plate camera.

238. Anti-Slavery Society archive. Bodleian Library, Oxford. MS Brit Emp s 19 D5-7/ D5-8 / D5-10. At the time of Casement's investigation no individual atrocities had been reported in the Baringa district. When, in January 1904, Harris first heard evidence of killings of local people he informed the Belgian authorities immediately. When Mrs Harris saw for herself evidence of murder and mutilation on 14th May 1904 she took the iconic photograph of the grieving father Nsala.

239. Christina Twomey, 'The Incorruptible Kodak. Photography, Human Rights and the Congo Campaign', in *The Violence of the Image. Photography and International Conflict*, eds. Liam Kennedy & Caitlin Patrick, I.B.Tauris & Co. Ltd., 2014.

240. Mark Twain, *"King Leopold's Soliloquy"*, PR Warren Co., Boston, 1905, pp. 73/74.

241. Ruth Slade, 'English Missionaries and the Beginning of the Anti-Congolese Campaign in England', Revue Belge de Philologie et d'Histoire, vol. 33-1, 1955, pp. 37-73.

242. *Ruth Slade, English-speaking Missions in the Congo Independent State 1878-1908*, Académie Royale des Sciences Coloniales. Brussels, 1959.

243. Dean Pavlakis, *British Humanitarianism and the Congo Reform Movement*, 1896-1913, Ashgate Publishing, 2015.

244. David Kagergren, *Mission and State in the Congo*, Gleerup-Lund, 1970.

245. Jean Omasombo Tshonda et al., Mai-Ndombe. Mosaique de peuples établie sur un patrimoine naturel. (Monograph of the province of Mai-Ndombe (DRC). Royal Museum of Central Africa, Teruven, 2019, pp. 269-336. (See also www.africamuseum.be)

246. Dean Pavlakis, *British Humanitarianism and the Congo Reform Movement*, 1896-1913, Ashgate Publishing, 2015, pp. 169-173.

247. William H. Sheppard Papers, RG 457, Presbyterian Historical Society, Philadelphia, Pennsylvania.

248. C. W. MacKintosh, *Dr Harry Guinness: The Life story of Henry Grattan Guinness, MD FRGS*, Regions Beyond Missionary Union, 1916.

249. Letter from John Harris to ED Morel 16th & 18th September 1905. John Hobbis Harris archive, London School of Economics. F8/75: 192, 195.

250. Letter from John Harris to ED Morel 7th September 1906. John Hobbis Harris archive, London School of Economics. F8/76: 268.

251. H. Grattan Guinness, *The Congo Crisis*, Pub. Regions Beyond Missionary Union, 1908 (Quoted by CWM.4 p. 77)

252. Brian Stanley, *The History of the Baptist Missionary Society 1792-1992*, T&T Clark, Edinburgh, 1992, pp. 134/139.

253. Ruth Slade, *English-speaking Missions in the Congo Independent State 1878-1908*, Académie Royale des Sciences Coloniales. Brussels, 1959, p. 162.

254. Seamas O Siochain, *Roger Casement: Imperialist, Rebel, Revolutionary*, Lilliput Press, 2008, p. 159.

255. Letter from John Harris to ED Morel 22/07/1904. John Hobbis Harris archive, London School of Economics.

256. Letter from John Harris to ED Morel October 8th 1904. John Hobbis Harris archive, London School of Economics.

257. Ruth Slade, *English-speaking Missions in the Congo Independent State 1878-1908*, Académie Royale des Sciences Coloniales. Brussels, 1959, p. 161.

258. Brian Stanley, *The History of the Baptist Missionary Society 1792-1992*, T&T Clark, Edinburgh, 1992, p. 138.

259. Nancy Rose Hart, *A Nervous State: Violence, Commerce, Remedies, and Reverie in Colonial Congo*, Duke University Press, 2016.

260. Ruth Slade, *English-speaking Missions in the Congo Independent State 1878-1908*, Académie Royale des Sciences Coloniales. Brussels, 1959, p. 36.

261. Jean Omasombo Tshonda et al., Mai-Ndombe. Mosaique de peuple établie sur un patrimoine naturel. (Monograph of the province of Mai-Ndombe (DRC). Royal Museum of Central Africa, Teruven, 2019, p. 282.

262. Ruth Slade, English-speaking Missions in the Congo Independent State 1878-1908, Académie Royale des Sciences Coloniales. Brussels, 1959, pp. 140/1.

263. Ruth Slade, English-speaking Missions in the Congo Independent State 1878-1908, Académie Royale des Sciences Coloniales. Brussels, 1959, p. 145.

264. Ruth Slade, English-speaking Missions in the Congo Independent State 1878-1908, Académie Royale des Sciences Coloniales. Brussels, 1959, p. 304.

265. Ruth Slade, English-speaking Missions in the Congo Independent State 1878-1908, Académie Royale des Sciences Coloniales. Brussels, 1959, p. 373.

266. Ruth Slade, English-speaking Missions in the Congo Independent State 1878-1908, Académie Royale des Sciences Coloniales. Brussels, 1959, p. 394.

267. Home Council Minutes 4 October 1910. RBMU archive, University of Edinburgh.

268. Ruth Slade, English-speaking Missions in the Congo Independent State 1878-1908, Académie Royale des Sciences Coloniales. Brussels, 1959, p.337.

269. Home Council Minutes 10 January 1911. RBMU archive, University of Edinburgh.

270. Ruth Slade, English-speaking Missions in the Congo Independent State 1878-1908, Académie Royale des Sciences Coloniales. Brussels, 1959, p. 245.

271. Letter from Morel to Wilkes, 24 June 1912, ED Morel archive, London School of Economics.

272. H. Grattan Guinness, *Not Unto Us: a record of twenty-one years missionary service* – Primary Source Edition. Regions Beyond Missionary Union, 1910, p. 73.

273. H. Grattan Guinness, *Not Unto Us: a record of twenty-one years*

missionary service – Primary Source Edition. Regions Beyond Missionary Union, 1910, p. 63.

274. Muriel Davey, The Story of Maka, 1957. RBMU archive, University of Edinburgh.

275. W. D. Armstrong, 'Sunrise on The Congo. A record of the earlier years of the Congo Balolo Mission', pp. 23/5. Unpublished. RBMU archive, University of Edinburgh.

276. W. D. Armstrong, 'Sunrise on The Congo. A record of the earlier years of the Congo Balolo Mission', p. 206, Unpublished. RBMU archive, University of Edinburgh.

277. Alice Seeley Harris interview: "BBC women of influence. Alice Seeley Harris". Soundcloud online. 1970.

278. W. D. Armstrong, 'Sunrise on The Congo. A record of the earlier years of the Congo Balolo Mission', pp. 40/1. Unpublished. RBMU archive, University of Edinburgh.

279. C. W. MacKintosh, *Dr Harry Guinness: The Life story of Henry Grattan Guinness, MD FRGS.* Regions Beyond Missionary Union. 1916, p. 45.

280. Dora McKenzie. How we Entered the Land. In H. Grattan Guinness, *Not Unto Us: a record of twenty-one years missionary service* – Primary Source Edition. Regions Beyond Missionary Union, 1910, pp. 71/78.

281. Regions Beyond. 1905. p. 174. RBMU archive, University of Edinburgh.

282. Regions Beyond. 1901. p. 38. RBMU archive, University of Edinburgh.

283. Charles Bond. Regions Beyond. 1902. p. 311. RBMU archive, University of Edinburgh.

284. Regions Beyond. November 1901. RBMU archive, University of Edinburgh.

285. Regions Beyond. 1902. pp. 32/4. RBMU archive, University of Edinburgh.

286. Regions Beyond. 1902. p. 55. RBMU archive, University of Edinburgh.

287. Regions Beyond. 1905. p. 159. RBMU archive, University of Edinburgh.

288. W. D. Armstrong, 'Sunrise on The Congo. A record of the earlier years of the Congo Balolo Mission', p. 233. Unpublished. RBMU archive, University of Edinburgh.

289. W. D. Armstrong, 'Sunrise on The Congo. A record of the earlier years of the Congo Balolo Mission', p. 248. Unpublished. RBMU archive, University of Edinburgh.

290. Regions Beyond. 1905. p. 4. RBMU archive, RBMU archive, University of Edinburgh.

291. 2 Corinthians. 10;16

292. Letter from J. Harris to Rev. J. Howell 22 May 1912. Anti -Slavery Society archive. Bodleian Library, Oxford. MS Brit Emp s 19 D3/5 503.

293. Letter from J. Harris to F.B. Meyer, 4 September 1912. Anti -Slavery Society archive. Bodleian Library, Oxford. MS Brit. Emp. s. 19 D3/6 428.

294. Congo Balolo Mission Record. January 1919. RBMU archive, University of Edinburgh.

295. Regions Beyond. November 1919. p.81. RBMU archive, University of Edinburgh.

296. Regions Beyond. November 1919. p.82. RBMU archive, University of Edinburgh.

297. Joseph F. Conley, *Drumbeats that Changed the World. A History of the Regions Beyond Missionary Union and the West Indies Mission.* William Carey Library, Pasadena, CA, 2000, p. 129.

298. Elizabeth Pritchard, *For Such a Time*, Victory Press, 1973, p. 46.

299. Congo Balolo Mission Record. January 1926. pp.8/9. RBMU archive, University of Edinburgh.

300. Letter from Wilkes to Wilson 18th February 1919. RBMU archive, University of Edinburgh.

301. Field Committee correspondence to Home Council. Field Conference 1938. RBMU archive, University of Edinburgh.

302. Minutes of Congo Field Conference 1950. RBMU Archive, University of Edinburgh.

303. Letter from E R Wide to Watkin Roberts & Toronto Council 16/3/1952. Personal papers in possession of the author.

304. Letter from Wright to Watkin Roberts 18/3/1952. Personal papers in possession of author.

305. Congo Balolo Mission Record. January 1935. RBMU archive, University of Edinburgh.

306. Congo Balolo Mission Record. 1934. p.4. RBMU archive, University of Edinburgh.

307. E. R. Wide, Graph of Statistics of Baringa Leper Camp 1962. Personal papers in possession of author.

308. Regions Beyond. Annual Report 1955/6. p.25. RBMU archive, University of Edinburgh.

309. Letter from Wright to American Leprosy Mission 5 August 1950. Personal papers in possession of author.

310. Yoseki Hospital report 1950. RBMU archive, University of Edinburgh.

311. Colin Legum, *Congo Disaster*, Penguin Books Ltd, 1961.

312. Isobel Wide diary entry 20 January 1960. Personal papers in possession of author.

313. Isobel Wide diary entry 1 July 1960. Personal papers in possession of author.

314. Isobel Wide Prayer Letter No.8. 30 January 1960. Personal papers in possession of author.

315. Letter from Wide to Walling 11 August 1960. Personal papers in possession of author.

316. Isobel Wide diary entry 10 July 1960. Personal papers in possession of author.

317. Regions Beyond October 1960. p.4.

318. Rev L. Hanson. Missionary Biography. 1972. Family papers in possession of Mr & Mrs W Snowball, 2012.

319. H. J. Hall. Regions Beyond. Spring 1965. RBMU archive, University of Edinburgh.

320. Isobel Wide Prayer letter no. 9. 17 October 1960. Personal papers in possession of author.

321. E. L. Walling. Congo Fellowship Letter. October 1960. pp. 6/8. RBMU archive, University of Edinburgh.

322. A Ivimey. Congo Fellowship Letter. October 1960. p 3. RBMU archive, University of Edinburgh.

323. Lokuli Simon. Congo Fellowship Letter. Oct 1960. pp. 9/11. RBMU archive, University of Edinburgh.

324. Elongi Michel. Congo Fellowship Letter. Oct 1960 pp. 12/13. RBMU archive, University of Edinburgh.

325. Mokalo Simon. Congo Fellowship Letter. Oct 1960 pp.5/6. RBMU archive, University of Edinburgh.

326. Tim Shenton, *Audrey Featherstone I presume? The amazing story of a Congo Missionary*, Evangelical Press USA, 2008.

327. Isobel wide diary entry 1960. Personal papers in possession of author.

328. Isobel Wide Prayer letter no. 9 17 October 1960. Personal papers in possession of author.

329. Letters from Walling to Wide; Wide to Wrights, 14 August 1960. Personal papers in possession of author.

330. Letter from Audrey Featherstone to Wide June 1968. Personal papers in possession of author.

331. Letter from Agnes Walling to Wide. Personal papers in possession of author.

332. Letter from Wide to Fred Dean. 23 September 1960. Personal papers in possession of author.

333. Regions Beyond. October 1960. p. 5. RBMU archive, University of Edinburgh.

334. Arthur Wright, letter January 1961. Personal letters in possession of Dr Josephine Higgs.

335. Regions Beyond. October 1960. pp. 7,17. RBMU archive, University of Edinburgh.

336. Letter from Wide to Oliver 2 November 1961. Personal papers in possession of author.

337. Horizons. Hand in Hand. Autumn 1981. p. 6. RBMU archive. University of Edinburgh.

338. RBMU Bulletin. January 1964. pp. 7,17. RBMU archive, University of Edinburgh.

339. Audrey Featherstone. Regions Beyond. April 1962, pp. 10/12.

340. Isobel Wide diary entry 1960 and various correspondence, Wide, Walling, Featherstone. Personal papers in possession of author.

341. E. W. Oliver. Widening the mission family. Regions Beyond (Winter) 1965. pp 2-3. RBMU archive, University of Edinburgh.

342. Letter from Wide to Oliver 22 November 1961. Personal papers in possession of author.

343. Elsa Morgan. Secondary School opens in Baringa. Regions Beyond (Autumn) 1965. RBMU archive, University of Edinburgh.

344. RBMU Bulletin. February 1962. RBMU archive, University of Edinburgh.

345. RBMU Bulletin. May 1964. RBMU archive, University of Edinburgh.

346. David van Reybrouck, *Congo. The Epic Story of a People*, Harper Collins Publishers, 2014, p. 322.

347. John Bruce. Personal correspondence. 2019, 2020.

348. Linda Devereux, Narrating a Congo Missionary Childhood (1958–1964): memory and meaning examined through a creative non-fiction text and exegesis.
https://openresearch-repository.anu.edu/handle/1885/14806/b37811393_Devereux_L_M.pdf

349. Professor Louis Denis, Antwerp. Personal communication. 2020.

350. David van Reybrouck, *Congo. The Epic Story of a People*, Harper Collins Publishers, 2014.

351. David E. Reed, *111 Days in Stanleyville*, Harper & Row, 1965.

352. Elsa Morgan, *Comings and Goings*, Owl Printing Company.

353. Letter from Featherstone to Wide, 28 April 1966. Personal papers in possession of author.

354. Joyce Fergusson, *Now what? Twenty years in Congo*, J& J Publishing, Calgary, Canada. 2002, p.55.

355. Joyce Fergusson, *Now what? Twenty years in Congo*, J& J Publishing, Calgary, Canada, 2002, pp.134; 213/4.

356. Bob Hunt. Personal communications 2020.

357. Richard Martin. Personal communications 2021.

358. Cath Ingram. Personal communication. 2020.

359. Shirley Bull, personal communications. 2020.

360. Dr David Pouncey. Personal communication. 2020.

361. Richard Tiplady. www.internationalbulletin.org › issues › 2005-01-038-tiplady.

362. Bernard Schmidt circular letter 27 February 1996. Papers in personal possession of the author.

363. David Carlson, personal communication. 10 August 2020.

364. Lucy E. Guinness, *Across India at the Dawn of the 20th Century*, The Religious Tract Society, London. 1898.

365. Joseph F. Conley, *Drumbeats that Changed the World. A History of the Regions Beyond Missionary Union and the West Indies Mission*. William Carey Library, Pasadena, CA, 2000, pp. 227/8.

366. Joseph F. Conley, *Drumbeats that Changed the World. A History of the Regions Beyond Missionary Union and the West Indies Mission*. William Carey Library, Pasadena, CA, 2000, pp. 317/8.

367. Joseph F. Conley, *Drumbeats that Changed the World. A History of the Regions Beyond Missionary Union and the West Indies Mission*. William Carey Library, Pasadena, CA, 2000, p. 478.

368. Joseph F. Conley, *Drumbeats that Changed the World. A History of the Regions Beyond Missionary Union and the West Indies Mission*. William Carey Library, Pasadena, CA, 2000, p. 480.

369. Geoffrey Larcombe. Personal communications 2019, 2020.

370. Joseph F. Conley, *Drumbeats that Changed the World. A History of the Regions Beyond Missionary Union and the West Indies Mission*. William Carey Library, Pasadena, CA, 2000, pp. 318/321.

371. Home Council Minutes 8 September; 10th November; 8th December 1922. RBMU archive, University of Edinburgh.

372. Judith Hymer, personal conversation 10 January 2020.

373. Horizons. Autumn 1990. RBMU archive, University of Edinburgh. p.6.

374. The Charity Commission. 7 April 2008.

375. Communaute Association des Eglises Evangelique de la Lulonga. https.//www.cadelu.cd

376. "Facing the Challenge. Sudan United Mission. 1904-2012". Sudan United Mission – Action Partners Pioneers UK, 2012, pp. 43,49.

377. Jesuit Refugee Service, Servir, No.27 November 2002. p. 5.

378. Jesuit Refugee Service. The Wound of the Border, 25 Years with the Refugees. October 2005, p. 209.

379. Elizabeth Pritchard, *For Such a Time*, Victory Press, 1973, p. 102.

380. Venture. March 1963 No.31. Evangelism success. RBMU archive, University of Edinburgh.

381. Chinua Achebe, *Things fall apart*, Heinemann Educational Books Ltd., 1958, p.134.

382. Botele Bo-Ekwela Kelly. Oeuvre Missionnaire Protestante dans la Congo Balolo Mission (CBM) 1887-1967. Institute Pedagogique National, Section des Lettres et Sciences Humaines, Kinshasa, 1990.

383. Catherine Guinness, *Rubber Justice*, Catherine Guinness. 2017, pp. 208/215.

384. Nancy Rose Hunt, *A Colonial Lexicon of Birth Control, medicalization and mobility in the Congo*, Duke University Press, 1999, p. 227.

385. Congo Field Conference report. 1930. RBMU Archive, University of Edinburgh.

386. P. P. Augouard and. H. Bentley, quoted by Ruth Slade in *King Leopold's Congo*, Oxford University Press, 1962, p. 32.

387. Ruth Slade, 'English Missionaries and the Beginning of the Anti-Congolese Campaign in England', *Revue Belge de Philologie et d'Histoire*, vol. 33-1, 1955, p. 66.

388. E.W. Oliver. Congo Mission Dies. Regions Beyond (April) 1967. RBMU archive, University of Edinburgh.

389. Congo Field Conference report. 1942. RBMU Archive, University of Edinburgh.

390. Congo Field Conference report. 1953. RBMU Archive, University of Edinburgh.

391. Brian Stanley, *The Bible and the Flag: Protestant Missions and British Imperialism in the Nineteenth and Twentieth Centuries*, Leicester: Apollos, 1990, pp. 78/84.

392. Jan Briffaerts. When Congo wants to go to school – Educational Organisation in the Belgian Congo (1908-1958). www.rozenbergquarterly.com. 2014. Para 2.1.

393. Jan Briffaerts. When Congo wants to go to school – Educational Organisation in the Belgian Congo (1908-1958). www.rozenbergquarterly.com. 2014. Para 2.1.2.

394. Brian Stanley, *The History of the Baptist Missionary Society 1792-1992*, T&T Clark, Edinburgh, 1992, p. 444.

395. Arthur Wright. Yoseki Hospital Report 1964. RBMU archive, University of Edinburgh.

396. Brian Stanley, *The History of the Baptist Missionary Society 1792-1992*, T&T Clark, Edinburgh, 1992, p. 460.

397. Brian Stanley, *The History of the Baptist Missionary Society 1792-1992*, T&T Clark, Edinburgh, 1992, p. 503.

398. Geoffrey Larcombe. Horizons 1987 (Spring). RBMU Archive, Edinburgh University.

399. Robert Dear. Horizons 1989. RBMU Archive, Edinburgh University

400. Brian Stanley, *The History of the Baptist Missionary Society 1792-1992*, T&T Clark, Edinburgh, 1992, pp. 502/516.

401. Francis Hannaway personal communications 2020.

402. Bokombe Imboko Jean Denis. Personal communications 2020.

403. Edgar Wallace. An Outsider's View. In H. Grattan Guinness, *Not Unto Us: a record of twenty-one years missionary service* – Primary Source Edition. Regions Beyond Missionary Union, 1910, pp. 106/112. (Reprinted from The Congo Balolo Mission Record, June 1907).

404. Seamas O Siochain, *Roger Casement: Imperialist, Rebel, Revolutionary*, Lilliput Press, 2008, p. 165.

405. Dr Onesimus Ngundu personal communication.

406. Glenn Schwartz. The Transformation of a Mission Hospital.

407. Christian Health Service Medical Corps.
https://www.healthservicecorps.org

408. Denis Mukwege, *The power of women. A doctor's journey of hope and healing*, Flatiron Books, New York, 2021.

409. Rene Lingofe. Personal communication 2022. See also www.lingofe.com.

410. H. Grattan Guinness, 'The white baby', In H. Grattan Guinness, *Not Unto Us: a record of twenty-one years missionary service* – Primary Source Edition. Regions Beyond Missionary Union, 1910, pp. 169/174.

411. Stephen Tomkins, *David Livingstone. The unexpected story*, Lion Books, 2013, p. 81.

412. RBMU archive, University of Edinburgh. File CSCWW.33/26/4. p. 392.

413. Regions Beyond. 1924. p. 77. RBMU archive, University of Edinburgh.

414. Regions Beyond. 1925. p. 90. RBMU archive, University of Edinburgh.

415. Regions Beyond. 1935. p. 30. RBMU archive, University of Edinburgh.

416. Regions Beyond. November 1935. p. 76. RBMU archive, University of Edinburgh.

417. Vyvyen Brendon, *Children of the Raj*, Weidenfeld & Nicolson, London, 2005.

418. Vyvyen Brendon, *Children of the Raj*, Weidenfeld & Nicolson, London, 2005, p. 198.

419. Bethany L. Mooradian. Going Home When Home Does Not Feel Like Home. California State University. 2008.https://_www-s3-live.kent.edu – › file › 04-Bethany-L.-Mooradian.pdf

420. Ruth Hill Useem & Ann Baker Cottrell, 'Adult Third Culture Kids', In *Strangers at Home: Essays on the effects of living overseas and coming "home" to a "strange land*, Aletheia Publications, 1996, pp. 22-25.

421. David C. Pollock, *Third Culture Kid: Growing Up Among Worlds*, Nicholas Brearley Publishers, Boston, Revised edition, 2009.

422. Margaret Newbigin Beetham, *Home is Where. The Journeys of a Missionary Child*, Darton, Longman & Todd, 2019.

423. Marylin R. Gardner, *Worlds Apart. A Third Culture Kid's Journey*, Doorlight Publications, 2018.

424. Faith Cook, *Troubled Journey. A Missionary Childhood in War-torn China*, Banner of Truth Trust, 2004.

425. Henry Morton Stanley, *Through the Dark Continent; Or, The Sources of the Nile: Around the Great Lakes of Equatorial Africa and Down the Livingstone River to the Atlantic Ocean*, London Sampson Low, Marston, Searle & Rivington, 1878.

426. Henry Morton Stanley, *In Darkest Africa; Or, The Quest, Rescue, and Retreat of Emin, Governor of Equatoria*, Scribner, 1890.

427. 'Benight', in The Shorter Oxford English Dictionary, 3rd Edition 1972.

428. 'Darkness', in The Shorter Oxford English Dictionary, 3rd Edition 1972.

429. Chinua Achebe, 'An Image of Africa: Racism in Conrad's "Heart of Darkness"', *Massachusetts Review*, 18, 1977.

430. Liverpool Everyman Theatre. "Heart of Darkness" Adapted and Directed by Andrew Quick and Pete Brooks. 2019.

431. Joseph Conrad, *Youth: A Narrative and Two Other Stories*, Typhoon, New York, 1902, p. 132.

432. J. H. Stape, *Conrad's Congo*, The Folio Society, 2013, pp. 122/3.

433. Bertrand Russell, 'Portraits from memory. V: Joseph Conrad (1956)', quoted by H. Stape, *Conrad's Congo*, The Folio Society, 2013, p. 153.

434. Daniel Podgorski, 'A Controversy Worth Teaching: – Joseph Conrad's – Heart of Darkness – and the Ethics of Stature', *Art Reviews and Articles*, 6 October 2015
https://thegemsbok.com/art-reviews-and-articles/book-reviews-tuesday-tome-heart-of-darkness-joseph-conrad

435. David Olusoga, *Black and British. A Forgotten History*, Pan Macmillan,2016.

436. Catherine Guinness, 'A Haunting Silence. Henry Reed and the First Tasmanians', Unpublished, 2020.

437. Fanny E. Guinness, *The New World of Central Africa*, Hodder and Stoughton, 1890, p. v.

438. H. Grattan Guinness, in H. Grattan Guinness, *Not Unto Us: a record of twenty-one years missionary service* – Primary Source Edition. Regions Beyond Missionary Union, 1910, p. 77.

439. Fanny E. Guinness, *The New World of Central Africa*, Hodder and Stoughton, 1890, p. 31.

440. H. Grattan Guinness, in H. Grattan Guinness, *Not Unto Us: a record of twenty-one years missionary service* – Primary Source Edition. Regions Beyond Missionary Union, 1910, p. 91.

441. W. D. Armstrong, 'Sunrise on The Congo. A record of the earlier years of the Congo Balolo Mission', Unpublished, p. 276. RBMU archive, University of Edinburgh.

442. Letter from Wright to American Leprosy Mission 5 August 1950. Personal papers in possession of author.

443. 'Savage', in The Shorter Oxford English Dictionary, 3rd Edition 1972.

444. John Dryden, *The Conquest of Granada*, 1672.

445. Nicholas Wadley, *Noa Noa. Gaugin's Tahiti*, Phaidon Press, Oxford, 1895, pp. 19-20.

446. William E. Phipps, *William Sheppard. Congo's African American Livingstone*, Geneva Press, Louisville, Kentucky, 2002, pp. 1/2.

447. T. Jack Thompson, 'The Camera and the Congo: Missionary Photography and Leopold's Atrocities', in *Light on Darkness*, Wm B Eerdmans Publishing Co., Michigan 2012, p.179.

448. William E. Phipps, *William Sheppard. Congo's African American Livingstone*, Geneva Press, Louisville, Kentucky, 2002, pp. 11/13.

449. John G. Turner, 'A Black-White Missionary on the Imperial Stage: William H Sheppard and Middle-Class Black Manhood', *Journal of Southern Religion*. Vol. IX.

450. Presbyterian Historical Society. The National Archives of the Presbyterian Church in the USA. www.history.pcusa.org.

451. Walter L. Williams, *Black Americans and the Evangelization of Africa, 1877-1900*, University of Wisconsin Press, 1982, pp. 124, 138. Quoted by William E. Phipps in *William Sheppard. Congo's African American Livingstone*, 2002, p. 216.

452. Grenfell, George (A) 1849-1906', Dictionary of African Christian Biography, Center for Global Christianity Mission..

453. M. A. Smith, 'Peace and Goodwill. George Grenfell on the Congo – 1', *The Baptist Quarterly* vol. 35, 1993. p. 143. Published online at www.biblicalstudies.org.uk.pdf.

454. Home Council Minutes 14 September 1893. RBMU archive, University of Edinburgh.

455. W. D. Armstrong, 'Sunrise on The Congo. A record of the earlier years of the Congo Balolo Mission', Unpublished, p. 114. RBMU archive, University of Edinburgh.

456. Oli Jacobsen, *Daniel J. Danielsen and the Congo: Missionary Campaigns and Atrocity Photographs*, BAHN (Brethren Activists & Historians Network), 2014, p.174.

457. Acts chapter 13 verse 4.

458. Fatih Cimok, *Saint Paul in Anatolia and Cyprus*, A Turizm Yayinlari, 1999.

459. John chapter 14 verse 6.

460. Dean Pavlakis, *British Humanitarianism and the Congo Reform Movement*, 1896-1913, Ashgate Publishing, 2015, p. 14.

461. Charles Freeman, *A.D.381. Heretics, Pagans and the Dawn of the Monotheistic State*, Peter Mayer Publishers, Inc., p. 1.

462. Kevin Grant, *A Civilised Savagery. Britain and the New Slaveries in Africa, 1884-1926*, Routledge, New York & London, 2005, pp. 1/26.

463. Brian Stanley, *The Bible and the Flag: Protestant Missions and British Imperialism in the Nineteenth and Twentieth Centuries*, Leicester: Apollos, 1990.

464. Andrew Porter, 'Cultural imperialism and Protestant Missionary Enterprise, 1780-1914', *The Journal of Imperial and Commonwealth History*, vol. 25 No 3, September 1997, pp. 367-391.

465. Dana L. Robert, *Converting Colonialism. Visions and Realities in Mission History, 1706-1914*, William B Eerdman's Publishing Company, 2008.

466. Andrew Wingate. Our Indian Empire. In H. Grattan Guinness, pp. 154/157.

467. John A Hobson. *Imperialism: A Study*. James Pott & Company, N York. 1902.

468. Mark A. Sealy, *Decolonising the Camera: Photography in Racial Time*, Lawrence and Wishart Limited, 2019. Also, http://etheses.dur.ac.uk/11794.

469. Nesrine Malik, 'Badenoch and the mentality of colonialism', The Guardian 27 September 2021, p. 4.

470. Regions Beyond. See numerous personal vignettes published prior to the departure of new missionaries. RBMU archive, University of Edinburgh.

471. Denis Mukwege, *The power of women. A doctor's journey of hope and healing*, Flatiron Books, New York, 2021, pp. 16/17.

472. Chinua Achebe, *Things fall apart*, Heineman Educational Books Ltd. 1977, p. 124.

473. Albert Luthuli, *Let my people go*, Collins, Fontana Books, 1962, p. 19.

474. Regions Beyond. May 1917. p. 38. RBMU archive, University of Edinburgh.

475. S. Gilchrist. Letter to Home Council 12 November 1917. RBMU archive, University of Edinburgh.

476. Albert Schweitzer, *My Life and Thought*, 2nd Edition, 1954, Guild Books, George Allen & Unwin, p. 89.

477. Albert Schweitzer, *On the Edge of the Primeval Forest & More from the Primeval Forest*, Adam & Charles Black, London, 1951, pp. 103/109.

478. Venerable Bede. *Ecclesiastical History of the English People (Historia ecclesiastica gentis Anglorum)* AD 731. Book III ch.5 & ch.14. Translation by Leo Sherley-Price. Penguin. 1955. pp. 151; 166/7.

479. Norbert Mbu-Mputu. *Cent ans d'évangélisation du Mai-Ndombe (Diocese d'Inongo) par les Pères de Scheut.* Éditions du Jour Nouveau – (Kinshasa). 1998.

480. Mbu-Mputu Norbert X. *L'Autre Lumumba. Un assassinanat sur la ligne de front de la Guerre froide.* LULU COM. 2019.

Index

ABIR (Anglo-Belgian Rubber Company), 63, 64, 65, 72
Aborigines' Protection Society (APS), 67
Achebe, Chinua, **193, 200**
Action Partners, **150, 156**
Africa Inland Mission, **90**
All Nations Bible College, **104**
American Baptist Missionary Union (ABMU), **32**
American Congo Reform Association, **85**
American Leprosy Mission, **117**
APS, see Aborigines' Protection Society, 67
Armée Nationale Congolaise (ANC), **132**
Armée Populaire de Liberation (APL), **132**
Arthington, Robert, **5**
Association Internationale du Congo, 57

Balolo, **30, 49**
Bantu, **20**
Bantu languages, **15, 105**
Bantu society, **15**
Baptism, **47**
Baptist Missionary Society, see also BMS, **5**
Baringa, **91, 94**
Baringa Hospital, **114, 141**
Basankusu, **122, 131, 161, 166**

Bentley, W Holman, **20, 82**
Berlin Conference, **59, 63**
BMS, 27, **47, 82, 85, 86, 105**
BMS Yakusu, **134**
Bofaso Davide, **144**
Bolanga Joseph, **118**
Bolobo, 29
Boma, 13, 29
Bompole, **49, 50, 51**
Bondjembo, Judith, **168**
Bongandanga, **91**
Bonginda, **53, 91, 94, 101**
Bourne, Henry Fox, **67, 70**
Brazzaville, **10, 27**
British National Free Church Council, **85**
Broom, Trixie, **118**
Brown, Margaret, **118**
Buelaert, Father, **87**
Bula Matari, **58**
Burton, Richard, **12**

C P Goerz Anschütz, **83**
CADELU, **129, 138, 151, 166, 167**
Cannibalism, **17, 95**
Captain J. K. Tuckey, **11, 12**
Casement, Sir Roger, **69, 73, 79, 167**
Chevalier de Saint-Georges, **195**
Chrétianité, **160**
Christian Health Service Corps, **168**
Church Missionary Society, **38, 51, 90**
Colonialism, 198
Comber, Thomas, **6, 27**

Commission of Enquiry, 82
Communauté des Disciples du Christ au Congo, 166
Communauté des Eglise Evangélique de la Lulonga. See also CADELU, 126
Conference of the Great Powers, 59
Congo Balolo Mission, 1, 16, 51, 54, 63, 92, 128, 145
Congo Belge, 65, 88, 91
Congo Evangelistic Mission, 90
Congo Free State, 59, 63
Congo Inland Mission, 90
Congo Protestant Council, 83, 105, 111, 163
Congo Reform Association (CRA), 69, 82, 83, 90
Congo River, 10, 29, 109
Conley, Joseph, 66, 103, 157
Conrad, Joseph, 67, 193
Craven, Henry, 6, 9, 23
Crudgington, H E, 27

Danielsen, Daniel J, 77, 80, 81
Democratic Republic of Congo (DRC, RDC), 10
Dilke, Sir Charles, 67
Diogo Cão, 10
Doyle, Sir Arthur Conan, 68

East London Training Institute, 9, 23, 32, 50, 102
Education, 43, 112, 126, 130, 140, 162
Eglise Chrétienne Missionnaire Belge, 89
Eglise du Christ au Congo", 111
Ekwalanga Timoteo, 116, 144
Equator Station, 29
Evangelism, 110, 126, 164

Faith missions, 164
Fermes-chapelles, 160
Fiote, 41

First World War, 102
Fitzgerald, Fanny Emma (see also Guinness, Fanny), 7
French White Fathers, 88

Glave, Edward James, 69
Grenfell, George, 6, 30, 83, 197
Guinness, Dr Henry Grattan Jr, 48, 50, 75, 81, 85, 95
Guinness, Fanny, 32, 102
Guinness, Henry Grattan, 7, 102

Hannaway, Francis, 168
Harris, John, 19, 82, 83, 85, 90
Harris, Mrs Alice Seeley, 83
Healthcare, 114, 142, 163
Heart of Africa Mission, 90
Heart of Darkness, 67, 193
Holt, John, 69, 75
Home Council, 71, 74, 77, 86
Homelands, 172

Ikau, 91, 94
Imperialism, 198
Independence, 121
Institut Chrétien de la Maringa (ICM), 126, 130, 163
Institut Supérieur de Théologie, 167
Institut Théologique de Baringa (ITB), 139, 154, 163
Interserve International, 150
Ivory, 60

Jacobsen, Oli, 77
Jesuit Refugee Service, 155
Johnston, H H, 42
Joplin, Scott, 195

Kibanguism, 14
Kimpa Vita, Dona Beatriz, 14
King Dom João II, 10
King Leopold II, 27, 55, 56, 59, 60, 63, 65, 82

Kingdom of Kongo, **11, 14**
Kingsley, Mary, **23, 36, 69**
Kinshasa, **10, 28**
Kodak, **84**
Kole Philippe, **139, 144, 163**

l'Etat Independent du Congo, **59**
Larcombe, Geoffrey, **148**
Latin Link, **150**
Launda, **43**
Lavigerie, Cardinal, **88**
Leopoldville, **28**
Leprosy, **116, 118, 141, 167**
Leprosy Mission, **141**
Lifeta, **116, 130**
LIM, see Livingstone Inland Mission
    (LIM), **26**
Lingala, **105**
Lingofe, Jean-René, **169**
Livingstone Inland Mission (LIM), **3,
    6, 9, 22, 29, 34**
Livingstone, Dr David, **1, 37**
Lofinda Benjamin, **144, 157**
Lopori River, **63**
Louvanium University, **162**
Lulonga, **48, 52, 91, 94**
Lulonga River, **15, 63**
Lumumba, Patrice, **121**
Luthuli, Inkosi Albert, **200**

Malaria, **35**
Maringa River, **63**
Matadi, **22**
Mbu-Mputu, Norbert, **203**
McCall, Adam, **25**
McKittrick, Dora, **96**
McKittrick, John, **48, 50, 54, 95**
Methodist Episcopal Church South US,
    90
Mill Hill Missionaries, **168**
Missionaries, **71, 74, 129, 142**
Missionaries, Associate, **129**
Missionary Aviation Fellowship

(MAF), **153**
Missionary Children, **171**
Mobutu, President Sese Seko, **122, 124**
Moffat, Robert, **105**
Mompono, **100, 109**
Mompono Ecole Biblique, **110**
Mompono Training Institute, **105**
Morel, Edmund Dene, **68**
Morrison, William M, **85, 197**
Mount Vernon Ladies' College, **104**
Movement National Congolais (MNC),
    124
Mpenzele, **122**
Mukwege, Dr Denis, **168, 200**
Murphy, J B, **73**

N'dambi, **43**
Nganga, **16, 44, 46, 93**
Ngbenze, **110**
Ngombe, **95**
Nkisi, **21**
Nkoiyo, **44**
Nzambi, **21**

Oliver, Ernest, **147**
Onesimus Ngundu, **168**
Operation Red Dragon, **134**
Owen, Dr Margaret, **118**

Palaballa, **22, 29**
Pères de Scheut, **88, 89**
Polygamy, **19, 127, 158**
Polygyny, see also polygamy, **19**
Pope Leo XIII, **89**
Printing press, **99, 105**
PS Henry Reed, **30, 31, 49, 52**
PS Livingstone, **26, 27, 106**
Pukamoni, **43**

Quinine, **36**

RBMU, **146, 148, 152, 165**
RBMU Toronto Council, **117**

Reed, Henry, **194**
Régions Beyond, **71, 77, 83**
Regions Beyond Missionary Union. See also RBMU, **102, 147**
Ridgelands Bible College, **104**
Roman Catholics, **14, 27, 84, 88, 106, 112, 121, 160, 162**
Rubber, **61, 64, 203**
Ruskin, Mr & Mrs A E, **46, 98, 104, 105**

São Salvador, **47**
Schweitzer, Dr Albert, **202**
Schweizerische Missions-Gemeinschaft (Swiss Missionary Fellowship), **119, 163**
Sheppard, William H, **85, 196**
Simba-Mulele rebellion, **132**
Sims, Dr Aaron, **28**
Sjoblom, Edvard Vilhelm, **74**
Slavery, **95, 194**
Stanley, Henry Morton, **13, 27, 56, 57**
Stanleyville, **134**
Strom, Mr, **6, 9**
Synod of Evangelical Churches in Belgium, **89**

Talking drum (lokole), **46**
Tamudjumbe, **106, 109**
Taylor, James Hudson, **8**
Taylor, Samuel Coleridge, **195**

Tearfund, **143**
Third Culture Kids, **171, 173**
Tilly, Alfred, **4, 32**
Tippu Tip, **31, 58**
Twain, Mark, **68, 83**

Unevangelised Fields Mission, **150**
Université Libre du Congo, **163**
Université Officielle du Congo, **162**

Vanga Evangelical Hospital, **168**
Vemba, **44**
Vereinte Evangelische Mission, **151, 166**
Vine, Ebenezer, **147**

Wallace, Edgar, **167, 194**
Ward, Herbert, **16**
Washington, Booker T, **85**
West African Mail, **69, 80**
Wide, Dr E R, **104, 114, 116**
Williams, George Washington, **70, 196**
World Team, **148**
Wright, Dr Arthur, **117**

Yoseki, **101, 109, 117, 153**
Yoseki hospital, **117, 141, 163**
Yuli, **100, 109, 118**

Zaire, **11**

Lightning Source UK Ltd.
Milton Keynes UK
UKHW021654111222
413755UK00002B/7